THE CHANGING
MEXICAN-AMERICAN
A READER

EDITED BY

RUDOLPH GOMEZ, PROFESSOR

UNIVERSITY OF TEXAS, EL PASO

EL PASO, TEXAS

Library of Congress Catalog Card Number 72-78444

ISBN:0-87108-185-7

Printed in the United States of America

DEDICATION

For my father and mother: Jesús José Gómez and Guadalupe Navarro Ayala de Gómez, who instilled in their family love for a country that extended at least as far north as Rawlins, Wyoming, and continued as far south as Jacona, Michoacán, and La Barca, Jalisco.

Preface

The primary purpose of this book is to make more Americans aware of the presence, in their midst, of a racial-cultural minority heretofore largely ignored in the avenues of communication imposed on most of us in our formal educational process. In this book the reader is encouraged to recognize that, in most cases, recorded American history has omitted mention of what today are labeled Mexican-Americans, Spanish-surnamed Americans, or Chicanos, as we are increasingly calling ourselves.*

In examining the experience of this minority in the United States, we are offering selections here which fit no single traditional academic discipline found in American colleges and universities today. The selections are authored by educators, social scientists, historians, journalists, and writers. The one factor which binds all these authors is their concern for revealing and improving the lot of Chicanos. This shared concern, in our judgment, erases the national heritage of each author, and he becomes at one with his subject matter. He is not an Anglo writing about Chicanos or a Chicano writing about Chicanos. Each author, rather, is a concerned human being writing about those people for whom he has a concern. Any errors are human ones and not racially-inspired or racially-intended.

We are grateful to the publishers and authors of the works that are reproduced here for their permission to reprint. In selecting the materials we have tried to give the reader a representative collection of articles encompassing what is adjudged "scholarly" and "academic" as well as what is journalistic and literary. Together they offer a perspective which

*We will use the term "Chicanos" throughout our commentary when referring to this minority group.

we believe is broad and comprehensive, but which is not a single approach to the subject matter. We have tried to organize the material in a systematic way so that the student is led to explore all the important aspects of the Chicanos' pilgrimage through the United States.

The editor is grateful to Ted Shields of Pruett Publishing Company for his encouragement and for his willingness to undertake this venture. My department chairman and colleague W. R. Nelson thoughtfully arranged my teaching schedule so I could have abundant time for reflection and writing. Mrs. Laura Ingram and Miss Kathy Spruill assisted in many ways—they performed much of the drudgery associated with this sort of enterprise.

No family man can embark on this sort of enterprise without the support of his family. Such support has been forthcoming from mine. My wife, Polly, began years ago to encourage me to "do something" that would involve my ethnic background with my profession. Her encouragement has been instrumental not only in this venture but in other similar ones as well. My sons, Robert and Clay, have personified, figuratively and literally speaking, the emergence of the new Mexican-American in the United States. They are self-consciously proud of both their heritages but forget both in their concern for human beings as individuals. Their support has been constant, uncritical, and completely devoted. I am grateful, obviously, to each.

CONTENTS

Introduction

In order to learn more about Chicanos in the United States, one must consider the facts and the analyses which have been produced on the subject matter. The discussions presented here, which include both facts and analyses, have been arranged into categories that are somewhat arbitrary and perhaps artificial. Yet one must impose an order on discrete data if they are to convey the impression of a completed whole.

The literature on Chicanos is growing so rapidly that a full-time effort is required to stay abreast. Many of the selections offered here are recent publications. In addition, however, we have felt it necessary to include some classic pieces even at the risk of excluding more recent publications. The judgment of whether the number of classic selections exacts too high a toll of this book must rest with the reader.

A final word about the number of selections offered in this reader. The editor strove for representation from as many different facets of Chicano literature as possible, but he also strove for compactness. Therefore, no pretense toward being encyclopedic in the number of articles offered in the book is made here. The editor has excluded some articles which others might have chosen but which the editor felt would have added only incrementally to the selections included. While they may have added an insight here, a different point of view there, they were not sufficiently distinct to merit inclusion.

The articles that have been selected for this volume represent an overview of Chicanos in the United States as perceived by the editor. Each article offers a clear view of a particular facet of the Chicano experience. Together, the articles should serve to inform the reader of the scope, the complexity, and the unity of the Chicano Problem as perceived and understood by the editor.

Readers wishing to probe the subject matter more deeply, and perhaps more profoundly, are encouraged to consult the selected bibliography found at the book's conclusion. If the articles contained in this book stimulate one reader to investigate the subject matter more fully, then the intent of the book will have been fulfilled. For the value of a book need not necessarily be that it educates us completely, for few if any books can do that, but that it stimulates us to want to learn more.

The order in which the selections are arranged is developmental. The Chicano experience is conceived as having a beginning, a change, and a result, and the task of the book is to trace this development through each stage. Accordingly, Part I of the book is concerned with placing the Chicano in his environment and then spelling out some of the consequences of the interaction between environment and Chicano. The significance of this interaction is examined both for its implications on the individual Chicano and for that part of the environment we call the community or society.

Part II is concerned with an examination of some of the major economic, educational, and social problems confronting most Chicanos in the United States today. The contention of Part II is that Chicanos start life as members of a disadvantaged group and continue in that relative position as a result of the functioning of the political, educational, and employment systems.

Part III contains readings that trace some of the changes wrought in the life style of the Chicano by his increasing alienation from institutions and values he has not developed, or contributed to the development of, in any significant way.

Part IV identifies the concept of *la raza*, the people, as the rallying point around which Chicanos of all persuasions gather. Chicanos are convinced that *la raza* has resisted assimilation, prejudice, and discrimination in the past and that the time has arrived for *la raza*, bound closer together by the hardships of the past, to use the concept to create a group that will more effectively work to achieve the educational, economic, and social goals denied them in the past. A discussion of Chicano political activity is also included in this section. It will probably come as a surprise to some readers to note that Chicano forebearers engaged in organized political activity several generations ago although their efforts bore no significant political payoffs.

Part V offers an article on Chicano literature and an article on scholarship. The increase in consciousness of being Chicano has resulted in a growing body of literature which is unique. Perhaps it is the most exciting cultural payoff to have emerged from the Chicano Movement to date. In addition, Chicano social scientists are increasingly concerned with research about Chicanos which they challenge because of its alleged cultural bias in favor of the dominant Anglo majority. This problem is important not only because it is concerned with a genuine epistomological problem, i.e., cultural bias, but also because it reveals that Chicanos are becoming professional academics in the various disciplines and are using those disciplines to service the needs of the Chicano community.

The last section of the book contains portraits of some nationally-recognized Chicano leaders. The point of departure between the current leadership and that of the past is its radicalization. In the past the leadership was content to work through the system to achieve its aims. Today the leadership, in striving to achieve its aims, is also working to effect a twofold change in the system. First, it seeks greater systemic recognition of what it considers are unique Chicano problems, and, secondly, it seeks to place greater numbers of Chicanos in public office, both in electoral and administrative positions.

A selected bibliography is appended to guide the reader to other sources which can provide greater breadth and depth to the understanding of Chicanos today.

I/HISTORICAL PERSPECTIVE

The readings comprising Part I of the book were selected because they serve to place the Chicano in an historical framework.

Jack D. Forbes does a fine job on an exceedingly complex subject—fitting the Chicanos into United States history. Forbes places what he calls "the Mexican heritage of the United States" at a point long before the time of Christ. About 4000 B.C. Indians were living in southern New Mexico and learning how to raise corn. Readers unfamiliar with the subject will be surprised to learn that the ancient Mexicans excelled in city planning and in the arts and crafts long before Columbus discovered America. The ancient Mexicans had a written language which was used to produce poetry, religious works, and philosophical speculation. To illustrate the degree to which the old Mexicans mastered a science, Forbes notes that "Mayan scientists developed a calendar which is more accurate than the one we use today."

After the Spanish invasion of Mexico under the leadership of Cortes, some of the old Mexican cultures merged with the Spanish, while others have survived intact to the present day. The result is that the modern Chicano is the product of a heterogeneous culture; he has in fact added to this heterogeneity by contributing to the English language and American customs and institutions. Forbes lists the many contributions the Mexicans have made to the art, culture, and customs of the American Southwest. The point of his article is that the Mexican/Chicano contributions to United States culture should not be viewed as alien—coming from a foreign place; instead the contributions are indigenous, they are as native to the United States as the territory that today comprises the states of Texas, Arizona, New Mexico, Colorado, California, and probably parts of Nevada (which means *snowfall*—apparently applied ironically to the deserts of that state) and Montana (which means mountain in the Spanish use of the word montaña).

Manuel Gamio's selection, unlike that of Forbes,

concerns the immigration of Mexicans to the United States during and immediately after the Mexican Revolution (roughly from 1910 to 1920). These immigrants are the parents and grandparents of many Chicanos now living in an area that extends from the Southwest to the Midwest. Gamio indicates that these immigrants, for the most part, were working people who sought employment opportunities from the Mexican border to the Canadian border. This pattern of immigration explains why the distribution of Chicanos is as widespread as it is.

The data utilized to discover the home state of the Mexican immigrant, i.e., money orders mailed to home states, reveal that those immigrants, like those from other ethnic minorities, came to the United States *in search of work.* They did not arrive seeking a "free ride" from a benevolent welfare state. The fact that relatively large numbers of Chicanos are on general assistance welfare today in certain parts of the United States suggests that many are on welfare for want of employment opportunity. If this conclusion is empirically valid, one might argue that the stereotype of Chicano laziness, held by people who point to their numbers on welfare rolls, is unjust since it is possible that welfare rolls are swelled as much by lack of employment opportunities as they are by "inherent racial characteristics."

The late George H. Sánchez, long a spokesman for Chicanos seeking elementary social justice in the United States, explains why Chicanos have retained their unique cultural identity in spite of institutional attempts to assimilate them into the dominant Anglo majority. Sánchez points to three factors which in his judgment have contributed to the perpetuation of the Chicanos as an identifiable, more or less homogeneous and cohesive ethnic group. First, he argues that the geographic isolation imposed upon Chicanos by poor transportation and communications facilities in the nineteenth and early twentieth centuries helped them retain their uniqueness and worked against their assimilation. He also suggests that there is heterogeneity within the Chicano community due to the same factor of geographic isolation. For example, he lists differences perceived by the *Hispanos* of New Mexico and the *Texanos* along the Rio Grande and still others resulting from the isolation of the *Californios.* The point needing emphasis is that Chicanos are as diverse in their unity as are the Latin and North Americans.

The second factor binding Chicanos together is their use of Spanish as their mother tongue in spite of the concerted efforts of Anglo school authorities to teach them to learn English as their "first" language. The insensitive treatment of Spanish-speaking Chicanos has created a two-fold unity among their students. First, there is the unity resulting from the common lack of preparation in English when Chicano children enter school, and secondly, there is the "pariah unity" resulting from teachers' mistreatment of Chicano students because they cannot learn English. This problem tends to reinforce itself in that it is never broken at any stage of the formal educational process. High school teachers commit the same language crimes against their Spanish-speaking students that their kindergarten and elementary predecessors committed. The student, understandably, accepts the pariah label and clings to Chicano friends who are similarly abused. Thus a community based on shame and founded in misery is formed early and often endures for life.

Finally, according to Professor Sánchez, racial discrimination practiced against Chicanos has served to weld them into one group in spite of some of their manifest differences. Sánchez notes how the educational and employment systems, in the Southwest particularly, have been used to keep the Chicano "in his place." Sánchez suggests that some alleviation of discrimination has taken place of late but not enough to assuage or efface the discriminatory treatment experienced by virtually every Chicano at some phase of his life.

Sánchez concludes his article by prescribing certain reforms which could do much to correct the overt discriminations he describes. He says nothing, however, of how the psychological damage inflicted by past discriminations can be remedied. One infers that little can be done about that. One hopes that time and proper reforms will assuage and compensate the Chicano. But time passes at minute intervals so we must not be surprised if Chicano anger and hurt continue after the assuaging reforms have begun. A hundred years and more of discrimination cannot be forgiven by the election of a Chicano mayor, congressman, senator, or indeed president. Forgiveness will come when each Chicano is treated as an equal by each person he is associated with throughout his life. And with forgiveness will come a lessening of tension and hostility between Chicano and Anglo. Such a time will not signal the millennium in the United States, but it will signal that we have taken one more step toward fulfilling the ideals found in the Declaration of Independence and the Constitution of the United States.

The Significance of the Mexican-American People

Jack D. Forbes

Approximately five million persons of Mexican ancestry reside in the United States. Most live in the states of California, Arizona, New Mexico, Texas, and Colorado, but a large number have made homes in the greater Chicago area and in other industrial centers. In many sections of the Southwest, particularly along the border from San Diego, California to Brownsville, Texas Mexican-Americans are the majority population, and their language and culture serve to provide the entire region with much of its charm and distinctiveness.

Modern-day Mexican-Americans play a vital role in the industrial, agricultural, artistic, intellectual, and political life of the Southwest but the significance of this group cannot be measured solely in terms of present-day accomplishments. It is certain that the Southwest as we know it would not exist without the Mexican-Spanish heritage. That which sets New Mexico off from Oklahoma and California off from Oregon is in large measure the result of the activities of the ancestors of our fellow citizens of Mexican descent. Our way of life has been and is being immeasurably enriched by their presence north of the present-day international boundary.

Jack D. Forbes, "The Significance of the Mexican-American People," in *Mexican-Americans: A Handbook for Educators* (1967-68), pp. 1-13. Reprinted by permission of the Far West Laboratory for Educational Research and Development, Berkeley, California. Available only from the Superintendent of Documents, Government Printing Office, Washington, D. C., at 35¢.

THE MEXICAN HERITAGE OF THE UNITED STATES: AN HISTORICAL SUMMARY

What Is a Mexican?

Prior to 1821 (when the modern Mexican nation won its independence from Spain), a Mexican was usually a person who spoke the Mexican or Aztec language (Náhuatl). In fact, the early Spaniards almost always referred to the Aztec people as Mexicans. This practice has continued in modern Mexico where the Náhuatl language is called "Mexicano" by the common people and where writers usually speak of the Mexican Empire rather than the Aztec Empire. The modern people of Mexico, who are said by scholars to be about 80% native Indian in their ancestry, are proud of their descent from the ancient Mexicans and trace the history of their people back to the builders of the magnificent cities of Teotihuacán, Monte Albán, and Chichén Itzá.

Our Ancient Mexican Heritage

The Mexican heritage of the United States commences long before the time of Christ. About the year 4000 B.C. Indians living in southern New Mexico learned how to raise corn (maize) as a result of contacts with Mexico (where that remarkable plant was first domesticated after what must have been a long and tedious process.) Other crops, including squash and beans, were subsequently borrowed and still later (about 500 A.D.) Southwestern Indians began to develop the Pueblo Indian Civilization. This advanced way of life, which still flourishes in Arizona and New Mexico, was largely based upon Mexican influences in architecture, pottery-making, clothing, religion and government.

In about 1000 A.D., according to some scholars, a people known as the Hohokam moved from northern Mexico into what is now southern Arizona. They brought many advanced traits with them, including the construction of monumental irrigation systems, stone etching techniques, and, very possibly, new political concepts. The Hohokams constructed a large center at Snaketown, Arizona and spread their influence widely, apparently establishing a colony at Flagstaff and trading their pottery as far as the San Fernando Valley in California. During the same general period Mexican influences seem to have reached the Mississippi Valley and advanced cultures developed there. The Indians of the southern United States developed a Mexican-style religious and political orientation and constructed small pyramid-temples while the Ohio River Indians built fanciful effigy mounds, sometimes in the shape of serpents.

The Vitality of Mexican Civilization

It is not at all surprising that ancient Mexico had a great impact upon the area of the United States. The Mexican people were extremely creative, industrious, and numerous (perhaps number 20,000,000 in central Mexico alone in the 1520's). Great cities such as Teotihuacan were developed very early and at the time of the Spanish conquest Tenochtitlán (Mexico City) was perhaps the largest and certainly the most modern city in the world. In fact, our cities of today are not as well planned and are probably not as well cared for as was Tenochtitlán.

The ancient Mexicans excelled as artists, craftsmen, architects, city planners, engineers, astronomers, statesmen, and warriors. They also developed centers of higher education (called *calmécac* by the Aztecs), wrote excellent poetry, produced many historical and religious works, and were very interested in philosophical questions. One philosopher-king, Nezahualcóyotl, put forth the view that there was only one Creator-God, while Maya scientists developed a calendar which is more accurate than the one we use today.

Mexican traders (*pochteca*) traveled great distances, going as far south as Panama. They helped to spread Mexican culture and also prepared the way for colonists to settle in places such as El Salvador and Nicaragua and for the last Mexican empire (that of the Aztecs) to expand. By the 1520's the Mexican language was the common tongue of the region from north central Mexico to Central America.

The Spanish Invasion

In the 1520's the Spaniards commenced their conquest of Mexico. Although the Aztecs were conquered quickly, in spite of a noble defense of Tenochtitlán led by Cuauhtémoc (the present-day national hero of Mexico), the rest of what is now Mexico was subdued only very gradually. In fact, many Indian groups in northern Mexico and in the jungles of Yucatan-Guatemala were never conquered. Also, many of the Mexicans who were subdued never lost their identity and this explains why at least one-tenth of the people of modern Mexico speak native languages, often in addition to Mexican Spanish.

The Spanish invasion did not bring an end to the vitality of the Mexican people. Most Spaniards came to rule, not to work, and the magnificent churches, aqueducts, and palaces of the colonial period are essentially the result of native labor and craftsmanship. Educated Mexicans helped to record the history of ancient Mexico and for a brief period a Mexican university, Santa Cruz del Tlaltelolco, flourished, training many persons of native ancestry. The conquering Spaniards, if of high rank, often married native noblewomen and the common Spaniards married ordinary Indian women, in both cases contributing to the mixture of the Spanish and native Mexican races.

The Hispano-Mexican Northward Movement

The number of Spaniards who came to Mexico was always very slight and the growth and expansion of the Spanish Empire depended upon the use of native and mixed-blood (mestizo) servants, settlers, craftsmen, miners, and soldiers (the Tlaxcaltecos, Mexicans of Tlaxcala, were particularly relied upon as colonists and soldiers). The conquest of the north would have been impossible without Mexicans and every major settlement, from Santa Fe, New Mexico, to Saltillo, Coahuila, had its Mexican district (barrio or colonia). Many of the settlers taken by Diego de Vargas to northern New Mexico in the 1690's were called "Españoles Mexicanos," that is, "Aztec-Spaniards;" and Juan de Oñate, the first Spanish governor of New Mexico, was married to a woman of Aztec royal ancestry and their son, Cristóbal de Oñate, was the second governor of that province. Every major expedition, including these of Coronado and De Soto, utilized Mexicans and eight Mexican soldiers were stationed at San Diego, California in 1769 by Gaspar de Portolá. The northward movement of Spain into the southwestern United States was, therefore, a Spanish-Mexican affair. It was Spanish-led but depended for its success upon Mexicans and mixed-bloods. In California, for example, well over half of the Spanish-speaking settlers were of Indian or mixed ancestary and the forty-six founders of Los Angeles in 1781 included only two persons called Spaniards, and their wives were Indian.

The Creation of Modern Mexican Culture

Gradually the way of life brought to America by the Europeans became mixed with native Mexican influences, until the life of the common people became a blend of Spanish-Arabic and Indian traits, much as the culture of England after 1066 became a blend of French-Latin and Anglo-Celtic traditions. The Spaniards used the Mexican language for governmental, scholarly, and religious purposes for several generations and many Mexican words, such as *coyote, elote, jicara, tamale, chile, chocolate, jacal, ocelote,* and hundreds of others, became part of Spanish as spoken in Mexico. Roman Catholic religious practice was modified by many Indian customs and devotion to the Virgin of Guadalupe has had a lasting impact upon the Catholic faith.

Meanwhile, the Mexican people intermixed with diverse tribes and eventually began to absorb both the non-Mexican Indian and the Spaniard himself. This process of migration and mixture made possible the creation of the independent Mexican republic in 1821, after a ten-year struggle for freedom.

The Mexican Republic in the North

Independent Mexico was to have a lasting impact upon the southwestern United States. Many Mexican leaders were imbued with new republican and equalitarian ideals and they sought to implement these reforms. Legislatures and elected local councils were establishd in California and elsewhere, the Indians and mixed-bloods were granted complete legal equality and full citizenship, and foreigners were encouraged to take up a new life as Mexicans. On the other hand, many persons found it hard to break with the authoritarian legacy of Spain, and republican reforms were often subverted. Foreign settlers did not always choose to become good Mexican citizens, as for example the Anglo-Texans who refused to set their slaves free or to obey Mexican land-title and tariff regulations.

The early Mexican governments were often beset by financial difficulties and progress was difficult in the face of widespread illiteracy and an unequal distribution of wealth and power. Gradually, however, these negative conditions were overcome and the Mexican people advanced along the road of democracy, albeit with backward steps from time to time.

In what is now the United States Mexicans were active in the development of new mining regions (gold was discovered in California in 1842, for example), opening up new routes for travelers (as from Santa Fe to Los Angeles via Las Vegas, Nevada), founding schools (some twenty-two teachers were brought to California in the 1830's and a seminary was established at Santa Ynez), establishing new towns (Sonoma, California is an example), and setting up printing presses (as in California in 1835). The north was a frontier region and was, therefore, not in the forefront of Mexican cultural progress, but it did benefit from developments originating further south.

Mexican Miners and Colonists in the North

Commencing in the 1830's Mexican settlers began moving north once again. Some 200 craftsmen, artisans, and skilled laborers sailed to California in that decade, and soon overland immigrants from Sonora were joining them. Thereafter a steady stream of Sonorans reached California, only to be turned into a flood by the discovery of gold in the Sierra Nevada foothills in 1848. The Sonorans were often experienced miners and their techniques dominated the California Gold Rush until steam-powered machinery took over at a later date. Chihuahuans and other Mexicans also "rushed" to California by sea and by land and they too exercised an impact upon mining as well as upon commerce.

The United States-Mexican War of 1846-1848 did not immediately alter the character of the Southwest greatly, except in eastern Texas and northern California. The Gold Rush changed the language of central California after 1852 (when Mexican miners were largely expelled from the Sierra Nevada mines), but Mexicans continued to dominate the life of the region from San Luis Obispo, California, to San Antonio, Texas. Southern California, for example, remained a Spanish-speaking region until the 1870's with Spanish-language and bi-lingual public schools, Spanish-language newspapers, and Spanish-speaking judges, elected officials, and community leaders. The first Constitution of the State of California, created in part by persons of Mexican background, established California as a bi-lingual state and it remained as such until 1878. Similar conditions prevailed in other southwestern regions.

Anglo-Americans Become Dominant

Gradually, however, Anglo-Americans from the east who were unsympathetic toward Mexican culture came to dominate the Southwest. Having no roots in the native soil and being unwilling to become assimilated to the region, these newcomers gradually transformed the schools into English-language institutions where no Spanish was taught, constructed buildings with an "eastern" character, pushed Mexican leaders into the background, and generally caused the Mexican-American, as he has come to be termed, to become a forgotten citizen.

By the 1890's, on the other hand tourists and writers began to rediscover the "Spanish" heritage and "landmark" clubs commenced the process of restoring the decaying missions of the Southwest. A "Spanish" cultural revival was thus initiated, and soon it began to influence architectural styles as well as the kind of pageantry which has typified much of the Southwest ever since. Unfortunately, the Mexican-Indian aspect of the region's heritage was at first overlooked and the Mexican-American people benefited but little from the emphasis upon things Spanish.

Twentieth-Century Mexican "Pioneers"

In the early 1900's a new group of Mexican immigrants began to enter the United States, attracted by job offers from agricultural developers who wished to open up virgin lands in southern California, Colorado, Arizona, and south Texas. During World War I and the 1920's this movement became a flood, a flood which largely overwhelmed the older group of Mexican-Americans (except in northern New Mexico and southern Colorado) and became ancestral to much of the contemporary Spanish-speaking population in the Southwest.

These hundreds of thousands of new Mexican-Americans had to overcome many obstacles as they attempted to improve their life patterns. Anglo-Americans were prejudiced against people who were largely of native American, brown-skinned origin, who were poor, who of necessity lived in substandard or self-constructed homes, who could not speak English, and who were not familiar with the workings of a highly competitive and acquisitive society. Gradually, and in spite of the trauma of the Great Depression (when all sorts of pressures were used to deport Mexican-Americans to Mexico), *los de la raza*, as Mexicans in the United States frequently refer to themselves, climbed the economic ladder and established stable, secure communities in the Southwest.

The Internal Development of the Mexican-American Community

The Mexican-American community was not simply a passive force during this long period of transition. Everywhere mutual benefit societies, patriotic Mexicanist organizations, newspapers, social clubs, small stores and restaurants were founded, and artisans began to supply Anglo-American homes with pottery and other art objects (the first gift I ever gave to my mother was a pottery bowl made by a Mexican-American craftsman who fashioned ceramics in a shop behind his home on our street in El Monte, California).

Mexican-American mutual benefit organizations soon commenced the task of helping to upgrade the status of agricultural and industrial workers by seeking better wages and conditions of employment. During the 1920's and 1930's Mexican-American labor organizers, with little formal education and less money, traveled from region to region, helping in the unionization process. Ever since, labor leaders have played an important role in Mexican-American affairs and Spanish speaking union officers are a significant element in the structure of organized labor in the Southwest. Current efforts directed toward the unionization of agricultural workers and obtaining a minimum wage for agricultural laborers, from California to south Texas, are being led by organizers of Mexican ancestry.

During the past twenty years the cultural and political life of Mexican-Americans has advanced remarkably. Today, fine Spanish-language newspapers blanket the Southwest and Far West, some of which are daily periodicals with the latest dispatches from Europe and Mexico. Magazines, including bilingual ones, issue forth with slick paper and exciting photographs. Spanish-language radio and television stations reach much of the Southwest, and theatrical-musical productions of a folk or modern nature are frequently staged for the benefit of both *los de la raza* and Anglos.

Mexican-American civic, business and political leaders are now prominent in many regions, and they include within their ranks members of Congress, mayors, and all types of professional people. The image of the Mexican heritage has vastly improved due not only to the activities of individual Mexican-Americans, but also due to the cultural renaissance occurring in Mexico itself concurrent with the incredible richness of the Mexican past revealed by contemporary archaeological discoveries. Anglo-Americans have ceased emphasizing the Spanish legacy at the expense of the Mexican, and a more healthy climate of mutual understanding has evolved.

Educational Progress

Educationally, Mexican-American progress has been striking in individual cases but has been slow over-all. Generally speaking, whenever Anglo-Americans gained control over a particular state or region in the Southwest they chose to import the kinds of public schools developed in the Middle West or East. Hispano-Mexican and bi-lingual schools were replaced by English-language, Anglo-oriented schools from which Mexican-American children were sometimes excluded. After the turn of the century greater numbers of Spanish-speaking youth began to attend schools, but the latter were either irrelevant to the background, language, and interests of the pupils (as in New Mexico) or were segregated, marginal elementary schools (as in much of California and Texas). Normally, secondary-level education was not available to Mexican-American pupils except in an alien Anglo-dominated school (and even that opportunity was often not present in many rural counties in Texas and elsewhere).

During the post-World War II period segregated schools for Mexican-Americans largely disappeared, except where residential segregation operated to preserve the ethnic school. Greater numbers of Mexican-Americans entered high school and enrollment in college was increased, although slowly. Nevertheless, drop-out rates remain high, even today; and it is also true that the typical school serving Mexican-Americans makes little, if any, concession to the Mexican heritage, the Spanish language, or to the desires of the Mexican-American community.

A Six Thousand Year Old Heritage

In summary, the Mexican heritage of the United States is very great indeed. For at least 6,000 years Mexico has been a center for the dissemination of cultural influences in all directions, and this process continues today. Although the modern United States has outstripped Mexico in technological innovation, the Mexican people's marked ability in the visual arts, music, architecture, and political affairs makes them a constant contributor to the heritage of all of North America. The Mexican-American people of the United States serve as a bridge for the diffusion northward of valuable Mexican traits, serve as a reservoir for the preservation of the ancient Hispano-Mexican heritage of the Southwest, and participate directly in the daily life of the modern culture of the United States.

Sources of Mexican Immigrants and the Distribution of Immigrants in the United States

Manuel Gamio

. . . the money orders sent to Mexico, presumably by immigrants to their families, during July and August of 1926, were directed in large to the central plateau (*mesa central*) and in lesser proportion, to those of the northern plateau (*mesa del norte*). From these states, then, comes the larger part of the Mexican Immigrants. (Editor's note: Table [1] given below indicates the source of Mexican immigrants according to number of money orders sent to Mexico during July and August, 1926.)

These two large zones, which are bounded on the east and west by the Sierra Madre, on the north by the American Border, on the south by the southern escarpment, enjoy conditions of altitude, temperature, and rainfall which make an ideal climate for the development of human life . . .

One might suppose that the immigrants coming from the central tablelands would choose to go to California, Arizona, and New Mexico, where the climate is relatively the same, and that the immigrants from Chihuahua, Coahuila,

Manuel Gamio, "Sources of Mexican Immigrants and the Distribution of Immigrants in the United States," in *Mexican Immigration to the United States* (Chicago: The University of Chicago Press, 1930), pp. 13-29. Copyright 1930 by the University of Chicago.

Nuevo Leon, and Sonora would go to the states of the east and midwest where a more rigorous climate prevails. Nevertheless, this is not the case. An examination of the data on distribution by states and cities shows that in California, for example, there is a relatively high proportion of immigrants from Sonora, Chihuahua, Coahuila, and Nuevo Leon; while in the northern east and midwest states, especially Illinois, Indiana, and Michigan, the largest proportion of immigrants comes from the states of Michoacán and Guanajuato, which are in the mild central plateau.

Table [1]

Home State of Mexican Immigrants to the United States
as Determined by Money Orders Sent to Mexico,
July-August, 1926

States	No. of Money Orders Received	% of Total	States	No. of Money Orders Received	% of Total
Michoacan	4,775	20.0%	Yucatan	78	0.3%
Guanajuato	4,659	19.6	Mexico	66	.3
Jalisco	3,507	14.7	Queretaro	68	.2
Nuevo Leon	1,913	8.0	Guerrero	57	.2
Durango	1,400	5.9	Colima	55	.2
Distrito Federal	1,196	5.0	Vera Cruz	54	.2
Zacatecas	1,140	4.8	Nayarit	51	.2
Chihuahua	1,046	4.4	Oaxaca	48	.2
Coahuila	903	3.8	Hidalgo	45	.2
San Luis Potosi	860	3.7	Tlaxcala	13	0.1
Tamaulipas	484	2.1	Chiapas	2	0
Sinaloa	473	2.0	Tabasco	2	0
Aquascalientes	462	1.9	Campeche	1	0
Sonora	294	1.2	Morelos	1	0
Baja California	115	0.5	Quintana Roo	0	0
Puebla	78	0.3	TOTAL	23,846	100.0

The official weather reports complied by the Mexican and United States governments show that in states from which come most of the immigrants the mean annual variation in temperature is not 20° F, while in some parts of the United States to which the Mexicans go, it is almost 100°. The great difference in humidity is likewise to be considered. The scant economic means and the ignorance and inexperience of the

Mexican immigrants hamper them in their struggle with the hostile climate, and they frequently succumb to disease.

One might conclude that the simple fact is that the immigrants come from those Mexican states having the largest populations. But this is not true. Of the three states in the republic which have more than a million inhabitants, Jalisco is the only one which provides a high proportion of emigrants, while Puebla, on the central plateau, and Veracruz, on the east coast, contribute very small percentages, 0.32 and 0.22 respectively. Probably the reason for the high percentage of emigration from Jalisco, Guanajuato, and Michoacán lies in the fact that conditions there for agriculture are difficult, the land having always been in the hands of a small number of big proprietors. For this reason, the excess population of the prolific *peon* class has been obliged to emigrate periodically. This region, because of its fertility and great production of cereals, and its excess population, has rightly been called the granary and "*peon* purveyor" of Mexico. The same circumstance, in smaller degree, can be said of Aguascalientes, Durango, Zacatecas, and San Luis Pótosi.

From the escarpments and the coasts come the lowest percentage of immigrants, except in those states near the border, Lower California, Sonora, and Tamaulipas, which furnish 0.48, 1.23 and 2.01 per cent, respectively, and Sinaloa, from which the United States is easily accessible so that the percentage there rises to 1.98. The small amount of emigration from the coasts is probably due to the fact that the agrarian problem, so acute in the central plateau and in lesser degree on the northern plains, is much more important in the tropics; therefore there is not an excess population which must emigrate . . .

From 1910 to 1920 (the years of the Mexican Revolution) California continued to develop economically, but the increase in Mexican immigration was not proportionately great, the number 33,694 in 1910, was little more than doubled in 1920, reaching 88,771. This relatively small increase might be accounted for by the fact that the anti-Asiatic campaign vigorously carried on in this period also retarded

Mexican immigration. In Texas, New Mexico, and Arizona the demand for Mexican labor increased proportionately to the development of these states, and the numbers rose to 251,827, 61,580, and 20,272, respectively; that is, the 1910 figures approximately doubled. In Oklahoma and Louisiana about the same relative increase occurred, but in Colorado the 1910 figures were quadrupled, probably because of the great development of mining. In Utah the immigration reached a figure approximately seven times that of 1910, and in Nevada it was almost doubled, as also in the states containing distributing centers, that is, Missouri and Kansas. The demand for Mexican labor was intensified in this period, chiefly for the cultivation of beets, and for industries such as iron, cement, automobiles, and packing houses, in the East and Midwest. In 1920 Mexican immigration was twenty times greater in Michigan than in 1910; ten times greater in Wyoming and nine in Nebraska and Idaho; five times greater in New York, Pennsylvania, and Illinois; and four times in Iowa. . .

With the exception of Maine, Vermont, and North and South Carolina, Mexican immigrants sent money to Mexico during these months from all the states in the American union. These money orders came from 94 American cities of more than 25,000 inhabitants and from 1,147 cities of less than 25,000. This is a total of 1,511 post offices, and represents approximately 4 per cent of the total 36,970 populated centers in the United States. This distribution seems to indicate that a high proportion of the immigrants are engaged in rural labor, in smaller towns and cities, and that a smaller proportion was employed in industrial enterprises. Though it is true that a large number are doing agricultural work, in cities like Chicago, Los Angeles, San Antonio, and in the vicinity of Pittsburgh and of others of similar importance, large numbers of Mexican immigrants are employed in industry. . .

History, Culture, and Education

George I. Sanchez

There are nearly four million persons with Spanish-Mexican antecedents in five southwestern states: Arizona, California, Colorado, New Mexico, and Texas. Most of them speak Spanish and, considering the circumstances, remarkably good Spanish. Although most of them speak English also, it is quite surprising that there are many present-day Spanish-Americans whose families have been exposed to the English language since the American occupation about one hundred thirty years ago, and yet they speak only Spanish. When one compares this situation with that of European immigrants who came to this country much later—Italians, Germans, Poles, and so on— many of whom have lost their original vernaculars, it would seem to indicate an unprecedented cultural tenacity (except for some Indian tribes, the Eskimos, and the Aleuts).

Why have these Americans of Spanish-Mexican back- grounds been so stubborn in relinquishing *their* vernacular? What institutions and forces made this possible? One would expect to find some concerted effort of these people to retain their language, some source of cultural pride. Or, one would expect that the English-speaking dominant group had recog- nized the values inherent in preserving the Spanish language and had instituted programs to that end. That is, one would

George I. Sánchez, "History, Culture, and Education," in *La Raza: For- gotten Americans*, ed. Julian Samora (Notre Dame, Indiana: University of Notre Dame Press, 1966), pp. 1-26. Reprinted by permission of the author.

expect some positive reason—some wise head, institution, or policy that has conserved this cultural resource. Sad to say, the major factor is none of these but a complex of factors that are much more negative than positive. The conservation of the heritage of the Spanish language is an eloquent illustration that it is, indeed, an ill wind that does not blow someone some good! But let us approach the matter with circumspection.

We must understand both the positive factors in the development of the Spanish language, its introduction and perpetuation in this area, and the negative forces that have resulted in the failure to make this population monolingual and English-speaking. The former is, essentially, a matter of tracing historical antecedents; the latter is one of evaluating the failure of the schools in their obstinate persistence to make English the only language of this group. This failure, more than anything else, has preserved Spanish in a bilingualism of a wide qualitative range, although among the disadvantaged classes the Spanish is superior to the English, and there is also a large group of persons of Spanish-Mexican descent whose English is excellent and whose Spanish is very limited or nonexistent.

This dualism suggests that the paper be presented in three parts: first, a historical perspective of the positive features of the process; second, an attempt to evaluate, with historical and other evidence, why the schools have not succeeded in obliterating Spanish as the mother tongue of most Americans of Mexican descent in the Southwest; and third, a brief attempt to blend these two, seemingly disparate parts into a constructive summary. Each part will have a separate bibliography, and except where specific data from a source are quoted or paraphrased, there will be no footnotes.

SPANISH IN SPAIN, NEW SPAIN, AND THE AMERICAN SOUTHWEST

The Spanish language heritage of Americans of Spanish-Mexican descent has many historical, geographic, and ethnic facets, which we will try to present in logical separation in this part of the paper.

Spain and Spanish

We usually think of Spanish as a Latin language, *romance.* It is that, of course, but in some important ways it is not Latin, not even European. Spain has been a cultural cross-roads from the earliest days of recorded history. Prehistoric man, Phoenician, early Greek, Carthaginian, and other early peoples blended their genes and cultures to form the Spaniard that later the Romans and then their conquerors ruled. The languages of the people of Spain received infusions from all of these cultural contacts, especially from the Latin of the Romans. Then came the greatest invasion of all, that of the Arabic-speaking Moslems in 711 A.D.

The "Moors" were in Spain for almost eight hundred years, ruling virtually all of the Iberian Peninsula for a time, until they were slowly pushed southward by the Christian armies. During this long period a remarkable process of acculturation took place. Although at times the conflict was bitter and bloody, there were long periods when Christians, Sephardic Jews, and Moslems lived in comparative peace and tolerance. Cities controlled by the Moslems tolerated the subordinate Christian people; those controlled by the Christians, in turn, tolerated the subordinate Arabic-speaking minority. In both, the Jews played a leading role as businessmen, brokers, financial counselors. The effect of this strange coexistence on the Spaniard—and on the Spanish language—is incalculable. The Sephardic Jews and the Moslems brought to Europe the wisdom of the Middle East, of Egypt, of North Africa. They brought institutions, technologies, value systems, instruments, and formal learning that, blended with what they found on the peninsula, produced the Golden Age of Spain in the fifteenth and sixteenth centuries.

Although the effects of this acculturation are evident in many fields—architecture, religion, agriculture, educational institutions, political science, folklore, value systems, and so on—nowhere is it so clearly revealed as in the Spanish language. Today there are at least 4000 words in Spanish that are not Latin but Arabic. Many of the words for luxuries little known to the Iberian Christians before the coming of the Moslems are Arabic. The finest jewels are *alajas*, pillows are *almohadas*, fine carpets are *alfombras.* Although the Christian could say "Que Dios nos . . ." when he expressed a devout hope, he quickly adopted the Moslem prayer to Allah to the same effect that has become the Spanish word *ojala* ("would that . . ."); this expressing condition contrary to fact, necessarily requires the subjunctive mode. Then there are the words that refer to a process, such as *adobar* ("to conserve"). The word adobe, now a good English word, comes from this verb; and one may have, in Spanish, an *adobe* of meat or of vegetables just as one may have an *adobe* of clay and straw!

There are many other Spanish words that are written and pronounced virtually the same way in Arabic and in Spanish. The words for shoes, for trousers, for neckties, for socks, for shirts, and for many other articles are essentially the same in Arabic as in Spanish. It is not within the scope of this paper to point out the contributions of Visigoths and Greeks, and others, in the formulation of Spanish. Suffice it to note that although the foundations of Spanish are Latin, *romance*, the structure is a variegated one to which many tongues contributed.

Spanish and New Spain

When Spain, in the phenomenally expansive mood of its Golden Age, came to what today is Mexico, it did not come to a wilderness nor to a cultural vacuum. There were millions of people in the area that came to be known as New Spain, people who presented a kaleidoscope of cultures, of languages, and of degrees of civilization. Conservative estimates place their number at ten million, although there are authoritative sources that go far beyond this estimate. . . . Those reveal the wide scope of the cultural attributes of these peoples. More particularly, they reveal the great linguistic variety.

The Maya language, the language of the Aztecs, the languages of the Pueblos, the language of the Otomiés—these and many others differed from each other as much as Chinese differs from English! Peoples living in close proximity spoke vastly different languages. Some, like the Navajos, had linguistic relatives only far away—the closest relatives of the Navajos (and their cousins, the Apaches) were in the interior of Alaska! These variegated tongues have had a tremendous influence in the development of Spanish in this part of the New World. In the three colonial centuries, less than one million Spaniards came to New Spain—one million Spanish-speaking people among ten or more million native peoples who spoke diverse languages.

Also, in New Spain the Spaniard came upon flora and fauna, processes, and customs, for which he had no terminology and so had to accept native designations. Although that strange, wonderful new bird, the turkey, could be described as *gallina de la tierra* (as people in New Mexico still call it), or the Spanish word *pavo* could be used (as it is in some places), it was very easy to fall into calling it a *guajolote*, or a *cócono*, or some other Indian name. In many instances there were alternatives, but what to call a "ring-tail cat"? It had to be *cacomistle* (which now is the proper English word for that beautiful creature). In the nomenclature of birds and animals, regionalism and a great deal of confusion prevail because of the variety of native languages and the application of Spanish names to creatures that were unknown in Spain. So the raccoon is a *tejón* (Spanish for badger) to some, *mapache* to many others, whereas *tejón* is still a badger in places like New Mexico! In many instances, however, alternatives were virtually impossible. A *quetzal* could hardly be called by any other name, nor could a mocking bird (*sinsontle*), although one can stretch things a little and call him a *burlón* (which really means "mocker" and has an unkindly connotation). The names of plants (*mesquite*, for a simple illustration), the names of foods (*nixtamal, tamales, chile, et cetera*), and the names of many objects in Mexican Spanish are Indian. The centuries of contact between the invaders from the Iberian peninsula and the peoples they conquered gave a wondrous flavor to the language of New Spain. It is this well-seasoned Spanish that is the heritage of the Americans of Mexican descent in the Southwest.

The Spanish-Speaking in the Southwest

Spanish-speaking people have been settled in the Southwest for more than 350 years. The villages north of Santa Fe, New Mexico, founded in 1598, are second only to St. Augustine, Florida, settled in 1565, as the oldest settlements of Europeans on the mainland of the United States. The New Mexico settlements, followed a century later by those in Texas and later by those in California, represent a Spanish colonial effort that left an indelible imprint upon the history and culture of the Southwest and the United States. More important, that colonial endeavor left people from California to Texas whose descendants constitute a part of the group we now refer to, very loosely, as Spanish-speaking.

The colonial Hispanos were not culturally homogeneous. The Nuevo Mexicanos, settled in the region as early as 1598, were different from their cousins, the Californios and the Texanos, who arrived much later. The date of migration and settlement, the attendant cultural concomitants, geographic isolation, natural resources, the number and kind of Indians among whom they settled, and many other factors resulted in not one Spanish-speaking people but several, each with distinctive cultures. The outlook on life and the values, the allegiances, the biology, the very speech of these colonial settlers varied greatly; and though all were Spanish-speaking, they can be thought of as different peoples.

Until about the mid-nineteenth century, the Californios, the Nuevo Mexicanos, and the Texanos went their separate cultural ways, held together only lightly by, first, the slender threads of Spain and, later, for a brief time, the uncertain bonds of independent Mexico. The annexation of Texas and the occupation of the rest of the Southwest by the United States changed the course of human affairs in the region, but the change was a slow one, unplanned and haphazard. The United States had not developed the social and cultural institutions to carry out an effective program of acculturation among her new citizens. The new states and territories were left to shift for themselves, with an understandable lack of success. The Spanish-speaking peoples of the Southwest remained Spanish-speaking and culturally isolated—unassimilated citizens, subject to the ever increasing dominance of a foreign culture.

Other things being equal, time alone would have had its influence, and the Hispanos would have become full-fledged English-speaking Americans. However, not only were the social institutions inadequate, but also changing conditions made it impossible for time alone to bring about their assimilation. After 1870 the southwestern scene changed rapidly. The coming of the railroad brought new economic opportunities and made old ones more attractive. The region ceased to be the "Wild West." It became instead a land where minerals and lumber, cotton and corn, cattle and sheep, fruits and vegetables gave rise to new economic empires.

These developments in themselves were not hindrances to acculturation. On the contrary, they should have done much to aid it, just as economic expansion in the East accelerated the Americanization of the heterogeneous masses from Europe. However, in addition to the fact that southwestern developments were based largely in rural life and on the production of raw materials, in contrast to the urban-industrial situation in the East, this area was sparsely populated and, insofar as the "American Way" was concerned, culturally immature and insecure. Worse still, since labor for the new enterprises was not available from the East, the Southwest had to turn to Mexico and the Orient. As a consequence, the region, already suffering from cultural indigestion, added to its troubles by importing thousands of Mexican families, again postponing the day for the incorporation of its Spanish-speaking population.

Even thus enlarged by immigrants from Mexico, the Indo-Hispanic group could have been assimilated had the United States taken time to assess the cultural issues and the increasingly complex socioeconomic problems—particularly those of this ethnic minority. But before 1910 almost no one seemed aware that there were far-reaching issues and problems. Virtually no thought was given to the educational, health, economic, or political rehabilitation of the Hispanos. And after 1910 the opportunity had passed. Until then the issues and problems were still of manageable proportions. They were soon to grow beyond all hope of quick solution.

The Mexican Revolution of 1910-1920 and World War I combined to bring many thousands of Mexicans to the Southwest. Large numbers came as displaced persons, driven across the border by a chaotic civil war. Even larger numbers came as contract laborers, recruited by the trainload to work the beet fields of Colorado, the gardens and groves of California, the railroads of the entire West, the copper mines of Arizona, the cotton fields of Texas, even the iron works of Chicago and the coal mines of West Virginia.

The consequences of this free and easy dipping into the cheap labor reservoir of Mexico are not difficult to observe. What for brevity I choose to call "cultural indigestion" can be documented by health and educational statistics, by pictures of the slums of San Antonio, and by depressing socioeconomic data from all over the Southwest. Suffice it to say that once again the Southwest pyramided problem upon problem, burdening itself with a situation for which sooner or later there would be a costly reckoning.

In a way, World War I served a good purpose. Full employment, good wages, and the educative results of military service stimulated acculturation in the Southwest. However, the issues were much too large and complex to be met adequately by the by-products of war. More research, more planning, and more well thought-out action programs were needed.

The "boom and bust" days of the twenties and the slow recovery during the thirties saw a little alleviation of the socioeocnomic difficulties confronting the Southwest. Thousands of Mexican nationals were repatriated through the joint efforts of the United States and Mexico. However, natural increase soon more than made up for their loss. Then the depression years bred more misery, more problems. During these critical times there was a growing interest in the plight of the unemployed, of out-of-school youth, and of common people in general. This interest was first expressed by state and national surveys. President Hoover's Committee on Social Trends, California Governor Young's Committee on Labor, and the Texas Educational Survey are examples. The "New Deal" reforms helped to relieve some of the most acute problems and stimulated the nation to a greater consciousness of its socioeconomic defects. In particular, more attention was given to studies of underprivileged groups and of cultural and "racial" minorities.

The condition of the Spanish-speaking people in the Southwest was not completely overlooked. Taylor's studies in California and Texas called attention to the plight of the agricultural worker, particularly the migrant Mexican. Manuel, at the University of Texas, was inaugurating educational studies of the Spanish-speaking group. Sanchez was working in the fields of bilingualism and of school finance and administration in New Mexico. Tireman, also in New Mexico, was addressing himself to the teaching problems presented by the bicultural situation. Other researchers concerned themselves with a variety of spot studies.

Some reform measures looking toward the effective acculturation of its population (50 per cent Spanish-speaking) were undertaken by New Mexico in the thirties. These involved far-reaching changes in the sources and distribution of school funds, improvement of public health services, more scientific land use, increased and more effective political action by Spanish-speaking voters. As a result, by 1940 the Spanish-speaking people of New Mexico were more nearly assimilated than those of any other southwestern state.

There were similar improvements during the same period in parts of Colorado, Arizona, and California. Texas, on the other hand, lagged far behind. The educational and health levels of the Texas-Mexican were the worst in the region. There fundamental civil rights were most flagrantly violated. Effective Spanish-speaking leadership was lacking. Conditions of employment and standards of living were woefully low. In a manner of speaking, Texas had become the "horrible example" in the acculturation of Spanish-speaking people. However, there was a growing realization there as elsewhere that none of these states could attain its potential cultural stature until the maladjustments were overcome, and in the last few years Texas has begun to buckle down to the long-postponed task of incorporating the Spanish-speaking one-sixth of its population.

World War II had its good effects also. As in World War I, military service and improved economic conditions gave a great boost to the assimilation of Spanish-speaking people. In addition, largely in response to pressure from Spanish-speaking groups, the federal government began to sponsor programs designed to improve the bicultural situation in the Southwest. More important, Mexico and the United States agreed to regulate the flow of Mexican labor northward across the border.

Whether the two governments realized it or not, this struck at one of the roots of the overall problem. As noted, time and again, just as we have been on the verge of cutting our bicultural problems to manageable proportions, uncontrolled mass migrations from Mexico have erased the gains and accentuated the cultural indigestion. Now, when the entire Southwest is inaugurating large-scale programs of acculturation, the control of Mexican immigration is most necessary. It would be short-sighted and tragic indeed if the two governments were to deviate from this sound path toward acculturation.

The most serious threats to an effective program of acculturation in the Southwest have been the population movements from Mexico: first, by illegal aliens, the so-called "wetbacks," then by the _bracero_ program, and finally by the commuters. . . . Unless we can end the legal or illegal entry of large numbers of Mexican aliens, much of the good work that state and federal agencies are doing will go for naught; much more time and effort and many more millions of dollars will be required to bring Texas and her sister states to a desirable cultural level.

BILINGUALISM IN THE SOUTHWEST: A TRAGI-COMEDY

In trying to assess both the teaching of English in the Southwest to children whose mother tongue is Spanish, and the persistence of Spanish, we are torn between two ways of getting across a basic point: current practice doesn't make sense. One could use the "academic" approach, muster an unassailable array of evidence—historical, experimental, comparative, and the like—and, by prolific footnoting of authoritative sources, make a case for the thesis implied in the heading above. This thesis, that we have been foolish in dealing with the English-Spanish dichotomy of the southwestern cultural reality, can be documented easily. One could with equal confidence appeal to common sense and simple logic, and in plain English, to puncture the balloon that has been blown up with the hot air of "language handicap," the perils of bilingualism and all the other clichés with which educators cover their lack of preparation and understanding. I will use both approaches, emphasizing the former at first and the latter subsequently.

Historical Perspective

The place of vernacular languages in education has been a concern for many centuries. The influence of language development upon personality, the function of language in our thinking process and the implications of bilingualism have occupied thinking men profoundly. The subject is a vast one in which distinguished contributions have been made over a long time.

It is not the shrinking world that justifies the study of foreign languages and demands the conversation of the foreign home-language resources of our peoples; the wisdom of the ages dictates it. The recorded history of foreign home-language in education goes back four thousand years to the time when the Semitic Akkadians conquered Sumer and gradually imposed their tongue, Hebrew, upon the Sumerians.[1] In turn, Aramaic supplanted the old Hebrew language, and just as Sumerian had become a "sacred language" when Hebrew became the vernacular, so Hebrew became the "sacred language" and Aramaic the vernacular. Time after time through the ages a foreign home-language has become the medium of religious instruction as a new language became the vernacular—for Hebrew, Greek, Latin, Arabic; in India, China, Europe, Russia, in our hemisphere; in the spread of Buddhism, Christianity, Judaism; in the Hellenization of Rome, the Latinization of Europe, the Westernization of the Americas; in the rise and fall of imperialistic colonialism—in each of these we find bilingualism in education.

These examples point to the unquestionable value of the vernacular in education, particularly when the mother tongue is not the language of instruction. For further support for our conclusion we can turn to the great thinkers of modern history who have expressed their views on this topic—Juan Luis Vives, Pedro de Gante, John Amos Comenius, John Locke, Johan Heinrich Herbart, John Dewey—and to contemporary psychologists, linguists, and philosophers such as Frank Laubach, who have concerned themselves with the place of foreign languages in education. It is a shock, then, to observe in the schools of the Southwest how violence has been done to the lessons of history and the views of great thinkers.

These make it very clear that in teaching native and foreign languages, we are dealing with more than a twenty-minute period in the daily schedule, with more than superficial sophistication, with more than vocational advantage and financial profit. The works of Vives, Herbart, and Dewey (particularly *How We Think*) show the vital role of language in intellectual development, the overwhelming significance of a child's mother tongue in the process of education in a second language. These factors have been completely ignored in the teaching of Spanish-speaking children in the schools of the Southwest. Herein lies part of the explanation why many of these schools, particularly those of Texas, find teaching English to Spanish-speaking an almost overwhelming task and why their failure is excused by assigning to the child's home-language a deleterious influence upon his educational development.

A quotation from the careful historical study of vernacular languages in education mentioned earlier applies here.

From time to time in education the question has arisen whether a child should be taught in some language other than his native language. In those cases where some language other than the native language has been used as the vehicle of instruction, usually the results, if objectively viewed, were convincing enough from an empirical basis to bring about a change in policy. The effectiveness of using the native language is tied in with the interpenetration of emotion and language. For the preponderent group of children, emotional satisfaction and release accompany the use of the vernacular; while frustration accompanies the use of some other language. Neglect of the native language or, worse still, its suppression is damaging to the morale of the student, and results in rebellion against, or apathy toward the educational process. Especially in the beginning years of school, but later as well, facility in using verbal symbols is essential for facility of thinking. The processes of thought seem to be blocked by the awkward use of the language.

This in no way means that the introduction of a second language, with the goal of developing bilingualism, blocks the processes of thought. Where a second language is introduced at the proper time with sufficient motivation for the student, it might be considered distinctly a potential aid to thinking. The Iliolo experiment has given objectively derived information on the use of the vernacular and the introduction of a second language. The vernacular was shown clearly to have advantages as the language of instruction, and the students, with whom it had been so used, were able in six months of studying a second language, to catch up with a matched control group which had been studying the second language for two years, and using it as the language of learning for all school subjects.[2]

There is much evidence to support the conclusions reached in this historical research. Of telling significance also are the experiments and conclusions of modern psychologists and sociologists.[3] For instance, Maier relates an experiment in which a rat was rewarded with food when it jumped for a certain card and was not rewarded when it jumped for another card.[4] Then the cards and consequences were interchanged, with a resulting sense of failure and frustration for the rat. Maier says, "He soon restrains his tendency to jump, holding himself in a crouching position on the platform in a hopeless or defiant attitude." How many times have I seen this repeated by children with a foreign home-language! How many times have I seen a child cringe and crouch, physically and emotionally, because the language of the home was taboo at school and the language of the school was nonfunctional at home. Here is the genesis of the *pachuco*, the delinquent.

Social psychologists recognize the fundamental importance of esteem in personality formation and motivation. For example, Maslow, in a report on "A Theory of Human Motivation," emphasizes that "Satisfaction of the self-esteem need leads to feelings of self-confidence, worth, strength, capacity and adequacy of being useful and necessary in the world."[5] What can contribute more to self-esteem than the recognition and appreciation of one's vernacular? We all love to be addressed, even if brokenly, *en la lengua que mamamos* ("in the language we suckled," in our mother tongue). So in fiilling the esteem need, as well as in avoiding psychological confusion, the home-language of the child is a highly potent educational instrument. Cheavens, again summarizing, says:

Use of the vernacular languages of minority groups living among people of another language has usually sped up the process of acculturation and made easier the learning of a second language for communication with the majority group. Where this policy has not

*been followed and the vernacular language has been
neglected or suppressed, the result has been a continued
cleavage between the minority group and the majority
group.*[6]

A recent study at McGill University also supported the
idea that bilingualism is highly desirable.[7]

The Southwestern Reality

As stated earlier, this matter of a foreign mother
tongue can be approached in various ways. For us in the
Southwest it is a matter for simple language and simple logic.
Instead of operating in the abstract, we can use our everyday
circumstances as a basis for our convictions about the place of
a foreign home-language in our culture and the value of that
language in learning English. We do not have to defend the
merits of acculturation and bilingualism. We derive much of
our cultural substance from Spanish, a native "foreign" language, a language bequeathed by Cabeza de Vaca, de Niza,
Serra, Zavala, and a host of others. It takes only very elementary research to see how the Spanish-Mexican contribution
undergirds the culture of the Southwest.

Limiting our remarks to Texas, one cannot help seeing
how Texans identify with Spanish-speaking people. The terminology of the cattle country (rodeo, lariat, ranch, remuda),
the place names, the names of people, the every day words
(adobe, amigo, patio), and the customs of daily living all
evidence this acculturation. And all of this is capped by the
satisfaction of those Anglos who are bilingual and those Latins
who know English as well as they know Spanish. The Alamo
is as much a symbol of biculturalism as it is of political freedom. After all, it was a Mexican flag flying at the staff that the
heroes of the Alamo defended. So we in Texas do not consider
the problem of foreign home-language as remote, or of narrow
significance in educational psychology, in curriculum, and in
the teaching process. Foreign home-language is real to us,
and the prospects are just as real.

Contradictorily, because of unfortunate incidents in our past, a tradition of disparagement developed here toward "that Mexican" and all that the term stood for, including language. Along with that, the immature psychology of "speak American" and the defensive provincialism of "despise that furriner" have led to the downgrading of the Spanish language and of those who speak it. Otherwise competent scholars speak of the language of the people of the Southwest as "border Spanish," as a dialect to be avoided. Some, in their ignorance, even refer to it as "Mexican," distinguishing it from Spanish to avoid dignifying it (and ignoring the fact that the Mexican language is *Náhuatl!*).

We extoll the virtues of foreign languages in the development and the achievements of the educated man; we decry their decline in public education; we view with alarm our backwardness when we compare ourselves with the Russians and others; we subsidize the teaching of foreign languages. Yet in the Southwest, one of the world's great languages is suppressed. It does not make sense!

In Texas there are about 300,000 Spanish-speaking children in the public elementary schools, and more than 35,000 in the secondary schools. For only a negligible few of them is Spanish being used as an educational device; and, if they succeed (and many do not) in retaining and developing their home-language, it is not because the public schools have planned it so. What a waste of the assets of the vernacular in education.

Education and Reality

An annotated bibliography on the education of Spanish-speaking people in the United States,[8] although not all-inclusive, lists almost nine hundred items: books, articles, bulletins, and theses. I have been working professionally in this field for more than forty years, and I have been highly critical of our schools' efforts for at least three-fourths of those years; still I was amazed at the persistence of the assertion that bilingualism is bad, that a foreign home-language is a handicap, that, somehow, children with Spanish as a mother tongue were doomed to failure—in fact, that they were *ipso facto* less than normally intelligent.

This sounds like an exaggeration, but these views can easily be documented. For example, in the first draft of a recent handbook for teachers of preschool-age, non-English-speaking children, the Texas Education Agency says, in the second sentence of the introduction, "Solely because of the language barrier, approximately 80 per cent of the non-English-speaking children have had to spend two years in the first grade before advancing to the second."[9] The devastating fact is that Spanish-speaking children in Texas schools *do* spend two or more years in the first grade and then, frequently, more than one year in succeeding grades until in sheer frustration they drop out of school. But to attribute this educational tragedy to the fact that they begin school speaking only Spanish is a gratuitous conclusion not borne out by the history of education in this country or elsewhere. One of the most important facets of the genius of the American school has been that—without distincton as to caste, class, home-language, national origin, and the like—it has been able to process children from all over the world in its normal operations as they become, usually averagely well-educated English-speaking citizens. To excuse the failure of the Texas schools to do the usual job by accusing the Spanish-speaking children of virtually inherent fault reveals a professional blindspot so elementary that it is difficult not to question the professional competence and integrity of the educators responsible. As a result of my protest, the draft of the handbook was changed to read in the published version, "Through no fault of their own, many non-English-speaking children have had to spend two years in the first grade before advancing to the second."[10] I protested that too, of course, for the implication is that the fault lies in the fact that they were born into Spanish-speaking families; this is certainly not admission that the fault lies in the schools! This is pathetically demonstrated when . . . the bulletin suggests that one way of determining who is eligible for the preschool instruction can be discovered by "Noting all eligible children whose names indicate that they are of foreign extraction.''

In Texas, much more than in the rest of the Southwest (though the rest is not entirely blameless), Jim Crowism has extended into the educational system.[11] As late as the 1940's, some school systems segregated "Mexican" children throughout the twelve grades of the public school. This extension has served to blind school people, from those in highest authority to those at the classroom level, to the fact that they have used "language handicap" and "bilingualism" to justify "racial" discrimination and their failure to do the kind of teaching job with these children that the American school has done with hundreds of thousands of other children who were similarly situated. Somehow, too, the political effectiveness of the Mexican-American has been spotty, so that the educational policy in New Mexico (where the Spanish-American has carried political weight for generations) and that in Texas (where political awakening of the Latin-American is just now taking place) have stood out as contrasts. The other southwestern states fall between these extremes, with educational effort reflecting the Mexican-Americans' political effectiveness.

What should be emphasized is that factors other than professional considerations have determined what should be done in the education of Spanish-speaking children. In the process, language and language-teaching have been so distorted that only a resort to common sense and the fundamental principles of the teaching profession can shock us back to the conclusions that the pages of history and the research literature underline.

Much is being made in Texas of the efficacy of summer sessions for non-English-speaking children who will enroll in the first grade in September.[12] It is widely implied that these summer sessions constitute the solution to the perennial and frustrating problem of the child with a "language handicap," and statistics are offered to prove that the majority of the children who attend these summer programs do not have to spend two or more years in the first grade but make the grade in one year (many do not!). It is abundantly self-evident that the extension of good education downward is good for all children and that one should expect children who are fortunate enough to get a preschool preparation for the first grade to make better progress, at least during the first few years, than their less fortunate fellows. It stretches credulity, however, when it is alleged that a few weeks of vocabulary building during the summer can substitute for the extra one, two, or more years that (by implication) a Spanish-speaking child otherwise would have to spend in the first grade!

What is being argued is, in effect, that a forty to sixty day summer session program for Spanish-speaking children is the equivalent of the extra nine months (or more) that the children would have to spend in the regular school in the first grade if they did not have the summer program. There must be something radically wrong with the regular first grade operation if the schools can do in eight weeks (summer) plus nine months (regular year) what, otherwise, takes eighteen or more months of regular school instruction! Why not do the equivalent of the eight-week summer program at the beginning of the regular year? Then, even at worst, one could expect logically that at the end of the first grade the children would be no less than eight weeks short of competence for second grade work—and, of course, hardly proper subjects for the repetition (one, two or more times) of the entire first grade work.

This illogic is repeated in the "Texas Project for Migrant Children."[13] So-called pilot schools have been established, in South Texas, where children of agricultural migrants are arbitrarily segregated from the other children. All of the migrants there are of Mexican descent. There is great pride that the migrant children achieve as much in vocabulary and reading comprehension tests as the children in the regular schools. The fact is that the regular children, on the average, made only .58 of a grade progress per school year in comprehension.[14] Also, in the migrant schools 38 to 45 per cent (or more) of the time is allotted to "English Language Arts," a much higher percentage than in the regular schools.[15] This kind of statistical legerdemain by a state education agency is wondrous to behold.

Although Texas is probably the "horrible example," the other states are not thereby exonerated. One more illustration from the "migrant bulletin": on page 1 the statement is made that "Most of the migrant children are educationally retarded from one to three years." Maybe this is true, but no proof is offered. However, Table V on page 11 shows that, on the average, on the comprehension pretest, the migrants were only .10 of a grade behind the regulars in the second grade; only .05 of a grade in the third grade; .17 of a grade in the fourth; .16 in the fifth; and .43 of a grade in the sixth. Adding the statement above and these figures gives a resounding condemnation of the regular program.

In the only official statistical report of its kind for that state, the Texas Education Agency in 1957 revealed that there were 61,584 Spanish-surname children in the first grade in the public schools of the state, that only 15,490 reached the eighth grade, and that there were only 5,261 in the twelfth grade.[16] Add to this the previously quoted (under-) statement that "Solely because of the language barrier, approximately 80 per cent of the non-English-speaking children have had to spend two years in the first grade before advancing to the second." The statistical evidence is an eloquent indictment of the educational program, which goes far beyond the condemnation of errors that a 40-60 day summer session program in vocabulary building will eliminate or even make much of a dent. No complacency is warranted, and little satisfaction can be derived from the unquestionable good that the summer schools do. Unless drastic reforms are instituted in the programs of the regular schools, the pupil statistics of a few years hence will not be much different from those of 1957—even though, in the meantime, every child were to go to a summer school. The 1960 U.S. Census of Population bears this out.

As has been implied, indictments such as these are not as applicable to the schools for the rest of the Southwest as they are in Texas, but it is not difficult to find illustrations of the same faults in other states. Numerous practices would be funny if they were not so tragic. One school system, by regulation of its school board, required that all children with a Spanish surname spend three years in the first grade. A federal court changed that. A doctoral dissertation proved that Spanish-speaking children who had preschool instruction in English did better in school than those who did not have that advantage. There have been various "experiments" wherein the intelligence of Spanish-speaking children has been "measured" by partially or completely translated tests. One test publisher reports that the company's intelligence test (standardized in English) was administered in Spanish to Spanish-speaking children—without even token recognition of the fact that translation does irreparable damage to the test norms and that the Spanish of the children was untutored (unlike the situation of the English-speaking norm children). Other investigators, proud of their recognition of the "language handicap" of Spanish-speaking children, have chosen to test the intelligence of these children with "nonverbal" tests, overlooking completely that the nonverbal tests are as culturally based as the verbal tests and that neither can test what is not there.

Then there are the teachers who are so impressed with the "inherent" talent of the "Mexicans" in music and art that they beleive this supposed talent explains (and justifies) inferior achievement in less exotic fields—an inferior achievement that is a product not of the "artistic temperament" of the child but of the inadequacy of the educational program. One could mention the remarkably consistent positive correlation between "racial" prejudice and discriminatory practices that have used the excuse that the children had a "language handicap." Again, the federal court cases reveal some of the tragicomedy of the situation. In one case, the parents of a Spanish-name child were very happy that the little girl had to be sent to the segregated "Mexican" school because there she could learn Spanish.

One could go into a lengthy recital of the varied irrationalities that have characterized the "teaching of English" to Spanish-speaking children in the Southwest, irrationalities that have vitiated the thinking of both top-level experts and less "authoritative" workers. Such a recital would serve only a negative purpose. One can do better (with the negative features in mind) by trying to find out ways of doing a better job.

The Ways Out

The lessons of history, the experience of other countries, the dictates of ordinary judgment suggest various ways for the school to approach the education of children with a mother tongue other than that which is the language of the school. A number of these approaches will be summarized.

1. It is virtually impossible to avoid the conclusion that children should be started off in their formal education in the mother tongue. There can be argument as to when the second language should be introduced and to what extent it should supplant the mother tongue, but the evidence is overwhelming that the home-language should be the springboard for the proper development of the second language. This procedure, followed in some countries now and in the past, has demonstrated its merit. However, it has some serious disadvantages in our society. For instance, it would involve the "segregation" of the foreign home-language child, a practice with many features that are not only objectionable but intolerable under our philosophy of the "unitary" school and our denial of the "separate but equal" doctrine. This incompatibility of our way of life with what might be pedagogically ideal leads us to the contemplation of possible compromises or alternatives.

2. The first compromise would be that the mother tongue be used partially in the instruction program. This partial use of the child's vernacular could vary from the teaching of one or more subjects of the curriculum to an occasional and informal use in the everyday relationships between the teacher and the pupil. The advantages to the child with English as a mother tongue are obvious. This would call for teachers who are bilingual and so is not feasible, at the moment,

in many schools of the Southwest. However, the talent potential for large numbers of bilingual teachers is here, and it would require no great effort to recruit Spanish-speaking high school graduates to enter teacher education programs if there were reasonable assurance of employment.

With notable exceptions (New Mexico is probably tops in this regard), the teacher of Spanish-Mexican descent is seldom found in schools where the enrollment is predominantly of the dominant (Anglo) group. Further, that teacher (who is woefully in the minority even in schools where most of the children are Latins) usually is admonished that she must not use Spanish in dealing with Spanish-speaking children. Incidentally, Spanish-speaking children generally are forbidden to use their mother tongue, and it is not unusual for severe punishment to be meted out, even in high schools, if pupils resort to Spanish in their conversation. In a climate of this sort, language teaching and language development go out the window, and the teaching of English becomes bewildering, frustrating, and oppressive to the child, who sometimes rebels violently.

3. There is, as a natural consequence of the above rationale, the possibility that the schools, even without bilingual teachers, could give status to the vernacular of the Spanish-speaking child and employ teachers who would give him a sense of satisfaction and belonging in his accomplishment in the Spanish language and the culture it represents. In a recent publication I offer rules that will help non-Spanish-speaking persons to pronounce Spanish names, words, and phrases correctly.[17] This compromise fits in with everything the authorities in intercultural education advocate. Under this plan, the dominant group child benefits as much or more as does the child in the subordinate group. The procedure would involve only more professional sophistication and could be attained easily if the educators would concede that the schools are dismal failures in the education of Spanish-speaking children.

I am reminded here of the findings of Ginzberg and Bray.[18] They have shown that southern Texas, where the

Spanish-speaking people are concentrated, had an almost unbelievable rejection rate for "educational reasons" during the draft of World War II—a rejection rate that was, in terms of area and population, the worst in the nation, not counting the statistics on Negroes but including those on Indians. If these schools are doing such a poor job for the Spanish-speaking child, they cannot be doing justice even to the English-speaking youngster.

    4. There can be no argument that, speaking generally, the Spanish-speaking child in the Southwest is socially and economically disadvantaged. In health, wealth, and welfare he is at or near the bottom of the scale when compared with his fellow Americans.[19] This offers special challenges to the school, in the teaching of English as in all parts of the curriculum, for any child, regardless of mother tongue. The fact that his state of socioeconomic disadvantage is usually accompanied by a lack of knowledge of the English language is nearly always interpreted as "language handicap," or "bilingualism." As a consequence of this confusion, the school addresses itself to a fruitless hunt into the mysteries of the deleterious effects of being unable to speak English, instead of adapting its program to the requirements of children who are disadvantaged socioeconomically. An ordinarily good school, confronted with the challenge of handicapped children, would give special care to the selection of teaching personnel, would keep class size to a minimum, and would channel more of its special aids and services to them than elsewhere.

    There are various legitimate questions that can be asked about teaching English to Spanish-speaking children. To qualify, should the teacher know Spanish? The answer is, "To qualify, the teacher of Spanish-speaking children should be an unquestionably good teacher." It would help for such a good teacher to know Spanish (to have casual conversation with the child, to talk with parents, to appreciate the problems and virtues of bilingualism), but the important thing is that she be a good teacher and that she be given an opportunity to do her job (reasonable class size, at least average help from her superiors, and the like). If the teacher does not know Spanish, she should at least understand why some of her Spanish-speaking pupils have particular difficulties.

5. The importance of a reading readiness program for children in the first grade is hardly a subject of debate, though one might debate the duration of such a program. For English-speaking children such programs should extend beyond the middle of the first year; this may be a radical position, but let us agree that the English-speaking child should undergo a reading readiness program of six weeks at the beginning of the first grade.

If the English-speaking child, who has been acquiring facility in oral English for six years before enrollment in school, needs a six-week readiness program before starting to read, shouldn't the readiness program of the non-English-speaking child take longer? Should the Spanish-speaking child be expected to be as ready to read with six weeks of "readiness" as the child with six years and six weeks? This is not an argument for having the Spanish-speaking child spend more than one year in the first grade, for his language development is essentially the same as that of his English-speaking fellow student. But he does need extra time, before beginning to read, to acquire facility in the recognition and use of the new linguistic labels. This is not an argument, either, for separating the two groups of children in the first grade. It will not hurt the English-speaking child to extend his readiness program to eight or twelve weeks or more. In the process, the Spanish-speaking child will have a chance to get a good start in the catching up process that should be virtually complete by the end of the third grade. Criteria for judging progress and grade placement should be modified accordingly; for it is with the development and progress of the child that the school is concerned, not with seeing to it that predetermined standards are rigorously met. The assumptions upon which those standards are based are usually grossly inapplicable. Failure to take such matters into account is behind the failure of many schools to do an adequate job for the non-English-speaking child.

The "Teaching of English"

Stated or implied throughout this paper is the conviction that the schools of the Southwest are not faced really with a problem of language handicap, in the fact that large numbers of the pupils come to school speaking little or no English. The issues are not truly linguistic, but rather lie in the areas of social policy, of school organization and administration, of educational philosophy, and of pedagogical competence. There are many thousands of persons in the Southwest whose mother tongue was Spanish, who were socially and economically disadvantaged (that is, who were in the same environmental situation as that of the Spanish-speaking children who fail miserably in many public schools today) and who did "make the grade." To attribute this to the suggestion that "they were different does not accord with statistics on the distribution of intelligence. The fundamental difference between them and their unfortunate fellows was the quality of the school. Good schools—and by this we do not mean anything extraordinary, just good schools as judged the country over—take the "problem" of the Spanish-speaking child in stride. In the others we are confronted not with handicapped children but with handicapped schools.

CONSERVATION OF SPANISH IN THE SOUTHWEST

It should be clear that the retention of the Spanish language by Americans of Spanish-Mexican descent in the Southwest has been the function of default, rather than of any concerted popular or institutionalized effort. The Spanish-speaking whom the United States acquired through the American occupation of the nineteenth century were almost totally illiterate. As noted in *Forgotten People*[20] and in the works of numerous other students, little was done for the Americanization of this population group in the nineteenth century or in the twentieth, for that matter, in some of the areas where the Spanish-speaking population existed in large concentrations.[21]

The educational level of this group is extremely low, as reference to the latest figures of the United States Bureau of the Census will show. One would expect a fairly low level of linguistic proficiency among this population. Oddly enough, but not inexplicably so, their Spanish is of good quality. This is a result in large part of their isolation from the dominant, English-speaking group. In part, too, it is a result of the strange phenomenon that has made Mexico, as Don Federico de Onís once said, the country where, on the whole, the best Spanish is spoken.

The Mexicano, whether in Mexico or in the United States Southwest, has had a flair for the Spanish language, whether he were literate or not. Of course, many in the Southwest fall into barbarisms that are the result of a meager vocabulary, of English-named articles and practices for which there are no Spanish equivalents, and of the almost total lack of formal tutoring in the language. In some parts of the Southwest, as in the mountains of Kentucky and Tennessee, many archaic expressions are still common—for the same reasons in both places, isolation and lack of education.

One could point to the feeble efforts of the Spanish-language press, or to those of organizations of Spanish-speaking people, or to the fact that Spanish is an official language in New Mexico and was widely used in politics and in the Legislature until recent years. Credit is due these, of course, but the fact remains that, in the Southwest, Spanish has been retained as a major language primarily by the default of the institutions of social incorporation. This default, although producing unfortunate results in other spheres, could be turned to tremendous advantage. Some suggestions are made in this paper. Others will occur to those who recognize bilingualism and multilingualism as of great value not only in our relations with the rest of the world, but also in the enhancement of the human spirit, in the development of the highest order of humanism.

1. Sam Frank Cheavens, "Vernacular Languages in Education" (Unpublished doctoral dissertation, University of Texas, 1957).
2. *Ibid.*, pp. 50-51.

3. Bruce S. Meador, "Minority Groups and Their Education in Hays County, Texas" (Unpublished doctoral dissertation, University of Texas, 1959).

4. Norman R. F. Maier, *Frustration: The Study of Behavior Without a Goal* (New York: McGraw-Hill Book Company, 1949).

5. A. H. Maslow, *Motivation and Personality* (New York: Harper and Brothers, 1954).

6. Cheavens, "Vernacular Languages," pp. 516-517.

7. W. E. Lambert and Elizabeth Peal, "The Relation of Bilingualism to Intelligence," *Psychological Monographs: General and Applied*, No. 546, 76, 27 (1962).

8. George I. Sánchez and Howard Putnam, *Materials Relating to the Education of Spanish-Speaking People in the United States—An Annotated Bibliography* (Austin: The Institute of Latin American Studies, The University of Texas, 1959).

9. Texas Education Agency, "Handbook for the Instructional Program for Preschool-Age Non-English Speaking Children" (First Draft, 1960).

10. Texas Education Agency, *Preschool Instructional Program for Non-English Speaking Children* (1960).

11. George I. Sánchez, "Concerning Segregation of Spanish-Speaking Children in the Public Schools," Inter-American Educational Occasional Papers, IX, University of Texas, December, 1951.

12. Louis Alexander. "Texas Helps Her Little Latins," *The Saturday Evening Post*, August 5, 1961, pp. 30-31, 54-55.

13. Texas Education Agency, *The Texas Project For Migrant Children* (1964).

14. *Ibid.*, p. 11.

15. *Ibid.*, p. 4.

16. Texas Education Agency, *Report of Pupils in Texas Public Schools Having Spanish Surnames, 1955-56* (August, 1957).

17. George I. Sánchez and Charles L. Eastlack, *Say It The Spanish Way* (Austin: The Good Neighbor Commission of Texas, 1960).

18. Eli Ginzberg and Douglas W. Bray. *The Uneducated* (New York: Columbia University Press, 1953).

19. United States Bureau of the Census, *U. S. Census of Population: 1950*, Vol. 4, Special Reports, Part 3, Chapter 6, "Persons of Spanish Surname" (1953); United States Bureau of the Census, *United States Census of Population: 1960*, "Persons of Spanish Surname," Final Report PC(2)-1B (Washington. D. C.: U. S. Government Printing Office, 1963); Robert H. Talbert, *Spanish-Name People in the West and Southwest* (Fort Worth: Leo Potishman Foundation, Texas Christian University, 1955).

20. George I. Sánchez, *Forgotten People* (Albuquerque: University of New Mexico Press, 1940).

21. George I: Sánchez, "The American of Mexican Descent," *The Chicago Jewish Forum*, 20, 2 (Winter), 1961-62).

BIBLIOGRAPHY

Gilberto Cerda, Berta Babaza y Julieta Farías, *Vocabulario Español de Texas*, University of Texas Hispanic Studies, Vol V. (Austin: The University of Texas Press, 1953).

Ernesto Galarza, *Strangers in Our Fields* (Washington, D. C. Joint United States-Mexico Trade Union Committee, 1956).

Galarza, *Merchants of Labor* (Private publication: 1031 Franquette Street, San Jose, California, 1965).

Charles F. Marden and Gladys Meyer, *Minorities in American Society*, 2nd ed. (New York: American Book Company, 1962).

George I. Sánchez, *Mexico—A Revolution by Education* (New York: Viking Press, 1936).

George I. Sánchez, *Forgotten People* (Albuquerque: The University of New Mexico Press, 1940).

Carey McWilliams, *North from Mexico* (Philadelphia: Lippincott, 1943).

II / PROBLEMS

In this second part an overview of some of the major problems confronting Chicanos is provided in Herschel T. Manuel's selection "The Case in Brief." As he sees it the Chicano is handicapped by a number of interlocking factors. For example, we can begin with the language problem. Since the Chicano child is raised in a Spanish-speaking household, he is handicapped when he begins his education in a school in which the instruction is in English. Not only must the child learn the subject matter, he must also learn the language through which the subject is taught. This simultaneous task would be difficult for mature adults; it is all but impossible for the elementary school pupils. The education-cycle thus sets in: the Chicano pupil drops further behind the English-speaking students and never catches up. In the process he develops a sense of inferiority because he is not as "good a student" as his English-speaking counterpart in class. When his deficiencies in school are attributed to his race, he develops a sense of shame in himself and his heritage. Next, he seeks employment in a job market where there is a diminishing need for raw labor, his only marketable commodity, and he is not surprised to find himself engaged in menial jobs. It is Manuel's hope that a more sensitive approach toward the Chicano's problems by the country's educational systems will break the cycle described above.

George L. Farmer has formulated a proposal which he believes should be used as a starting point for educational reforms designed to assist Chicano students to take better advantage of their formal educational opportunities. His reforms go beyond the confines of the classroom and involve what he calls "recommendations to society." The specific recommendations in themselves are not as important as the recognition that significant educational reform must include the society outside the classroom.

The problem of residential segregation in the urban Southwestern United States is examined by Joan W. Moore and Frank G. Mittelbach. Using a variety of statistical techniques they develop an index of residential segregation for thirty-five cities. Their classification of cities by levels and order of segregation is important because it reveals high levels of residential segregation of Spanish-surnamed people from Anglos in Dallas, Fort Worth, Denver, Houston, Los Angeles, Lubbock, Phoenix, San Antonio, and Tucson. Equally important is the finding that there are low levels of segregation in Colorado Springs, Galveston, Laredo, Oakland, Pueblo, Sacramento, and San Jose. It is evident that there are both high and low levels of residential segregation found in the same states: Arizona, California, Colorado, and Texas. Comfort from these findings will be found by both Anglos and Chicanos— the former because they can "prove" that residential segregation is declining in the urban Southwest, and by the latter because they can "prove" that residential segregation exists, even if at low levels, in some cities of the Southwest.

Paul Bullock, using census aggregate figures, demonstrates that Chicanos in the United States have found the greatest employment opportunities in the blue-collar, skilled and unskilled labor fields. He argues that many American employers have "long regarded the Mexican population (domestic and foreign) as a source of cheap and 'dependable' labor."

The dogmatic classification of Chicanos as menials by prospective employers has created a self-fulfilling prophecy relative to their employment. Since employers view Chicanos as laborers, they hire them for only those kinds of positions and then aruge that Chicanos are "natural" laborers.

Bullock notes that one reason Chicanos have made little progress in broadening their employment horizons is because their labor movement has frequently been divided against itself. He states that "Fragmentation and internecine warfare have rendered many Mexican-American groups impotent." It may be that an improvement in this area has been made since the time Bullock wrote, but data to that effect are not overwhelming. Indeed the following selection argues that Chicano farm laborers still are at a tremendous disadvantage relative to employers in spite of the gain in that area of employment made by César Chávez's organization in California.

* struggling within a group

Donald Janson in an article written for *The New York Times* notes that in many parts of the country "farmers may violate minimum wage, health, housing, immigration and child labor laws without fear of losing the services of the federally funded, state-operated farm labor offices that recruit seasonal workers for them." This selection was included in this portion of the book to illustrate that seven years after the Johnson administration declared its war on poverty few battles have been fought that benefit Chicano laborers. One can thus understand why some Chicano leaders have become cynical about what they can realistically expect from "the establishment."

The final selection of Part II is potentially the most significant, for it deals with the question of ethnic assimilation of Chicanos into the dominant Anglo culture. Frank G. Mittelbach and Joan W. Moore using data drawn from Los Angeles offer some tentative conclusions about the rate Chicanos in that city are assimilating through marriage to non-Chicanos. Briefly, their data permit them to speculate, cautiously, that Chicanos, particularly the women, are marrying non-Chicanos in significant proportions in Los Angeles. The authors are understandably reluctant to overgeneralize from their data, which they characterize as sparse, but they do hint that there is a significant assimilative process by marriage at work in the United States.

The factors they believe are most conducive to marriage outside the ethnic group include age, sex, and generation. Immigrants from Mexico (first-generation ethnic group members) are the least likely to marry outside their group. The most likely to marry outside the group are young third-generation females.

These conclusions, albeit highly tentative, are intriguing for they suggest that despite Chicano rhetoric, young Mexican-Americans are assimilating at a rate that is impressive. While lip service is being paid to *la raza* by increasing numbers of Chicano leaders, many of their young compatriots are apparently rejecting *la raza unida* (the united people) by marrying outside it. One could paraphrase Lenin here and state that many Chicanos are voting for assimilation with their bodies. What impact this movement toward assimilation will have on the total Chicano Movement is impossible to predict. Yet it does hint that the supposed "gap" between the Chicanos and Anglos is in many instances more verbal than real. The answer will not be forthcoming, if it is to come, for at least a generation.

The Case in Brief

Herschel T. Manuel

The population of the five states of the Southwest consists primarily of two intermingling groups, Spanish-speaking and English-speaking, with smaller but significant numbers in other groups. Together they face the task of building and maintaining a democratic society with benefits and responsibilities which are shared by all. The task is not easy anywhere, but it is especially difficult in the Southwest because of differences in language, culture, and economic status, and because of antagonisms deeply rooted in the past.

As a matter of both individual rights and public welfare, the people are committed to a policy of education for all children. The democratic process demands educated citizens. Even actual survival as a great nation requires careful attention to human resources. Education is equally vital for individual welfare, for only through education can latent possibilities be realized. The primary concern in this book has been the problem of educating Spanish-speaking children.

THE HEAVY HAND OF THE PAST

Until recently, as history goes, the English-speaking people and the Spanish-speaking people of the world have been rivals in the strife for economic welfare and political power and at times even enemies in battle. The struggle for

Herschel T. Manuel, "The Case in Brief," in *Spanish-Speaking Children of the Southwest* (Austin: University of Texas Press, 1965), pp. 186-195. Reprinted by permission of the publisher.

position in the New World at the time of its discovery and colonization continued in one form or another for centuries. The Spanish-speaking people were the first of the two groups in the territory which became the Southwestern states, coming into this area from what is now Mexico. In time the spread of the English-speaking people from the north and east reached the Southwest, and they rapidly became the majority group in the region as a whole. First the Texas Revolution, then the annexation of Texas, then the war between the United States and Mexico, and finally the purchase of a small strip of land changed the Southwest from being a part of Mexico, with its Spanish language and Spanish-Indian culture, to being a part of the United States, with its English language and North European culture. But the transfer of national sovereignty did not change the nature of the populations. The problem of building the two groups into a united community remained. Only the direction of the movement was changed. The task had been to assimilate English-speaking people into a Spanish-speaking, Mexican community. With the change in national sovereignty the Spanish-speaking people had to become part of an English-speaking nation. More than a century has passed and the people of the Southwest, both English-speaking and Spanish-speaking, are still struggling with the problem.

The solution to the problem of building and maintaining a democratic society in the Southwest cannot be found in a kind of federation of Spanish-speaking and English-speaking states. The representatives of the two cultures live together, not in districts from which separate states can be carved. To be sure, in some communities and subcommunities there are concentrations of population which are almost wholly either English-speaking or Spanish-speaking, but in larger units the peoples are inextricably mixed. Even in smaller sections segregation is breaking down, though not nearly as fast as would serve the common welfare.

DIFFICULTIES OF SPANISH-SPEAKING CHILDREN

Cultural differences and enmities inherited from the past tend to keep the two peoples divided, but the most serious

enemy - hatred - rivalry

handicaps to building one society out of these diverse elements and the most troublesome problems in the education of Spanish-speaking children are those of language and of low economic level, with its accompanying cultural deficiencies.

There are extreme differences in the Spanish-speaking population as the term is used in this report. Some members speak only English and some speak both English and Spanish, but for most of the group, English is still to be learned as a second language. Again, some Spanish-speaking people are wealthy, and many are of the middle class economically. Likewise, many are of superior cultural level. The great majority, however, are of the lower economic levels, and a large number have the cultural traits associated with long-continued poverty. Additions to the original population by immigration from Mexico in this century have in overwhelming proportion been persons of relatively low economic status and cultural level. Spanish continues to be the home language of most families because of the nearness to Spanish-speaking Mexico, because of constant migration across the border, because of social pressures exerted by the older members of the population, and because of the inherent difficulties of establishing new language habits.

In general, Spanish-speaking children at school entrance have more to learn: a second language and also the knowledge and skills of which they have been deprived by poor home opportunities. They cannot start their schooling at the level already reached by English-speaking children. Starting behind and facing greater handicaps, the Spanish-speaking children tend to fall farther and farther behind with advance in grade. The progress of many is hindered by poor attendance resulting from the poverty of the home and the ignorance of their parents. Many find the going too hard, in part because the school program is not adapted to their needs, and drop out when age permits them to do so. There are exceptions to this trend; many make satisfactory progress, and a large number are even outstanding.

The difficulties of Spanish-speaking children extend beyond the learning of a second language and the acquisition of knowledge. It is difficult also for them to develop normal interests, healthy emotional habits, and helpful patterns of action. Some observers would refer to this problem as one of emotional and social adjustment. Every child faces hazards to his mental health, but the hazards of large numbers of Spanish-speaking children are almost overwhelming. They are caught in the conflict of two groups and two cultures in the same community. As they try to find a place in the larger community, they are often criticized by their own people and rejected to some extent by others. If not rejected, at least they have no easy way to establish the associations which would lead to acceptance. Many of them have no adequate mastery of either the Spanish or the English language. The Spanish of their culture-deprived homes is adequate for little more than basic community associations, and their English lags behind, often far behind, that of others of their age level. Large numbers of these children are unable to compete on an equal basis with other children in material possessions, in the social status of their families, and in that part of their school work which depends heavily upon experience and mastery of English. The poor quality of their spoken English handicaps them in securing employment. Even those who rise above these handicaps and those who have never been so handicapped are sometimes confronted by an attitude which tends to overlook individual merit. This of course is unjust, but it is a reality. Finally, the Spanish-speaking child shares the historical antagonisms and attitudes of his family.

PERSONALITY DEVELOPMENT

These difficulties tend to produce abnormalities of personality and behavior which are in themselves undesirable and which interfere with learning. For one thing there is a feeling of insecurity. The child is not comfortable, and he cannot give his full attention to learning activities. Then there is frustration and disappointment, often resentment. Sometimes a child who cannot face his real deficiencies finds an escape in blaming the other group, developing a chip-on-the-shoulder attitude which may continue through adult life. In his thinking, it is the prejudice of others, not his own deficiencies, which seems to stand in his way. Another child becomes submissive, overwhelmed by failure. He gives up and quits struggling. He *assumes* the inferior position which the less fortunate of his group seem to occupy, and he accepts the inferiority which others unjustly ascribe to him. In his own thought, feeling, and behavior he puts himself in an inferior position. He feels that there is nothing much ahead for him; and because of this feeling, not because of actual inferiority, there probably is not anything very inspiring in his future. One of the great problems of the school and the community is to prevent discouragement, to inspire hope, and to stimulate the development of normal traits of personality.

The tendency of many to think too much of their own misfortunes rather than to give undivided attention to the situations with which they must deal leads toward defeat. A vicious circle is created: a person's attitudes work against accomplishment, and resulting failures increase his maladjustment. Participation in the larger community is hindered by antagonisms developed in his home and nourished by his own experiences. Sometimes the maladjustment takes the form of antisocial behavior and in extreme cases, of actual delinquency.

HELPING CHILDREN WITH THEIR PROBLEMS

The solution is easy in principle: remove as far as possible the conditions which handicap the children, provide educational opportunities adapted to their needs, and help them develop normal personal and social traits in spite of the extreme difficulties with which they must deal. In practice, none of these is easy, but there are definite things which can be done. Many of them in fact are being done in various places —slowly to be sure, but, in the testimony of educators and other observers, progress is being made.

First and foremost as a prerequisite to progress is a dedication to the principles of democracy and a firm will to educate all children. Despite our ready affirmation of democratic principles, there are still many who give consideration to very little beyond the welfare of their immediate group. They are almost totally blind to the fact that even their own welfare is intimately tied to the welfare of all. Many also do not realize that the world is changing. They cling tenaciously to the old familiar ways and resist even constructive change. To meet this situation powerful leaders are needed within the subgroups, leaders to help the people see their problems more clearly and to move ahead more rapidly.

Compulsion may enforce legal rights, and sometimes it challenges people to new ways of thinking, but much more is needed. To bring about fundamental changes of thought and feeling, to inspire a new consciousness of the brotherhood of man, to create an awareness of how the democratic ideal may be realized—all of these call for the aggressive leadership of persons of prestige and vision.

As the Spanish-speaking and English-speaking people of the Southwest continue to intermingle and to live under the same environmental influences their cultural differences will become less and less. People will become more tolerant of the differences which remain, and it is to be hoped that in the conflict of cultures the best aspects of each will survive. Historical antagonisms will diminish with increased understanding and with participation in common tasks.

The improvement of general economic conditions will be a long-term process, depending on many factors and requiring the cooperation of agriculture, industry, and government. Fortunately, there are enough materials and human resources to support the population at a high level. The economy in the United States is clearly moving upward, and it is moving upward also in Mexico. But progress should be speeded up and adjustments made which will achieve a better distribution of the fruits of common effort. Here again leadership is needed.

Although language is becoming less of a problem as more and more children learn English at home, it is still a major difficulty with thousands of children. Because of migration and because of nearness to a Spanish-speaking nation, there is no likelihood that the language problem will disappear at any time which can be foreseen. The tragedy is that the Spanish-speaking group handicaps its own children to the extent that it refuses or neglects to help teach them English. Hearing only Spanish at home, the children enter school with a handicap, and continuing to hear only Spanish at home they fall farther behind in their unequal struggle with an English-speaking environment.

EDUCATIONAL ADJUSTMENTS

One of the greatest single steps which the public can authorize the school to take—a step which many schools have already taken—is to extend its work downward to the five-year-old child, with a program skillfully directed, in the case of Spanish-speaking children, toward the teaching of English, and toward building up basic experiences and concepts for those who come from culture-deprived homes. A summer program preceding enrollment in the first grade helps, but it is not enough. Five hundred English words are better than none, but they are not equivalent to two or three thousand. Three months can add something to a child's experience, but they cannot make up for six years of privation. For that matter, neither can nine!

The Spanish language is an asset of Spanish-speaking children which should not be wasted through neglect. At some point in their lives these children should have an opportunity to become literate in their spoken language. To provide such an opportunity requires careful and realistic planning. It should be realized that only the more able and those with unusually favorable opportunities to learn the two languages in a natural setting may be expected to develop a high level of ability in both English and Spanish. For most children there simply is not enough time in the school day and in the years which will be spent in school to learn two languages to a high level of efficiency and at the same time learn the other things which life in the modern world demands.

It is possible for overanxiety about learning a language to hinder the learning process itself by robbing it of content. Language grows out of the need for communication, and drill which is normal and necessary can easily be dull and barren when it has no other motive than learning forms which are said to be correct.

The general objectives and problems in the education of Spanish-speaking children are precisely the same as they are for all children. All need an opportunity to develop their capacities and to become useful and productive citizens. Like other children, Spanish-speaking children are widely different among themselves. The special problems of the schools they attend arise from the large numbers who must learn English as a second language and who must be instructed in other fields of study in this second language, from the large numbers who are of low economic level with its accompanying deprivations, from certain differences in cultural traits, and from the fact that the Spanish-speaking and English-speaking people are as yet imperfectly united in a single cooperating community. It is to meet these conditions that the schools need to mould their policies and programs.

Schools need all the devices which can be accumulated to give children who are learning English more contacts with spoken and written English than the teacher can provide in the class period. Filmstrips, tape recorders, television, interesting reading material suitable for different degrees of learning are of inestimable value. Television programs skillfully designed, presented with the help of children, and broadcast at out-of-school hours could help a whole community.

Many children need help in securing adequate food, clothing, and school supplies. In a well-organized community, various agencies can share this responsibility, but in some places the school itself must become a relief agency as well as an educational institution. Whatever the source of aid, one of the central problems is to give it in such a way that it will not damage the child's self-respect or tend to perpetuate and increase his dependency.

The satisfaction of material needs is only part of the problem. The school must adjust its program to large numbers of children who have had less than normal opportunity to learn outside of school. At the same time it must make provision for extreme differences in capacity. The ideal in the development of human resources is to provide such opportunities that the only factor limiting the development of a child will be his capacity. At every level of ability obstacles to progress must be removed, opportunities for learning provided, and children guided in making the most of these opportunities. Efforts to help the slow learner should be balanced by a "Project Talent" which will rescue gifted children whose progress is now hindered by unusual difficulties and by discouragement.

The education of the migrant child presents special problems which can be met only by the cooperation of school, home, employer, and related community agencies. Although there is hope for a lessening of the need of migratory labor through automation and the development of opportunities for year-round employment in a given community, the migration of agricultural laborers to and from areas of peak employment will continue to create major social and educational problems for many years.

MODERN SCHOOLS FOR A MODERN WORLD

So much is at stake in the education of children that no one should be satisfied with less opportunity than a modern world can provide. "Opportunity" implies buildings, equipment, and materials of the kind which will make educational effort most productive. It is not enough that children be enrolled, housed, and taught without prejudice. Equal treatment may also be inferior treatment for all.

Even more important in the educative process is the professional staff: those who administer, supervise, teach, or engage in the special services which modern education requires. The devotion and professional competence of the staff determine in large measure the kind of school which a community will have. It is a heavy responsibility to interpret the needs of children, to provide appropriate learning opportunities for them, to help them overcome difficulties, to inspire them to do their best, to lead them toward happy and effective living, and to prepare them for citizenship.

COMMUNITY SUPPORT

The kind of schools which a community has is a responsibility of the whole community—local, state, and national. The community must provide the material support and the climate in which superior schools can flourish. Since a child learns from his total environment, the community owes it to its children not only to provide excellent schools but to maintain out-of-school conditions which will be favorable to growth in intellect and character. All the institutions and agencies of a community are part of the teaching environment and thus influence what children learn. In addition to this incidental teaching, many give direct assistance to the schools or conduct educational activities of their own.

The home occupies a unique place in relation to the school and is an educational agency in itself. There the child gets his start in language and in knowledge of the world. There he develops his basic emotional trends. There he is given support or denied it as he makes his way through the school. There his future is profoundly influenced in many ways. Whatever makes the home a better place for children contributes to education.

The church shares with the home the primary responsibility for religious education. Often also it conducts a significant program in general education. Its ministry to physical and economic needs improves the educational opportunity of many children. Its teaching of the brotherhood of man is a powerful influence toward friendship, sympathy, and cooperation.

The government of a community is responsible for the organization and support of public schools as well as for many other activities which serve the general welfare. These activities may include, as in Denver, a definite program for the promotion of understanding and cooperation among the people of different groups.

Parent-Teacher Associations, luncheon clubs, and other voluntary organizations add to the educational resources of a community. Their contribution includes cooperation with schools, promotion of interest in education, cultivation of understanding and good will, and assistance to individuals who need help. Such organizations can make one of their best contributions to education and to the community by including both English-speaking and Spanish-speaking persons in their membership and demonstrating effective cooperation in their own activities. The climate of understanding and good will developed in this way will spread to the larger community and will be reflected in the relations of children in and out of school.

The school itself can be a laboratory in which children prepare for a better community. In such a laboratory both the activities in which the children engage and the climate in which they work are significant factors in such preparation. The fifth grade of a semi-rural school which was visited in California provided an impressive illustration of this point. Of the thirty pupils enrolled, seven were from Spanish-speaking families. The class was working on a unit of study dealing with the colonists of New England. "These people," the memorandum which was given to the visitor recorded, "came with an ideal of personal freedom, both social and religious. As such an ideal inspired and nurtured a concept of complete democracy, it will also develop a deep appreciation and understanding of our democratic way of life." The class was engaged in varied "laboratory" activities, some of which obviously were designed to give a background of experience for their study. A few of the children were dipping candles and in that group was a little girl who seemed to express the spirit of all. It was near Christmas, and as she was dipping her candle she was singing softly "Silent night, holy night."

A FINAL WORD

The education of Spanish-speaking children is a problem of concern to all, English-speaking and Spanish-speaking alike, and all share the responsibility for dealing with it effectively. It is partly a technical problem for the educator who must find and apply better ways of dealing with children handicapped by differences in language, culture, and socioeconomic status. It is partly a problem of obtaining support for research and for the practical work of the schools. It is partly a problem of strengthening the constructive forces of the community. It is partly a problem of developing a better economy.

But it is more than these. The education of Spanish-speaking children is part of the problem of building and maintaining the democratic society to which the nation aspires. It is part of the worldwide problem of building communities, nations, and international organizations in which persons and groups of different origin, language, and culture will participate on an equal basis for the common welfare. The isolation of many centuries developed group differences which tend to keep peoples of different heritage apart, but migration has brought them together, and modern transportation has made all the world neighbors. The problems of living together must be solved or our civilization will perish. There is no choice.

Education

George L. Farmer

The biggest problem to date in the Mexican-American community is that of education. It can be said without generalizing too much that whatever progress in education and community consciousness has been achieved, can be attributed to (1) the Mexican-American becoming realistically aware of his non-acceptance in American society, as the majority in the community will; (2) not accept him as a bonafied citizen with all its attributes; finding personal dignity and worth in his ethnic and cultural background, sacrificing immediate ethnic integration and assimilation by excelling in education and the professions.

In most schools the educational program is directed toward the Anglo student, who has a minimal language and cultural problem and has completely ignored the Mexican-American (who has a maximum language and cultural problem) in that the life of the Mexican-American is molded by the stark reality of living in two worlds: a cultural dichotomy not touched or tapped by the actual methods in curricula construction. This, in part, accounts for the low intelligence scores as typical tests are not adapted to language differences or differing cultural backgrounds. Teachers, counselors, and administrators often tend to categorize the Mexican-American as, at best "a vocational pupil, unfitted for academic training."

George L. Farmer, "Education," in *Education: Dilemma of the Spanish Surname American* (Los Angeles: University of Southern California, 1968), pp. 43-48. Reprinted by permission of the author.

The 1960 census showed that, on the average, the Mexican-American student had completed fewer years of school than any other group in the Los Angeles area. He averaged less than a ninth grade education (Table 12). In metropolitan Los Angeles, ten per cent had less than four years of school. The drop-out rate in two Los Angeles senior high schools, predominantly Mexican-American, averaged 18.6 per cent in the 1961-1962 school year compared with an average of 9.8 per cent for all the schools.

RECOMMENDATIONS TO SOCIETY

The plea throughout this writing has been for constructive long-range planning. The schools can no longer function as an isolated unit, or continue to carry on practices based on tradition; formulate its program, or much less fill its role as an educational institution for the bicultural community, under the present "all or none" concept as an educational philosophy.

It is, therefore, *first* strongly recommended that educational philosophy, theory, and practice, in order to be better equipped to guide and direct Mexican-American youth and fulfill the complex needs arising from a bicultural life, should:

1. Incorporate intelligently the sociological process of acculturation, diffusion and assimilation.

2. Embrace a functional theory of culture and culture's relation to the growth of human personality.

3. Establish within the existing educational objectives a positive corollary by means of which the Mexican-American society can be made a smoother and a far more stable process.

Second, it is strongly recommended that the purposes of education in American democracy, as defined by the Educational Policies Commission in 1938: (1) self-realization, (2) economic efficiency, (3) human relationships, and (4) civic responsibility to be fully implemented.

1. To strengthen the underpinnings of these principles and make the acculturative process a smooth and more stable process, the following concepts are offered as imperatives:

Table 12

*Median Years of School Completed by Spanish-Surname
Persons of 25 Years and Over, Compared with Other
Population Groups in 35 Metropolitan Areas, 1950 and 1960*[a]

Standard Metropolitan Statistical Area	1950 Total pop.	1950 Spanish-surname	1960 Total pop.	1960 Anglo Anglo	1960 Spanish-surname	1960 Non-white	Schooling Gap 1960(%) Spanish-surname	Schooling Gap 1960(%) Non-white
Abilene	10.1	n.a.	11.7	12.0	4.0	8.8	67	27
Albuquerque	11.7	7.7	12.2	12.5	8.7	10.9	30	13
Amarillo	11.3	4.7	12.1	12.2	8.1	9.5	34	22
Austin	10.9	3.5	11.7	12.3	4.4	8.6	64	30
Bakersfield	9.9	6.5	10.8	11.4	7.3	8.5	36	25
Beaumont-Pt. Arthur	9.7	7.0	10.8	11.7	8.7	7.1	26	40
Brownsville-Harlingen-San Benito	6.3	2.7	7.9	12.3	3.9	9.5	68	23
Colorado Springs	11.7	8.4	12.3	12.4	10.1	12.1	19	2
Corpus Christi	9.4	3.2	10.1	12.2	4.5	8.0	63	34
Dallas	11.0	4.4	11.8	12.1	6.4	8.6	47	29
Denver	12.0	8.0	12.2	12.3	8.8	11.4	28	7
El Paso	9.2	5.2	11.1	12.4	6.6	11.7	47	6
Ft. Worth	10.7	5.4	11.4	11.9	7.7	8.7	35	27
Fresno	9.8	5.6	10.4	10.7	6.1	8.8	43	18
Galveston	9.4	4.9	10.3	11.3	6.9	8.3	39	27
Houston	10.4	5.2	11.4	12.1	6.4	8.8	47	27
Laredo	6.1	5.2	8.7	n.a.	5.4	n.a.	n.a.	n.a.
L.A.-Long Beach	12.0	8.2	12.1	12.3	8.9	11.1	28	10
Lubbock	11.0	1.7	11.6	12.1	3.1	8.3	74	31
Midland	12.1	1.8	12.4	12.6	3.7	8.8	71	30
Odessa	10.4	3.9	11.4	11.8	4.6	8.8	61	25
Phoenix	10.6	5.3	11.6	12.1	6.1	8.5	50	30
Pueblo	9.1	6.3	10.2	11.0	8.1	9.2	26	16
Sacramento	11.3	7.9	12.2	12.3	9.1	10.9	26	11
San Angelo	10.2	2.9	10.7	11.5	4.0	8.0	65	30
San Antonio	9.1	4.5	10.0	12.1	5.7	9.4	53	22
San Bernardino-Riverside-Ontario	10.9	6.7	11.8	12.1	8.0	9.8	34	19
San Diego	12.0	8.1	12.1	12.2	8.9	10.7	27	12
S.F.-Oakland	12.0	8.9	12.1	12.3	9.7	10.2	21	17
San Jose	11.4	8.0	12.2	12.4	8.3	12.0	33	3
Santa Barbara	11.8	7.0	12.2	12.4	8.3	9.9	33	20
Stockton	9.1	7.2	10.0	10.7	7.5	8.2	30	23
Tucson	11.2	6.5	12.1	12.3	8.0	7.8	35	37
Waco	9.4	2.9	10.3	11.0	5.5	8.2	50	25
Wichita Falls	10.3	4.5	11.4	11.7	6.3	8.7	46	26

[a]No data for the Spanish-surname group are available for 2 of the 37 metropolitan in the Southwest, which are omitted, and no non-white data are available for one of the areas shown in the table. Sources: 1950 U.S. Census of Population.

a. Accept the [reality] of the Anglo-Saxon and Hispanic ethnic as they exist in the Western Hemisphere. They
have been meeting and throwing circles of influence over
one another in the southwest, creating a permanent and
perpetual historical cultural continuum through the movement of people.

b. This cultural buffer area forms the framework for
the process of acculturation affecting both groups, from
which emanates the subconcepts; the culture within a culture concept, and the function of the school having to
perpetuate the national core of values, traditional and
emergent.

c. Within this framework any "long or short term
goal" educational program to be effected has to be based
on the values, traditional and emergent, of the Anglo and
the Hispanic communities, together with the needs of all
individuals, including ages, abilities, interests, cultural
differences and socio-economic status. This is the motivation, the "glue" that will hold the problem together.

d. Embrace a functional theory of culture and its
relation to the growth of human personality and investigate
how such a person adjusts to the demands of the two cultures (bilingual in the true sense), and the proud inheritor
of both the Anglo Saxon and Hispanic traditions, thus per-
mitting greater social mobility, participation and acceptance
as a useful citizen to his community and the nation. This
entails a broader acceptance of the acculturation process
as an educational concept.

Third, it is highly recommended that the school-
community idea be given greater depth in meaning and better
purposes in implementation. These two entities have long been
goemetrical parallel lines; lines which never meet to explore
and exploit their potential.

1. The creation of a core of counselors to serve as
liaison workers between school and community, establish and
supervise programs in which the leadership of both school
personnel and community are to be utilized to a maximum.
Wherever possible these counselors should be bilingual, espe-

cially where the demand for Spanish exists as the communication and problem function.

Fourth, to strengthen cultural awareness and self-
image.

1. Spanish should be taught as early as possible on
the elementary level and coordinated with the English program
and made a "must" or a strong elective for non-academic
students in the junior and senior high schools.

2. Units on History, Literature, Art, Music, regional
dress and foods concerning Spain, Mexico and other Latin-
American countries should be developed in the present courses
in Social Studies, Home Economics, and Art, not only for the
purpose expressed above, but also to create a more informed
general citizenry.

Fifth, establish a definite and specific program for
compensatory education with the objective of supplementing
the normal education effort and preparing the Mexican-
American child to compete and achieve within the existing
education program.

1. Such programs whether in the elementary, junior
high, or senior high school, should have continuity as determined by:

    a. local needs and

    b. stipulations made by the Federal and State
authorities.

2. These programs can be extensive and costly as the
"Higher Horizon Program" in New York City, or smaller target
areas can be selected involving the community, curriculum
guidance, counseling, attendance, and tutorial areas as specific projects.

3. These projects can be constructed and written up
as a result of interaction at workshops within local schools, or
recommended directly by school personnel (Curriculum Director, School Psychologist, Principal, Vice-Principal, Teacher,
Nurse, Attendance Counselor) acting as a team.

4. While it is recommendable that such programs be
made available for the elementary, junior high and senior high
schools, it is strongly recommended that a great deal of con-

centrated effort be placed within pre-school, the elementary, and junior high schools. . . (Editor)

5. Promising educational practices already in effect within the local schools affecting Curriculum, Counseling, Guidance and School-Community relations may be expanded. For example, *The Handbook for the Los Angeles City Schools*, and other school districts could be utilized for ideas. A survey of these practices should be made and constructed, with permission, into a similar handbook.

Sixth, the total concept of education as to philosophy and program described above can certainly be extended and implemented in the area of adult education.

Seventh, it is strongly recommended that the potential leadership in the various schools as well as the community be utilized to effect any program within the district.

1. In-service training for teachers and community leaders is recommended, preferably in small groups with the technique of the workshop at its best.

2. Utilize panels, speakers, and seminars for this purpose, correlating any effort with compiled materials in a kit containing historical, socio-logical, and statistical materials, and recommendations as to philosophy and programs.

Eighth, develop continuing flexible programs of testing, guidance, and counseling which will permit the discovery as early as possible of the potential and creativeness of each child, the identification and development of the academically able student, the so called "slow gifted," and the culturally different child, motivating him toward definite educational goals, thus preventing him from becoming misplaced within the school as to ability and interest and thus becoming a dropout.

Ninth, expanding and modernizing the vocational program of the comprehensive high school so as to give adequate acceptability and adaptability to a technological changing community.

Tenth, in reference to community relations and communications it is urged that bulletins be developed which are more meaningful to the general public and more interesting in format especially when they are intended to be sent home, and that, Spanish on a communicative level be used in the appropriate areas.

Eleventh, recruit, hire, and place bilingual teachers who have an understanding of the Mexican-American child and his community.

Twelfth, consultants should be utilized to the fullest extent to:

1. Aid school personnel set-up projects; and

2. act as consultant for such, for teachers' in-service training and in-service training for community leaders.

Thirteenth, recruit, hire, and place counselors, bilingual or not, who have an interest, an understanding, a potential success ethic, patience, and the desire to get away from simply "stamping" programs.

Fourteenth, recruit, hire, and place counselors who are available to tell truths! The counselors should/must be the "cutting edge" in an improved-program plan. They should/must be the authority; neither the teacher nor the principal is able to individualize sufficiently to meet the counselor's "need"—the counselor must be available.

Fifteenth, encourage, recruit, and hire young, and older, Mexican-Americans to become educators. Presently, in a group that constitutes 8-10 per cent of the California population, the educator "image" for the Spanish surnames have _no_ administrators and _one_ to _two_ teachers, at best. Yet, they must stay in school and become educated.

RECOMMENDATIONS TO TEACHERS*

. . . The greatest limitation facing today's teacher of the Mexican-American student is lack of knowledge of the student's culture and background. . . . Many Mexican-American students are the descendants of an agrarian folk culture and, as such, have developed in a home where the parents have a reluctance to change, a limited experience in civic affairs, no real sense of social responsibility, a limited experience in handling money, a *lack of need for organization, and an attitude that encourages strong individualism. . . . Mexican-Americans are generally non-competitive. Competition is not in keeping with traditional folk values. The individual is all-important. . . . Many Mexican-Americans students are in conflict with traditional values and attitudes; therefore, they are in conflict with their parents. . . . These students question not only their identity but also their adequacy, for they are relegated to the position of second-class citizens by many members of the dominant society; as a result, they may develop hatred toward both groups. . . . These students find themselves straddling two cultures; (the Hispanic and Anglo) therefore, they have questions about their true identity. . . . The large number of Mexican-American students who are monolingual when they enter school are taught English by teachers who have no awareness of the student's native language or of the principles involved in teaching them English as a second language. . . . These youngsters are subjected to the values and mores of their teachers who generally come from a culture which is quite foreign to them. . . . Mexican-American students are not generally competitive yet they are expected to measure up against criteria which do not take into account their culture or heritage. . . . Most Mexican-American youngsters reflect a tight patriarchal family. . . . Most Mexican-American children grow up hearing and seeing the practice of two basic philosophies which underlie the entire social, economic and educational structure of their world. These philosophies are constantly offered in such expressions: "Dios dirá," (literally, God will tell; or it is in the hands of God); and "Hay mas tiempo que vida" (literally there is more time than there is life). . . . that these students will respond to a reward given as soon as the job is completed. (Teachers should evaluate, grade, and return students' work as soon as possible). . . . Analysis reveals the student carrying by himself the burden of scholastic achievement. . . . The Mexican-American youngster wants the valued recognition of his parents and teachers. Unfortunately, neither of these sources offers the reassuring reaction; the response is one of negation, denial, disapproval. His parents cry "¡No somos así!"—We are not like that! The teacher declares, "No, you are not right. You look wrong. We do not accept you." Ironically, the disapproving teacher is a representative of the alien community which has forced into being this unacceptably dressed and groomed individual. For the Anglo school itself is an enclave into the Mexican-American community. It judges, it imposes, it demands: seldom does it approve or understand; rarely does it channel or guide these youngsters seeking their unique identities. In terms of values unfamiliar to him and dominant over him, the Mexican-American teenager is deemed inferior.*

. . . Mexican-American students, in some areas, using the negative denotation, are growing up and developing in what they call "Barrios," what we call ghettos. . . . Mexican-Americans who are born in the ghetto or who come to live there at an early age grow up understanding that this is their section, their part of town. Many reach their adolescence without ever having left their section of town. . . . The fear of unfamiliar surroundings is transmitted to the young people who in many cases refuse to leave the ghetto for any reason, as do the "old folks." . . . Our work has revealed that Mexican-American students are burdened by a language handicap which is far more subtle than of intonation, accent or usage. . . . They do not have the ability to communicate or to reflect confidence and self-assurance in their speech or appearance. . . . First impressions are still the great determiners of whether a young person is suitable for a job. . . . The Mexican-American youngster, not aware of what is expected of him often presents himself in clothes and hair-do that do not support the worth of the ability or skill he possesses. . . . Job candidates must have poise and carriage which connote self-confidence and assurance. . . . Mexican-Americans fail, in too great num-

---

*This entire section was abstracted from two excellent articles written by Luis F. Hernandez, a Consultant on the Oral English Project of the Los Angeles City School Districts' E.S.E.A., Title 1, program. The entire coverage is in the *Journal of Secondary Education* (February 1967). pp. 59-65 and (March 1967), pp. 123-128.

bers, to respond successfully here. They do not know how to answer personal questions; they do not know the answers and if they know them they are reluctant to answer them, particularly in front of non-family members. . . . Mexican-Americans fare no better in written examinations. Many businesses give some sort of writing test, which vary in form or degree of difficulty, and contain a section on vocabulary. Some Mexican-American candidates find the instructions an insurmountable task, do not read them thoroughly, under-read, mis-read, try to guess, and then give up in despair even though time and analysis would prove that they really know the answer. . . . The interviews and tests expect the candidate to demonstrate his initiative and sufficient aggressiveness to make decisions. For a Mexican-American youngster such demonstration is most difficult. His is a patriarchal environment where the father is the ultimate authority. The father makes all the decisions. The young man must submit, until he attains a position of authority in the family unit. . . . Rejection is one of the most damaging blows that can be dealt to a youngster who is weak in self-image. . . . It therefore becomes essential that in any classroom where a majority of the students are Mexican-American that a teacher must develop, within the established curriculum, a program meaningful to children of the majority group, not only in terms of the world in which they will eventually live, but also in terms of the world in which they already live. . . . The recommended approach to these children is the positive one. The teacher should not criticize or minimize, should not place value judgment on these students' means of seeking status, whether they be language, dress, or mannerisms. . . . The essence of the matter is that a teacher must identify with the individuality of each student in terms of Mexican culture. . . . Knowledge of the Mexican culture should indicate to the teacher that these children respond best to a disciplined situation, with overtones of formality. . . . A matter which could lead to complete breakdown of communications between the teacher and his students is the "embarrassment" of the child by the teacher. . . . When a teacher finds it necessary to discipline by heaping guilt on a youngster, he should never do it in front of the youngster's peers. . . . The solution to the teacher's problems is a broad understanding of the student's background and culture, accompanied by a specific appreciation of the individual student's place in that heritage. . . .

Measuring Residential
Segregation in 35 Cities

Joan W. Moore and Frank G. Mittelbach

Residential segregation means simply the separation of two or
more subpopulations. But segregation implies more than mere
physical distance; it implies social distance between those
populations. Social distance is not invariably accompanied by
physical distance: in some cities of the South, for example,
Negroes and whites live on the same block, the Negroes living
in the poor alley housing once reserved for slaves and the
whites occupying the old mansions. But in most American
cities, where social distance between subgroups is not so
thorouhgly embedded in all social institutions, residential
segregation reflects the realities of social distinctions.

There are some societies in which social distance
between populations has no negative connotations. These distinctive subpopulations may indeed occupy "separate but
equal" housing. This is not the case in the United States. Here,
social distance, whether expressed physically or otherwise, is
usually accompanied by social deprivation. Segregated ethnic
areas tend to be low-income areas with poor housing, reflecting
the generally subordinate position of large proportions of the

*By "all others" is meant nonwhites and persons of Spanish
surname.

Joan W. Moore, Frank G. Mittelbach, "Measuring Residential Segregation in 35 Cities," in *Residential Segregation in the Urban Southwest* (Mexican-American Study Project, Advance Report 4, Los Angeles:
Graduate School of Business Administration, University of California,
1966), pp. 15-22. Reprinted by permission of the University of California.

ethnic group. Chapter IV presents an analysis of some such correlates of residential segregation. In this chapter we will examine the patterns of segregation found in 35 central cities of the Southwest and discuss some of the processes leading to these patterns.

ANALYSIS OF INDIVIDUAL CITIES

Residential segregation is measured here by an "index of residential dissimilarity" (D).[1] The index ranges in value from 0 to 100. Crudely, a score of 0 means that there is no segregation of a subpopulation from the other—that the members of both populations are randomly distributed throughout the city. A score of 100 means that the two populations are totally segregated—that all of the members of each population are concentrated in separate areas. These indexes were calculated from Census tract data from the 1960 Census of Housing and Population. . . .

Table 2 shows the index scores for each of the 35 central cities included in the analysis. The first three columns present the segregation of the dominant Anglo white population—first from all others* in each city, and then from each of the two major minorities separately, Mexican-American and Negro. The data indicate that in every city, without exception, Mexican-Americans are less segregated from Anglos than are Negroes. In other respects, however, the table highlights sharp differences in the extent of segregation of various populations and wide variations from one city to another. For example:

1. Segregation of Anglos from all others ranges from a low of 39 in Laredo, Texas to a high of 83 in Dallas, Texas.

2. Segregation of Spanish-surname persons from Anglos ranges from a low of 30 in Sacramento, California to a high of 76 in Odessa, Texas.

3. Segregation of Negroes from Anglos ranges from a low of 57 in Pueblo, Colorado to a high of 94 in Lubbock, Texas.

The lack of uniformity is even more apparent when we examine the segregation of minorities from each other, shown

Table 2

Indexes of Residential Dissimilarity for 35 Southwest Central Cities, 1960

City	Anglo vs. All Others[a]	WPSS[b] vs. Anglo[c]	Negro vs. Anglo[c]	WPSS[b] vs. Negro	WPSS vs. Other NW[d]	WPSS[b] FB vs. NB[e]
	1	2	3	4	5	6
1. Abilene, Texas	68.3	57.6	85.1	55.7	64.8	28.1
2. Albuquerque, New Mexico	53.0	53.0	81.7	62.4	34.9	26.2
3. Austin, Texas	62.9	63.3	72.1	66.1	69.9	9.5
4. Bakersfield, California	72.4	53.7	87.7	61.4	49.3	24.6
5. Colorado Springs, Colorado	55.4	44.8	74.0	53.8	32.6	50.5
6. Corpus Christi, Texas	73.7	72.2	91.3	51.0	46.9	13.2
7. Dallas, Texas	83.2	66.8	90.2	76.1	63.4	23.9
8. Denver, Colorado	64.9	60.0	86.8	68.0	39.9	32.9
9. El Paso, Texas	52.9	52.9	79.2	59.5	52.8	17.9
10. Fort Worth, Texas	74.8	56.5	85.4	78.1	58.8	29.7
11. Fresno, California	64.4	49.0	92.0	55.2	38.8	19.5
12. Galveston, Texas	58.1	33.3	73.8	52.1	42.3	10.8
13. Houston, Texas	73.2	65.2	81.2	70.9	52.1	14.0
14. Laredo, Texas	39.3	39.4	60.1	43.9	44.7	12.7
15. Los Angeles, California	68.7	57.4	87.6	75.7	50.3	23.8
16. Lubbock, Texas	74.4	66.0	94.4	89.0	65.8	16.3
17. Oakland, California	60.0	41.5	72.2	56.4	40.5	21.0
18. Odessa, Texas	81.8	75.8	90.5	29.2	68.2	11.8
19. Ontario, California	52.6	50.6	80.1	32.6	44.3	27.0
20. Phoenix, Arizona	62.8	57.8	90.0	60.7	40.6	21.6
21. Port Arthur, Texas	81.7	45.9	89.7	76.3	50.3	26.6
22. Pueblo, Colorado	39.9	40.2	57.0	44.1	44.5	39.4
23. Riverside, California	67.7	64.9	80.8	45.6	48.9	33.8
24. Sacramento, California	39.5	30.2	61.9	47.8	38.8	31.4
25. San Angelo, Texas	67.2	65.7	77.5	75.6	70.6	12.9
26. San Antonio, Texas	63.7	63.6	84.5	77.4	49.9	17.0
27. San Bernardino, California	70.6	67.9	83.5	35.2	44.6	20.9
28. San Diego, California	55.9	43.6	81.1	55.2	34.6	27.5
29. San Francisco, California	46.8	38.1	71.5	65.9	60.0	18.8
30. San Jose, California	42.5	43.0	64.7	44.4	42.7	17.0
31. Santa Barbara, California	48.6	46.5	76.7	37.6	9.8	17.8
32. Stockton, California	59.3	52.6	73.0	31.0	39.8	22.0
33. Tucson, Arizona	63.9	62.7	84.5	64.1	39.0	18.2
34. Waco, Texas	65.7	59.7	74.3	60.6	53.4	20.7
35. Wichita Falls, Texas	76.8	64.8	86.1	47.6	67.8	30.8

[a]White persons of Spanish surname plus nonwhites
[b]White persons of Spanish surname
[c]Anglo whites, i.e., whites other than Spanish surname
[d]Nonwhites other than Negroes
[e]FB—Foreign born; NB—Native born

in columns 4 and 5 of the table. This is a very important, though largely neglected issue in most discussions of minorities. In a few cities, Mexican-Americans are less segregated from Negroes than they are from other non-whites, but in most places the reverse is true. Of course, the composition of the "other nonwhite" population differs from one area to another: it is predominantly Indian in Arizona and New Mexico, and predominantly Oriental in many California cities. In many parts of the Southwest, the "other non-white," together with the Mexican-American population formed the bulk of cheap labor supply. In various places, Mexican-Americans established symbiotic, economic, and other special relationships with these "others:" In Tucson and Albuquerque, for example, with the Indians,[2] in Phoenix with the Chinese merchants,[3] and in Los Angeles County with the Japanese. In most places in the region, Negroes are relative late-comers compared with these other minorities. The table shows that:

4. Segregation of Negroes from Spanish-surname persons range from a low of 29 in Odessa to a high of 89 in Lubbock.

5. Segregation of Spanish-surname persons from other nonwhites ranges from a low of 10 in Santa Barbara to a high of 71 in San Angelo.

Finally, the table shows the segregation *within* the Mexican-American minority—the foreign-born from the native-born persons of Spanish surname.

6. Intra-minority segregation of foreign-born from native-born persons of Spanish surname ranges from a low of 9 in Austin to a high of 50 in Colorado Springs.

Students of the Southwest will recognize that this last type of segregation reflects not only a generational split but an intra-minority cultural dissimilarity. The cultural differences are much sharper than the split between generations. We found in further analysis that a *high* order of segregation (dissimilarity index) is associated with a *low* proportion of foreign-born and with a low rate of increase in the Spanish-surname population. Thus, the highest 'Ds' emerged in two

Colorado cities of our universe of 35 cities and the lowest appeared in the cities of south Texas.

The Spanish-surname population of northern New Mexico (not included in our set of cities) and southern Colorado consists predominantly of the descendants of persons who settled in this area before 1848. More recent immigrants from Mexico (such as workers in the beet and melon fields of eastern Colorado) often met hostility from these older "Spanish-Americans." The higher 'Ds' in Colorado cities may well reflect this cultural rift. On the other hand, the lower 'Ds' in the cities near the Mexican border probably reflect the fact that little if any generational cleavage has developed. Mexican-Americans living in border cities seem to visit Mexico a great deal on a routine basis, and Mexicans come to the U.S. side with equal ease. This probably tends to reduce any sense of distance between Americans of Mexican descent and the Mexican-born.

SEGREGATION PATTERNS

A more systematic analysis of the variation in these indexes is presented in Table 3, which shows both the average scores for each type of segregation and the average variability in the scores.

Table 3

Indexes of Residential Dissimilarity (D) for 35
Southwestern Cities, 1960: Means and Standard
Deviation for All Cities

	Mean D	Standard Deviation
Anglo-white vs. all others	62.5	12.2
Anglo-white vs. Spanish-surname	54.5	11.4
Anglo-white vs. Negro	80.1	9.5
Spanish-surname vs. Negro	57.3	15.1
Spanish-surname vs. other nonwhite	48.4	12.9
Spanish-surname foreign-born vs. native-born	22.6	8.7

These data express in more condensed form observations drawn earlier from the vast array of figures in Table 2 and permit generalizations obscured by the wide range of variations from one city to another. Anglo segregation from Negroes is higher on the average than segregation of Anglos from the total non-Anglo population, and it is substantially higher than their segregation from Mexican-Americans. Also, the variability around the mean of segregation of Anglo-whites from Negroes is quite small compared to the other indexes.

Further, Table 3 shows a general pattern of inter-minority segregation. The segregation of Mexican-Americans from Negroes is greater (though more variable) than the segregation of Mexican-Americans from other nonwhites. Segregation of Mexican-Americans from Negroes is also slightly greater on the average than the segregation of Mexican-Americans from the dominant population, though far more variable.

Is the segregation of one population systematically related to the segregation of another population in the same city? Yes and no. As Table 4 indicates, segregation of Mexican Americans from Anglos is highly correlated with segregation of Negroes from Anglos across the 35 cities, that is, where one minority is highly segregated, the other is likely to be highly segregated also. Neither one, however, is very highly correlated with inter-minority segregation—that is, segregation of Mexican-Americans from Negroes. In contrast to what might be observed in a few isolated cases, the extent of a minority's segregation from the dominant group has little to do with the extent of its segregation from another minority. Negroes and Mexican-Americans do not necessarily form one big ghetto where either or both are separated from Anglos. nor do they necessarily separate into possibly hostile or competing ghettos where one or both are segregated. Finally, with respect to intra-minority segregation—of foreign-born from native-born persons of Spanish surname—there tends to be an insubstantial but inverse correlation with the other forms of residential segregation.

Table 4

Simple Linear Correlation Matrix Comparing Segregation of Various Subpopulations from One Another, 35 Southwest Central Cities, 1960

	1	2	3	4	5	6
	(Items are the same as for numbers in rows)					
1. Anglo-white vs. All Others	1.00	.83	.76	.38	.53	-.12
2. Negro vs. Anglo-white		1.00	.67	.38	.24	-.10
3. Spanish-surname vs. Anglo-white			1.00	.20	.50	-.24
4. Spanish-surname vs. Negro				1.00	.38	-.08
5. Spanish-surname vs. Other Nonwhite (excl. Negroes)					1.00	-.25
6. Native-born vs. Foreign-born Spanish surname						1.00

Further inspection of the original array of scores in Table 2 suggests still other ways of viewing the data. Generally speaking, the segregation scores for the three principal types of segregation were found to rank as follows: the highest is that of Negroes' segregation from Anglos; the second highest is that of Mexican-Americans from Negroes; and the lowest score is that of Mexican-Americans from Anglos. This pattern exists in 26 of the 35 cities. It probably indicates the overall ordering of social as well as residential distance between the three subpopulations, in which Anglos and Mexican-Americans are generally closer to each other than either group is to Negroes, and Negroes are less remote from Mexican-Americans than from Anglos.

In 9 of the 35 cities, however, there is a different ordering of the indexes. In this second group of cities, Negroes' segregation from Anglos also scores the highest, but the second highest segregation score is that of Mexican-Americans from Anglos, and the lowest is Mexican-Americans from Negroes. The two minorities—Negroes and Mexican-American—are both relatively highly segregated from the dominant Anglos, but not from each other.

These differences call for further analysis. The patterning of relationships between the minorities and the dominant population is distinctively different from one type of city to another. These differences seem to indicate that the minorities affect each other's chances for residential and other mobility. In other words, if we want to understand the Mexican-Americans' residential segregation we must look not only at Mexican-Americans' cultural and economic position in each city, but also at that of the Negroes. It seems likely that the processes producing segregation—especially of Mexican-Americans—differ in the two types of cities discussed. And it is likely that the consequences of segregation are different as well.

Though there are too few cities for elaborate analysis, we have classified these two types of cities into further subtypes (Table 5). In these subtypes we have tried to take account of the level of segregation in addition to the order of each type. Thus, if the score for segregation of Negroes from Anglos is above the mean, we call it "high"; if it is below the mean we call it "low." The type HHH means that all three major types of segregation scores are above average, and LLL means that all three scores are below average.

This new arrangement of the data shows that, generally, cities of second type where Mexican-Americans and Negroes are relatively unsegregated from each other are middle-sized or smaller communities. Almost all of them—6 of the 9—fall into one type—HLH—in which segregation of both minorities from Anglos is above average, while their segregation from each other is below average.

The large number of cities where Mexican-Americans are more segregated from Negroes than they are from Anglos present much greater diversity. This group includes not only all of the very large communities in our study but smaller cities as well. Most of the larger cities are of type HHH, in which all three types of segregation are above average. Nine cities are in this category. However, an almost equally large number, 7, are in LLL type. This order of segregation scores tends to prevail irrespective of the levels of segregation.

Little is known about the general images of these cities held by members of the minority groups. It is clear that certain

Table 5

Classification of Cities by Level and Order of Segregation

Level of Segregation*			Order of Segregation	
Negro vs. Anglo	Spanish-surname vs. Negro	Spanish-surname vs. Anglo	Spanish-surname more segregated from Negroes than from Anglos	Spanish-surname more segregated from Anglos than from Negroes
H	H	H	Dallas, Ft. Worth, Denver, Houston, Los Angeles, Lubbock, Phoenix, San Antonio, Tucson	None
H	H	L	Albuquerque, Bakersfield, Port Arthur	None
H	L	L	Fresno, San Diego	Ontario
H	L	H	None	Abilene, Corpus Christi, Odessa, Riverside, San Bernardino, Wichita Falls
L	H	L	El Paso, San Francisco	None
L	H	H	Austin, San Angelo, Waco	None
L	L	H	None	None
L	L	L	Colorado Springs, Galveston, Laredo, Oakland, Pueblo, Sacramento, San Jose	Santa Barbara, Stockton

*The designations H and L in columns 1, 2 and 3 indicate whether the level of segregation is above (H) or below (5) the mean.

cities are known as particularly "bad" for Mexican-Americans or Negroes, and other cities are known as relatively "good." There seems to be a general, though not perfect relationship between the minority image of the city and the pattern of segregation present in the city. Exploratory interviews suggest that many highly segregated cities tend to have a bad reputation among minority group members for many other reasons in addition to residential segregation. The HLH cities also seem to have a bad reputation. These are the towns where the minorities are more or less in the same boat, and remote from the dominant Anglos. Several such communities have a recent history of inter-minority conflict. It may well be that the ecological situation indicated in this pattern represents a distinct factor in the generation of inter-minority tensions. However, the task of relating our subtypes of cities more systematically to their reputations among various minorities and to the prevalence or absence of conflict must be left to future research.

In this chapter, we have presented an overview of residential segregation in the Southwest. We have discussed the segregation of several ethnically distinctive populations, focusing on the three major subpopulations—Anglo white, Mexican-American, and Negro. In sum, segregation of these populations from each other is not random but follows general patterns throughout the region, with special variants. We have attempted to formulate a typology of cities in which the major variations in segregation patterns are embodied. Finally, we have suggested that the overall life of minorities reflects and is reflected in the particular pattern of segregation in each city, and that this special quality finds expression in each city's reputation among the minority.

1. This index was developed by the Duncans and utilized in Otis Dudley Duncan and Beverly Duncan, "Residential Distribution and Occupational Stratification," *American Journal of Sociology*, LX (March, 1955), 493-503.
2. Harry T. Getty, "Interethnic Relationships in the Community of Tucson," University of Arizona, unpublished Ph.D. dissertation, 1950, Department of Anthropology.
3. Discussion with the late Rose Hum Lee, a Phoenix sociologist of Chinese descent, sketched the occasionally hostile relationships between the two ethnic groups.

Employment Problems of
the Mexican-American
Paul Bullock

The appearance of this article in a symposium on minorities and employment is perhaps symbolic of the changing and expanding role of the Mexican-American in our society. It is unlikely that even as late as a decade ago, a journal editor would have considered the Mexican-American worthy of such attention. An appalling and almost universal indifference to the problems of this group has been reinforced, until recently, by the general inaccessibility of data on employment, educational, and the cultural patterns of Americans of Mexican descent. Only in 1950 did the Bureau of Census initiate a consistent series of reports on the "Spanish surname" population, a category which only approximates the Mexican-American totals for the five southwestern states. The few researchers toiling in this area have been lonely and isolated.

The lack of knowledge and information concerning the Mexican-American population is all the more remarkable in view of its size. In California, Mexican-Americans outnumber other "minority" groups (including Negroes and Orientals) by a substantial margin. A total of 1,426,538 white persons of Spanish surname lived in this state in 1960, compared with 880,486 Negroes and 159,545 Japanese. The pattern within

Paul Bullock, "Employment Problems of the Mexican-American," *Industrial Relations*, vol. 3, no. 3 (May 1964), pp. 37-50. Reprinted by permission of the Institute of Industrial Relations, University of California, Berkeley, and by the author.

the Los Angeles metropolitan area is essentially the same, with Mexican-Americans outnumbering Negroes by about a 3 to 2 margin. Negroes in Texas numbered 1,185,476 while the Spanish surname population totaled 1,417,810. Yet this vast group seemed obscure or at least remote to most Anglos until recent events forced a degree of recognition (Table 1).

The reasons for this neglect are not always clear. It is likely, however, that forces within both the Anglo and Mexican-American communities are responsible. Many Anglos, and many Mexican-Americans, have never regarded the urbanized Mexican-American as being "disadvantaged" in any significant way, though most would concede that the lot of migratory farm workers is less than ideal. In Southern California particularly, an aura of sentiment, history, and romance has often surrounded the Mexican-American population, effectively obscuring the realities.

Urban Mexican-Americans with the lowest levels of income and education and the highest rates of unemployment are usually concentrated in ghettos (barrios) where they are hidden from the sight of their more prosperous Anglo and Latin compatriots. Financially successful Mexican-Americans situated in other parts of the community and well integrated into the larger culture, do not identify with the disadvantaged and evince, a best, only a token concern with their problems.

Perhaps a critical reason for community insensitivity to Mexican-American problems lies in the traditional inability of the Mexican-Americans to organize into effective political and economic groups. Many other minorities have secured a redress of their grievances through a skillful use of votes and economic strength, but cultural factors, among other things, have heretofore prevented the Mexican-Americans from achieving the unity required for organizational effectiveness. Individualism and distrust of organizations (even of government itself) are characteristic of the Latin community.

Even the relative advantages enjoyed by this minority —for example, less intensive housing discrimination—have conspired to weaken its political cohesiveness, since the absence of overt repression and the greater dispersal of the

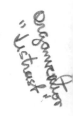

to show or demonstrate; manifest; prove

Table 1

Distribution and Growth, Spanish Surname and Negro
Population, Five Southwestern States, 1950 and 1960

	1950		1960	
State	Spanish surname	Negroes	Spanish surname	Negroes
Arizona	128,318	26,298	194,356	43,585
California	760,453	462,576	1,426,538	880,486
Colorado	118,131	20,198	157,173	39,827
New Mexico	248,880	8,423	269,122	17,109
Texas	1,033,768	977,458	1,417,810	1,185,476
Totals	2,289,550	1,494,953	3,464,999	2,166,483

Sources: *Persons of Spanish Surname*, U.S. Census of Population: 1960,
Final Report PC(2)-1B; and *Nonwhite Population by Race*, U.S. Census
of Population: 1960, Final Report PC(2)-1C.

population reduce the possibility of bloc voting which could
command respect for the group's demands. Growing political
awareness, however, is one of the most striking changes now
in process throughout the Mexican-American communities of
the Southwest.

It is impossible to describe the role of the Mexican-
American in the labor market without giving attention to some
of the cultural forces which influence him. The Mexican-
American, especially the youngster, is in a sense a person between cultures, neither fully a Mexican nor fully an "American." He is asked by many of his Anglo associates to reject
the cultural heritage of his family, a demand which places
overwhelming (and, in the author's judgment, unnecessary)
psychological pressures upon him. The predominant values of
Anglo society come into conflict with many of those which
characterize the Mexican culture.

Economists have rarely focused on the relationship of
cultural values to employment patterns, probably because most
regard this as a sociological problem and therefore out of their
jurisdiction, but it is certain that the model of a coldly rational
income-maximizing worker, so familiar in economic theory,
bears little resemblance to reality. Values and motivations differ from one person to another and, a fortiori, from one culture

to another. In the case of the Mexican-American traditional values have been strongly influenced by a folk or rural culture in which organized and continuous striving for future monetary gains plays little part. Satisfaction of present wishes and needs tends to take precedence over long-range planning which requires immediate sacrifices.

This pattern of living, particularly among the poor, involves a mixture of individualism and family unity which leaves little room for an interest in the community. Youngsters have a primary obligation to the family and its welfare, which often requires them to leave school early and contribute to the family's support. Little concern is expressed for those large and impersonal factors which are of critical importance to the urbanized Anglo: law, government, politics, social organization.

If ever in the native culture there is frequent suspicion of hostility toward social institutions such as government, the police, and the schools, and if there is a deep conviction that those institutions "belong" essentially to other persons and other classes, those feelings will be exacerbated in an alien culture. The overt and subtle discriminations against Mexican-Americans, the expressed antagonism to Mexican culture, the prohibitions in schools and elsewhere against the speaking of Spanish, the assignment of Mexican-Americans to low-level jobs, and the callous exploitation of the unskilled and the uneducated to serve the economic interests of particular employers have only served to heighten the alienation of the Mexican-American.

In addition, the male has traditionally played the dominant role in the Mexican family. Machismo—the expression of masculinity and male dominance—can lead to an emphasis on physical strength and a suspicion of an interest in education as unmasculine. Occupations requiring muscular prowess may have greater appeal than those associated with intellectual effort. Women are actively discouraged from participating in community activities or taking jobs usually identified as male jobs. All major decisions are left to the male members of the family.

However strong these influences may have been in the past, there is evidence that an acculturation process is now taking place which is infusing the Mexican-American family structure with many "Anglo" characteristics and is, in turn, increasing the awareness by Anglos of the needs and contributions of the Mexican-Americans. The role of the Mexican-American woman may be changing. Available statistics suggest that more and more Mexican-American women are employed in traditionally male occupations, that the emphasis on education is increasing drastically, and that women are assuming a more active role in both family and community affairs.

Perhaps of greatest significance, there is a growing willingness to form and join organizations, though the Mexican-Americans still lag far behind the Anglos and the Negroes in this respect. Several unions, notably those in the garment trades and unskilled construction work, have high percentages of Mexican-American membership. New community organizations have sprung up in recent years, one of which succeeded (with the help of the Teamsters Union) in winning full control of municipal government in Crystal City, Texas. Mexican-American Congressmen now represent constituencies in California, Texas, and New Mexico. Ad hoc Mexican-American committees on employment and education, under the aegis of the Los Angeles County Commission on Human Relations, are presently active in the Los Angeles area. Political awareness has increased enormously, and government agencies and legislative bodies are responding more sensitively to the needs and demands of the Mexican-American community.

Among the interstate or interregional Mexican-American organizations which have received particular attention are the League of United Latin American Citizens (LULAC), the GI Forum, and the Community Service Organization (CSO). Local Mexican-American groups throughout the five states are too numerous to list.

Contrary to some impressions, Mexican-Americans in Arizona, California, Colorado, New Mexico, and Texas are

Patronage

Table 2

Nativity of Spanish Surname Population, Urban and Rural,
Five Southwestern States, 1960

	Total	%	Urban	%	Rural Nonfarm	%	Rural Farm	%
Total	3,464,999	100.00	2,740,950	100.00	541,659	100.00	182,390	100.00
Native-born	2,930,185	84.6	2,309,852	84.3	476,235	92.2	144,098	79.0
Native parentage	1,899,402	54.8	1,464,942	53.4	338,085	62.4	96,375	52.8
Foreign or mixed parentage	1,030,783	29.7	844,910	30.8	138,150	25.5	47,723	26.2
Mexican parentage	917,614	26.5	750,909	27.4	126,120	23.3	40,585	22.2
Other and not reported	113,169	3.2	94,001	3.4	12,030	2.2	7,138	4.0
Foreign-born	534,814	15.4	431,098	15.7	65,424	12.1	38,292	21.0
Born in Mexico	468,684	13.5	373,918	13.6	59,946	11.1	34,820	19.1
Other and not reported	66,130	1.9	57,180	2.1	5,478	1.0	3,472	1.9

Source *Persons of Spanish Surname,* U.S. Census of Population: 1960, Final Report PC(2)-1B.

concentrated overwhelmingly in the cities and towns. About 80 per cent of all white persons of Spanish surname in these five states are urban dwellers. Furthermore, almost 85 per cent are natives of the United States, and 55 per cent have native-born parents (see Table 2). Even in California, which has the lowest percentage of natives, 80 per cent of all residents of Spanish surname are native-born.

There is evidence of considerable migration from one area to another, particularly to California and more specifically to Los Angeles County, but the available statistical data provide little insight into precise patterns. The increase of Mexican-American population in the Los Angeles area has been especially striking: the Spanish surname total for the metropolitan area doubled between 1950 and 1960 and made up almost 10 per cent of the total population in the latter year. The combined Mexican-American and Negro populations now equal close to one-fifth of the total. In all probability, close to two-thirds of the 318,000 increase resulted from in-migration. The birth rate for Mexican-American families exceeds the average for Anglos, further stimulating population growth.

Like the Negroes, the Mexican-Americans are heavily concentrated in the blue-collar job categories and have made comparatively little headway in the managerial, professional, clerical, and sales occupations. Over 76 per cent of all males with Spanish surnames were employed as craftsmen, operatives (semiskilled), private household workers, service workers, farm laborers and foremen, and "other laborers" in 1960, while only 49 per cent of Anglos held such jobs. Mexican-Americans were located in large numbers in the semiskilled category: about 23 per cent of the men and 25 per cent of the women were operatives. About 16 per cent of the males were farm laborers, approximately the same as the percentage for craftsmen and for "other laborers" (see Table 3).

The Mexican-American, typically, is better off than the Negro and worse off than the Anglo in terms of income and rate of unemployment. The intermediate position of the Mexican-American may be attributable, at least in part, to the relatively greater penetration of men into the craftsmen

✗ manual labor

(skilled) category and of women into the clerical. The rigid discriminatory barriers which have prevented entry of Negroes into these jobs do not seem to apply in the same degree to Mexican-Americans. On the other hand, Mexican-Americans do no better than Negroes in the high-income professional categories. Only 4.5 per cent of employed Spanish surname males, identical with the percentage for employed Negro males, were defined as professional, technical, and kindred workers.

It is impossible to determine, with any precision or confidence, the extent to which the occupational distribution of Mexican-Americans has been influenced by the direct or indirect discrimination which has undeniably occurred. One fact is clear: many American employers, particularly those in agriculture, have long regarded the Mexican population (domestic and foreign) as a source of cheap and "dependable" labor. The flow of Mexican nationals into and out of this country has been regulated (or unregulated, as in the case of the "wetbacks") in accordance with the needs of domestic employers. The inflow has increased enormously in wartime and during other periods of labor shortage and, in turn, many Mexicans were returned to Mexico by force during the Great Depression. In 1954-1955, prior to inauguration of the bracero program, public pressure forced the return of thousands of illegal entrants to Mexico. At this writing, the bracero program appears doomed to well-earned extinction at the end of its current term; however, the complex and specialized problems of agricultural labor are beyond the scope of this article.

A particularly disturbing trend in urban areas is the increasingly widespread employment of Mexican-Americans, often women, in low-paying service or semi-skilled jobs. Small firms, such as laundries and garment manufacturers, in highly competitive industries employ Mexican-Americans in large numbers. Union officials charge that many employers take advantage of language barriers, low levels of education, and unfamiliarity with legal rights to exploit these workers. Some garment trades unions in Texas have been decimated by such tactics. The Amalgamated Clothing Workers, among others,

a group of related persons

Table 3

Distribution by Sex and Occupation, Spanish Surname and "Anglo" Populations, Five Southwestern States, 1960

Occupation	Spanish surname				"Anglo"*			
	Male	%	Female	%	Male	%	Female	%
Professional, technical, and kindred	28,955	3.9	14,683	5.5	805,595	13.6	433,769	15.4
Farmers and farm managers	16,442	2.2	482	0.2	253,603	4.0	12,759	0.4
Managers officials, and proprietors, exc. farm	32,010	4.3	6,744	2.5	806,000	13.6	153,416	5.4
Clerical and kindred	33,866	4.6	54,362	20.4	411,234	6.9	1,031,662	36.6
Sales	24,933	3.4	20,183	7.6	481,467	8.1	252,075	8.9
Craftsmen, foremen, and kindred	116,578	15.8	3,273	1.2	1,221,760	20.7	32,740	1.1
Operatives and kindred	68,497	22.9	66,212	24.8	933,176	15.8	251,215	8.9
Private household	878	0.1	28,514	10.7	5,925	0.1	125,197	4.4
Service, exc. private household	52,749	7.2	41,189	15.4	305,734	5.2	347,942	12.3
Farm laborers and foremen	117,688	16.0	10,319	3.9	131,818	2.2	17,792	0.6
Laborers, exc. farm and mine	106,409	14.4	3,006	1.1	281,317	4.8	8,864	0.3
Occupation not reported	37,763	5.1	17,688	6.6	266,519	4.5	149,499	5.3
Totals	736,768		266,655		5,904,148		2,816,930	

Sources: *Persons of Spanish Surname*, U.S. Census of Population: 1960, Final Report PC(2)-1B; *General Social and Economic Characteristics: Arizona, California, Colorado, New Mexico, and Texas*, U.S. Census of Population: 1960, (PC)1 Series.

*"Anglo" represents the total employed in each category *minus* the Spanish surname and Negro totals.

has launched a campaign to organize these employees in the Los Angeles area. The difficulties are great and it is still too early to judge how successful the program will be.

Overt discrimination against the Mexican-American (or Latin-American) is more common in Texas than in California, although California is not blameless. Fair Employment Practices laws have provided a degree of protection to the Mexican-American in California which does not exist in Texas, a state characterized by antiunion laws and an absence of civil rights measures. Testifying before a subcommittee of the U.S. Senate Committee on Labor and Public Welfare in late 1963, Congressman Henry B. Gonzalez of San Antonio declared that Mexican-Americans in that state suffer discrimination both in employment and in education. He pointed out that Mexican-Americans are often concentrated in types of industry, such as agriculture and small firms, which are not covered by minimum wage and other protective laws and are usually nonunion: "It is not uncommon to find Latins in Texas who earn less than fifty cents an hour, or even less. Laundry workers, for example, often make less than fifteen dollars for a forty-four to forty-eight hour week." Noting the absence of an FEPC law in Texas, Congressman Gonzalez cited specific examples of discriminatory job specifications, taken from employment ads in San Antonio newspapers. Among the examples cited are these: "Maintenance: 30-45 Anglo, local, married, $250 . . ."; "Neat, dependable Anglo short order cook . . ."; "Waitresses, Colored or Latin . . ."; Latin tire changer . . ."; "Counter Attendants, under 35 . . . Anglo. . . ."

The testimony of Congressman Gonzalez contains further examples of discriminatory treatment in pay scales, housing, and education. He cited the case of a young Mexican-American woman who held a clerical position at a local library, was highly skilled and educated, and spoke only English. Yet she was paid $25 per month less than her coworkers doing the same job. Her employer explained that "the other girls would quit if I paid her as much as they make."

Congressman Gonzalez and many others emphasize the critical role of poor education in blocking the economic progress of the Mexican-American. Two problems confront most Mexican-Americans in Texas: (1) school districts with high Mexican-American concentrations tend to be poor and thus offer inferior and oftentimes segregated facilities, and (2) cultural factors and unenforced school attendance laws make it especially difficult for Mexican-American youngsters to benefit from a school program directed to the English-speaking. The result is that the illiteracy rate among the Texas Latins is extremely high.

The Mexican-American would be at a disadvantage in the labor market because of the inadequacy of his education and training, even were there no discrimination. Mexican-American youngsters drop out of high school at an alarming rate, and their lack of a diploma disqualifies them from apprenticeships and other training programs. A high, though indeterminate, proportion of the dropouts actually are pupils who have been categorized as ill-behaved or unmotivated and have been invited to leave. In addition, Mexican-American schools experience relatively high transiency rates, which impair the quality of instruction received by the youngsters.

Unfortunately, in all too many cases the pupil receives little encouragement to stay in school. Parents and peers alike pressure him to drop out (sometimes for economic reasons), and the school itself may consider him "burdensome" for one reason or another. He does not fit easily into the mold created for the Anglo student, nor does the typical school program offer special help to youngsters having difficulty because of language problems or cultural differences. Employers and school officials have remarked to the author, on several occasions, that the problems of the Mexicans would vanish if only they became "Americanized," i.e., exactly like the Anglos. The author, of course, does not share this naive view.

Programs of vocational education and training have had little impact thus far on Mexican-Americans. Most unemployed Mexican-Americans fall into those age and education brackets which are proportionately under-represented in the training programs inaugurated under the Manpower Development and Training Act. Existing classes do not enroll many young people who have dropped out of high school, have little or no employment experience, and do poorly on standard examinations. When language problems are added, it becomes clear that the Mexican-American is not yet in a position to benefit significantly from such programs.

Nor is there consensus either among experts or among Mexican-American families as to the value to Mexican-Americans of vocational programs in the public schools. A few parents undoubtedly resist the assignment of their children to vocational courses because academic or college-oriented programs have greater prestige. It is a commonly held belief within both the Mexican-American and Negro communities that minority youngsters, including many with college potential, are unfairly categorized as vocational pupils. Others feel that the school system does not offer enough vocational training. Whatever the merits of these respective claims, most specialists agree that vocational counseling and the teaching of vocational subjects in nearly all schools are seriously deficient, largely because there is inadequate liaison between industry and the schools and pitifully little awareness by counselors of job requirements and trends in the labor market.

Mexican-American spokesmen, employers, and educators generally agree that education is the key to a solution of the Mexican-American's employment problems. However, there is little agreement on how responsibility for such improved education should be divided or on the proper function of the educational process in serving the particular needs of a bilingual youngster. The schools tend to blame Mexican-American parents for allegedly failing to motivate the children to take advantage of educational opportunities, while Mexican-American spokesmen charge the schools with failure to meet the needs of students other than the favored Anglos.

The predominant view among employers, as expressed to the author, has been suggested previously: that the Mexican-American must be persuaded to drop his attachment to the Spanish language and Mexican culture. It is undeniable that the Mexican-American who speaks English fluently and exclusively and adopts "American" (Anglo) customs has a considerable employment advantage over his less American-ized compadres, especially if he is also light-skinned. But two important questions arise here: is this single-focus approach realistic for the vast majority of disadvantaged Mexican-Americans, and quite aside from realism, is it genuinely de-sirable to subvert a cultural heritage simply because its values may sometimes conflict with those of an Anglo majority?

So far, the most concrete programs for improvement of Mexican-American employment opportunities have been aimed at young people. Probably the largest and most noteworthy single project yet undertaken is the "youth employability" program financed initially by a half-million dollar grant from the Office of Manpower, Automation, and Training of the U.S. Department of Labor and administered by the Youth Oppor-tunities Board of Greater Los Angeles in the overwhelmingly Mexican-American East Los Angeles area. The purpose of the project is to provide training, counseling, and guidance for youngsters, particularly high school dropouts, who otherwise might join the ranks of the hard-core unemployed.

Even at an early stage, project officials have had some success in persuading dropouts to return to school and in placing some of the unemployed, but the critical tests are yet to come. Based on interjurisdictional cooperation among the California State Employment Service, the city and county schools, the city and county governments of Los Angeles, and various community agencies, the program seeks to: identify youngsters in the 16-21 age bracket who are unemployed or underemployed and who meet certain other criteria; provide counseling by experienced staff of the State Employment Service and the schools; locate jobs which offer "reasonable expectation of employment;" and gear training and placement programs to such jobs.

Certain of the school districts are now initiating long-overdue programs to improve counseling and teaching of Mexican-American pupils, combat excessive dropout rates, develop and introduce books or materials directed to the non-

Anglo students as well as to the Anglo, and build closer ties with the Mexican-American community. The Los Angeles Board of Education has recently established an Office of Urban Affairs, empowered to undertake programs of this nature, and has adopted policy statements favoring increased instruction in Mexican history and culture, remedial English classes, and similar offers. Much remains to be done, however. Counseling is a major problem area, and the standard methods of communicating with parents continue to yield meager results in a community, like the Mexican-American, which has little background of participation in school affairs. The problem is further complicated by a severe shortage of bilingual teachers, counselors, and administrators at all levels of the school system.

A significant aspect of the current push for more and better jobs for Mexican-Americans is that it coincides with, and probably has been stimulated by, the movement in the Negro community toward the same goals. This timing, in the context of an economy which has high levels of persistent unemployment, creates obvious problems. Some Mexican-American spokesmen seem uncertain whether the Negro push for equality of opportunity is a boon or a hindrance to the corresponding efforts of their community. Neither the Negroes nor the Mexican-Americans have yet resolved the question of how much they can or should work jointly in programs to break down employment barriers. Some Mexican-Americans strongly oppose any consolidation of efforts, while others urge further cooperation. The anomalous position of the Mexican-American, who is neither fully accepted nor fully rejected by the dominant Anglo community, makes this decision harder. There are some, fortunately a minority, within the Mexican-American group who deny the existence of serious problems and condemn all those who are organizing for action.

The degree of cooperation between the minority communities appears to differ from one state to another. In Texas, Negroes and Mexican-Americans have long tended to work

x irregular, abnormal

together, politically and otherwise, for common goals. In California, by and large, the two groups have acted separately. Tentative gestures to increase collaboration have been made on both sides, but political clashes have recently engendered antagonism and an occasionally expressed fear that Negroes may be getting jobs at the expense of Mexican-Americans. The evidence for this is tenuous and elusive at best. But despite signs of tension, no basic cleavage seems imminent at this writing.

The critical need for public programs which would increase the general level of employment is certainly clear in this context. The economic difficulties confronted by Mexican-Americans and by Negroes stem from the general unemployment situation as well as from specific problems of discrimination, cultural differences, and lack of training. It would appear that the two communities have a strong common interest in generating support for measures to restore full employment.

One major difficulty has been that the Mexican-Americans, unlike most other minorities, have not supported permanent, adequately financed organizations concerned with community problems. There is no Mexican-American equivalent of the Urban League, and no single organization which can legitimately claim to speak for a large segment of the community. Fragmentation and internecine warfare have rendered many Mexican-American groups impotent. Furthermore, those identified as "leaders" are often detached from those most in need of assistance and either cannot or will not back strong demands for action.

Basically the Mexican-American community faces the same problems as does the Negro, except in a more subtle form. Direct discrimination does not hit the Mexican-American as severely, but he has arrived at the same dead end by a different route. Like the Negro, the Mexican-American lacks the education and training to give him sufficient adaptability in a dynamic labor market. Like the Negro, the Mexican-American is found mainly in blue collar jobs, the category most vulnerable to automation. Like the Negro, the Mexican-

American suffers an excessive rate and duration of unemployment. And, even worse than the Negro, the Mexican-American is placed at a disadvantage by the absence of community organizations powerful and united enough to secure a redress of grievances. There is evidence, however, that the old order is changing and that the Mexican-American will no longer be a "forgotten man."

Many Farm Labor Offices Favor Growers

Donald Janson

In much of the country, farmers may violate minimum wage, health, housing, immigration and child labor laws without fear of losing the services of the federally funded, state-operated farm labor offices that recruit seasonal workers for them.

Many of the offices in the 38-state network, set up to aid workers as well as growers, have become strongly grower-oriented. County and local branches are often staffed by former growers or friends or relatives of growers. Some have no compunction about disregarding federal regulations and supplying labor to farms that chisel on the law.

VIEWPOINT OF GROWERS

Milton M. Eisley, until recently manager of California's Sonoma County office, says he made no effort in six years to cut off service to growers who hired Mexicans smuggled into the country illegally. Frank Valenzuela, former Mayor of Hollister, Calif., and a former employee of three farm labor offices, says the offices "knowingly refer workers to growers offering unsafe, unsanitary working conditions."

Nor do the offices require compliance with other key laws affecting farm labor. Interviews in this state, which grows 40 per cent of the nation's produce and is the leading user of seasonal farm workers with an average of 113,000 in the fields each month, turned up numerous questionable cases.

Not long ago, for example, Ernie Basurto, 10 years old, and his brother Ralph, 9, worked with their family in the powdery dust of the Michael Moran apple orchard near here, as part of a group sent by the Sebastopol Farm Labor Office. A state law prohibits employing children under 12.

And Mrs. Antonia Mendoza, working recently with her teenage sons and two neighbor girls in the sweet-smelling Albert Lunceford apple orchards, found none of the required drinking or washing water in the fields. Her pay at a piece rate of $5 a bin amounted to a dollar an hour. The state minimum is $1.65.

Growers usually deny intentionally hiring illegal aliens, sometimes even after repeated seizures by immigration agents. They often contend that the children in their fields are "just playing," that workers could go to the main house if they needed water and that workers not making the minimum could do so by speeding up their pace.

But some of the larger growers, who comply with the laws and pay enough to recruit workers without outside help, side with the workers. "The operation of California farm labor offices,'" said Thomas P. Driscoll of Los Angeles, secretary-treasurer of Driscoll Strawberries Association, Inc., "primarily benefits only those growers who either violate wage and working condition laws or pay the lowest wages."

Whatever the extent of the violations, almost everyone seems to agree that where they do exist it is someone else's job to stop them. The farm labor offices say they have no enforcement powers. The Federal Department of Labor's Rural Manpower Service, which allocates $23-million annually to the offices, says enforcement is not its primary concern either.

The manpower service has never used its basic enforcement weapon, the power to cut off funds, even though Federal regulations require that farm labor offices receiving

Federal funds may not refer workers "to a position where the services to be performed or the terms of conditions of employment are contrary to Federal, state or local law."

Officials of the service contend that the regulations are merely "suggestions" without the force of law. They also say that they do not want to encroach on state prerogatives and that migrants with complaints can seek relief either through the courts or through other agencies with specific enforcement functions.

MIGRANT AID GROUPS ACT

There are, indeed, a number of state and Federal agencies charged with separate responbility over such areas as sanitation, housing and minimum wages. But migrants often lack the legal aid, knowhow and facility in English necessary to find the right bureau in the right city to file a complaint. Many could not follow through on a complaint anyway, for they must move on to the next state and the next crop. And many others are too fearful of retaliation to complain at all.

Groups formed to aid migrants insist that the Federal regulations do have the force of law and charge that, by not enforcing them, the Government is "subsidizing the illegal exploitation" of workers it should be protecting. Aided by funds from the Office of Economic Opportunity, these groups are starting to file lawsuits in the workers' behalf. Affidavits they have collected challenge a wide range of practices.

Farm labor office employes in 18 southwest Idaho towns, for example, also operate growers' camps that house migrant labor, deciding which crews awaiting work will be sent to the fields and which will be passed over because of complaints about low pay and working and living conditions.

Richard A. Skinner, a lawyer with West Idaho Legal Aid, Inc., a pro-migrant group, called the dual positions "a blatant conflict of interest and a bar to the fair and impartial treatment of labor by the Department of Labor."

Michael Donnelly, also of the legal aid group, said: "The United States Department of Labor is subsidizing the maintenance and operation of labor camps, through payments to the managers, that do not even meet the minimum sanitary, building and health standards established by state or Federal law."

He said the use of Labor Department funds in this way gave the appearance of Labor Department "consent to or complicity in the practices and activities of the local managers and growers."

He said the practices included threatened evictions and increases in rent "to force the workers to desist in their legitimate complaints and employment practices."

Father Lorenzo Avila, a Roman Catholic priest, in personally checking on the legality of conditions on farms to which his parishioners were sent, asked for work and was referred by the Salinas, Calif., farm labor office to a grower whose fields had no toilet facilities.

"Other workers were forced as I was to urinate or defecate on the planted area," he said.

Complaints of workers often are given short shrift by farm labor offices. In Michigan, David Vasquez of Brownsville, Tex., and some of his migrant neighbors complained to the Keeler office that at the end of the harvest one grower began working them in empty fields where they could make no money at piece rates.

They said the idea was to induce them to leave without qualifying for the bonus they had been guaranteed if they stayed throughout the harvest. . . .

Carmen Olguin and 40 others were sent nearly 2,000 miles by the Calexico, Calif., office to Illinois to work for the Green Giant Company for $2 an hour. Less work and more deductions than expected cut this to 36 cents an hour, Mr. Olguin said, and when he complained to the Calexico office upon returning "they just laughed at us."

Such interstate recruiting often produces an oversupply on labor devastating to migrants. Esmeralda Sanchez, of Texas's Rio Grande Valley, was referred with a large group of workers to Ohio tomato fields but found little work on arrival because the grower had 4,000 harvesters on hand rather than the 1,000 he actually needed.

Terry Y. Feiertag of the Illinois Migrant Council says farm labor offices make no independent inquiry into the extent of labor needs. He says he has seen numerous orders for farm workers specifying such vague hours of employment as "zero to 14 daily."

DENOUNCED AS 'COVERUP'

He called this a "coverup" for such farm worker nightmares as "no guaranteed work, no minimum amount of work, no employment if the weather is bad or the crop is late, even if such conditions were expected by the employer."

"But none of these miseries is quite so unfair, he said, "as the chronic underemployment due to unconscionable over-recruiting by employers with the active cooperation of the Illinois State Employment Service and the Texas Employment Commission."

While giving the grower a free, tax-supported service, he said, the farm labor network "exhibits no awareness that it is to function in any way as a Government protection against exploitation of the worker, but rather acts as an all-too-willing partner of the employer in just such exploitation."

Last April, 398 farm workers and 20 migrant-oriented groups across the country sued the Secretary of Labor and the state farm labor offices . . . in a class action asking that the farm labor office network be reformed or abolished.

The complaint contends that farm workers, despite their relative powerlessness, would fare better and be exploited less if they dealt directly with farmers rather than through a public agency that sanctions illegality.

The suit charges that even if they wanted to the "vast majority of the 2,000 farm labor office employees could not help chicanos, a major segment of the farm labor force, because they speak no Spanish. Even in Spanish-speaking communities most offices post job lists only in English.

FEW TEST OR COUNSEL WORKERS

Pilar Saldivar of Windsor, Calif., said the Santa Rosa farm labor office would not consider his bricklaying and carpentry skills and would send him only to the fruit ranches because chicanos are looked upon in the offices as good only for stoop labor despite civil rights legislation guaranteeing equal opportunity.

Few offices follow the Labor Department regulation requiring placement in the best job available if that means testing or counseling a chicano or sending him to the industrial job office in the same building or elsewhere in town.

An investigation by the Labor Department's regional office in San Francisco found this to be ˣ de facto institutional discrimination." . . .

A study of the Stokely-Van Camp operations in Illinois last year found that Mexican-Americans did all the stoop labor and "anglos" were hired only as supervisors or operators of tractors and other machinery.

Dr. Daniel W. Sturt, director of the Rural Manpower Service for the Labor Department, testified before the Senate Subcommittee on Migratory Labor last year that he disagreed with those who saw such jobs as opportunities for upgrading migrants.

APTITUDE IS QUESTIONED

"I contend that most of the migrants do not possess the basic aptitude for acquiring mechanization skills," he said. "They are oriented toward picking and harvesting, but not toward the operation of machinery."

The suit by 398 farm workers, in the form of a petition to the Secretary of Labor, seeks equal opportunity for all. It asks abolition of farm labor offices or a farm worker voice in their operation to insure compliance with civil rights, minimum wage, housing and other laws.

In the era of John Steinbeck's "Grapes of Wrath," it says, "the grower exploited the migrant on his own without

ˣ from the fact or reality; actually
ˣ anger, violent

Federal subsidies. Today, the exploitation is accomplished with the monetary assistance of the migrants' legal guardian."

"Most of the local offices are staffed by and beholden to local growers who frequently refer migrants to their own ranches at the worst wages," said Robert L. Gnaizda, a San Francisco spokesman for migrants.

Here in the Napa Valley Cesar Chavez's United Farm Workers Organizing Committee won a contract last month for Hueblein grape harvesters of $2.40 an hour, raising pay to levels already achieved by the union in vineyards to the south.

But exclusion of farm workers from the right to collective bargaining guaranteed others in 1938 by the National Labor Relations Act has made organizing in most crops extremely slow and has stiffened resistance by many growers, particularly those with marginally profitable farms.

"We don't need unions," said Mrs. Lucille Nase at her prune ranch near Healdsburg. "Anytime we need labor we can give a quick call to the farm labor office and get all we want."

UNIONS SEEN AS PROTECTION

In a recent study for the Labor Department, Abt Associates, Inc., of Cambridge, Mass., found that "unionization would protect the migrants from unfair practices by employers."

It said employer orientation of farm labor offices in a number of Northern states was "reinforced by social connections" between growers and office employees.

Also, it found, a ready supply of labor and more stringent Federal housing regulations for migrants had so reduced the number of clearance orders processed by the offices that they "can often stay busy only by not enforcing housing regulations strictly and not alienating those employers who, though they could recruit without employment service help, do go through employment service channels to get their labor."

Frank Valenzuela, the former Mayor of Hollister who once worked for three farm labor offices in California, said the offices were aware that some of the growers to whom they were sending workers were not only offering unsafe, unsanitary housing but were also charging the workers for it by considering it part of their pay.

Mr. Valenzuela said that whenever vacancies occur in farm labor offices, local growers play a major role in determining who shall be selected to fill them. "For this reason," he said, "the farm labor office is often referred to as just another arm of the farm bureau." The American Farm Bureau Federation is a national organization of growers.

Because the reputation of the offices is so poor among farm workers, many migrants arriving in a community to seek field work go instead to "Mexican" bars or the home of acquaintances for reports on the availability of jobs and then deal directly with growers. In many areas, the offices have been reduced to filling out grower needs with applicants from local welfare rolls.

The feelings of many migrants were expressed by Esmeralda Sanchez of Texas. "The farm labor office is not protecting the farm worker and he is not benefiting from the service," she said. "If the farm labor offices were closed, I don't think the farm worker would be hurt. We could do just as woll in negotiating by ourselves. The only good farm labor office I remember in any state that we have been to—and that includes Arkansas, Missouri, Ohio, Indiana, Illinois, Michigan, Arizona and California—was New York."

As criticism of the farm labor offices was intensified, Federal officials have started to respond. "We do not intend to terminate the rural manpower service," said Secretary of Labor James D. Hodgson in a letter to the Migrant Legal Action Program, Inc., a petitioner based in Washington. But the Labor Department has begun a nationwide investigation of the allegations, with a report due soon.

James E. Bailey, deputy director of the special review staff conducting the inquiry, said some truth to the charges had been found in seven states visited so far. But Dr. Sturt deplored the petition's insistence on enforcement of the laws and regulations.

"It is very difficult to control what a state agency does," the Rural Manpower Service director said. "We can put out guidelines and suggestions, but we're not in a position to see that all these conditions are carried out."

Nor is Dr. Sturt eager to see enforcement by the courts. Migrant groups recently won a Federal District Court order forcing the Michigan Employment Security Commission and its farm labor offices to refuse to serve growers without checking to make sure they complied with housing, sanitation, wage and other regulations. Dr. Sturt said in a telephone interview that the Michigan agency had been cautious about providing service to anybody ever since.

He said such lawsuits were a "disservice," as would be attempts at enforcement through withholding allocations that over the years had become almost automatic.

"Withholding funds from states is not a good method of enforcement," he said. "Enforcement is not appropriate for our agency. I would like to get us out of the enforcement business."

'SOMETHING OUT OF KAFKA'

Some contend the agency has seldom been in. Senator Walter F. Mondale, Democrat of Minnesota, has called the situation "bureaucratic . . . insensitivity for illegality."

"Enforcement is practically nonexistent," said Senator Harrison A. Williams Jr., Democrat of New Jersey, at a recent hearing on the Federal minimum wage law.

He had just heard Felix Cruz, a former farm worker, describe a typical case in which the Sonoma County farm labor office sent a family of six to an apple rancher but named only the head of the family and listed only a single Social Security number.

"It looks like good pay when the record shows that one person got more than the minimum," Mr. Cruz said, "but it actually took six to do it."

While the farm labor office listed only one worker as receiving any pay, Mr. Cruz said, it listed all six on its job replacement records. These statistics figure in the amount the

Labor Department allocates each year to the states to run the farm labor offices.

Mr. Eisley, the former manager of the Sonoma County office, conceded in answer to a question for a deposition that anyone who came in to ask to use the rest room counted in his statistics as a "contact."

Mr. Gnaizda, the San Francisco migrant advocate, called totals compiled by many farm labor offices "deliberate frauds in an effort to continue funding at the present level."

And William H. Tolbert, orange grower who heads California's farm labor services agency, said under questioning for a deposition that statistics were "part of the game."

Senator Williams seemed taken aback by the combination of doubtful statistics on farm labor published by the Department of Agriculture and what he called "derelict" enforcement of farm labor law by the Department of Labor.

"It's like something out of Kafka," he said.

Ethnic Endogamy—The Case of Mexican Americans

Frank G. Mittelbach and Joan W. Moore

Theorists concerned with problems of social differentiation have generally taken the endogamy rate of a subpopulation as an indicator of the rigidity of boundaries around it. (Boundaries are, of course, due both to prejudice against the group and to the group's internal cohesiveness.) As Merton argues, this is justified theoretically because exogamous marriages disrupt the network of primary-group relationships that underlie the cohesiveness of any population. In some respects, this is a functional as well as a motivational explanation in that the threat of disrupting primary-group relationships acts as a deterrent to exogamous marriages.

Empirical studies of intermarriage between subpopulations in this country have in some cases emphasized the significance of external boundaries imposed by prejudice, as, for example, in the analysis of Negro exogamy. In other research, as in the analysis of upper-class endogamy and endogamy of European ethnic populations, much literature assumes the boundaries internally maintained by in-group solidarity to be the important factor.

This paper examines the Mexican Americans, the nation's second largest disadvantaged minority and a group

Frank G. Mittelbach and Joan W. Moore, *Intermarriage of Mexican-Americans* (Mexican-American Study Project, Advance Report 6, Los Angeles: Graduate School of Business Administration, University of California, 1966), pp. 7-16.

which has often been portrayed as distinctively unassimilated and unacculturated—that is, one which has unusually strong boundaries around it. Though these boundaries are most frequently attributed to in-group cohesiveness, Mexican Americans have also experienced considerable prejudice and discrimination. In short, analysis of patterns of intermarriage among this group, which shares minority status with Negroes and shares ethnic distinctiveness with other foreign immigrant groups, offers some promise of fruitful insight into the processes of boundary maintenance and dissolution.

The paper has two purposes. The first is to increase understanding of the current status and future prospects for assimilation of this population, and the second is to amplify general propositions about conditions under which exogamy occurs. The two purposes reinforce each other: Mexican American patterns of endogamy are best understood in a general context, and the analysis of this unusual case may help extend the theoretical frontiers slightly.

Previous studies of Mexican American endogamy are comparatively rare, but all show extremely low rates of exogamy, supporting the notion of the group as distinctively unassimilated. Panunzio's study of individuals born in Mexico and marrying in Los Angeles between 1924 and 1933 showed that only 9 per cent of the individuals (and 17 per cent of the marriages) were exogamous. An analysis of Spanish-surname persons in Albuquerque from 1924 to 1940 indicated that only 8 per cent of the individuals (and 15 per cent of the marriages) were exogamous. Finally, a more recent study of Spanish-surname persons in San Antonio marrying between 1940 and 1955 showed exogamy rates of no more than 10 per cent for persons (and 17 per cent for marriages) in any of the years sampled. Considering that many of these persons in Albuquerque and probably in San Antonio are native born of native parents, the image of this minority as distinctively unassimilated gains much support from these studies. And considering that these studies were prepared in different places and times, the notion that the low rate of assimilation is due to unusual strength of in-group bonds also gains much support.

Both social scientists and journalists have tended to emphasize the special strength of Mexican American ascriptive bonds—especially to kin and "la raza" (diffusely, the ethnic group)—in interpreting the slow rate of acculturation and assimilation in the population. However, this kind of interpretation does not help much in our analysis of intermarriage in contemporary Los Angeles. The Los Angeles patterns are understandable only in the light of general propositions about the process of assimilation. The data, for example, illustrate the effects of the considerable and growing internal differentiation within the population. They suggest that this differentiation has differentially weakened the holding power of the ascriptive bonds of "la raza."

In addition to pointing to the effects of this growing differentiation within the Mexican American population, the study—whose findings depart so notably from the three cited above—strongly indicates the importance of the environing social system. The contemporary Los Angeles milieu is far less hostile to Mexican Americans and offers far more economic opportunity than any of the other milieus studied. These data thus compel the analyst to give consideration to external-system as well as internal-system effects on boundary maintenance of this group.

DATA AND MILIEU

The data which form the basis for our analysis consists of 7,492 marriage licenses issued in Los Angeles County during 1963 from a total of over 47,000 licenses. These 7,492 licenses include all marriages in which one or both spouses carry a Spanish surname. By the definition adopted, a total of 9,368 Mexican American individuals were identified. Of these 2,246 (or 24.0 per cent) were first generation or born in Mexico; 3,537 (or 38.2 per cent) were second generation, with one or both parents born in Mexico, and 3,585 (or 38.2 per cent) were third generation, defined as Spanish-surname individuals whose parents were born in one of the five South-western states where Mexican Americans are concentrated.

The Mexican Americans hold a very special position in southern California, both as the major local minority and as compared with Mexican Americans elsewhere. In many respects they appear to be a "typical minority." Mexican Americans constituted slightly less than 10 per cent of the total Los Angeles County population in 1960, but more than 80 per cent were born in the United States. Though it is thus no longer an immigrant population, it is one which has been locally defined as a problem for more than two generations. Memories of the zoot-suit riots of the 1940's are still alive, and segregation from both Anglo whites and Negroes is sharp, great enough so that three Los Angeles area high schools are predominantly Mexican American—a factor certainly important in the availability of marriage partners. However, prejudice against the population in Los Angeles is comparatively low and opportunities for status advancement quite high in comparison with other parts of the American Southwest. From the point of view of the environing social system, then, Los Angeles is an environment which facilitates interaction with the larger system.

FINDINGS

A. *Sex and generational differences.*—The over-all rate of exogamy in these data was much higher than anticipated. Forty per cent of the marriages involving Mexican Americans were exogamous, and 25 per cent of the Mexican American individuals married outside their ethnic group. Although statistics in the field are notably difficult to find, it is clear that exogamy in Los Angeles today is much higher for Mexican Americans than in the past or in other urban areas. Interestingly, the Mexican American exogamy rate is roughly that of the Italian and Polish ethnic populations in Buffalo, New York, a generation ago. Both of these populations are now assimilating rather rapidly.

Table 1

Percentage of In-and Out-Group Marriages of Mexican Americans, Los Angeles County, 1963

Spouse	Mexican-American Grooms			Mexican-American Brides		
	Foreign born, Mexico	Foreign or mixed parentage, Mexico	Natives of native parentage	Foreign born, Mexico	Foreign or mixed parentage, Mexico	Natives of native parentage
	1	2	3	4	5	6
Foreign born, Mexico	*51.9*	13.8	6.8	*48.5*	14.5	6.9
Foreign or mixed parentage, Mexico	22.8	*34.5*	23.8	21.8	*36.7*	27.0
Natives of native parentage	12.2	28.4	*38.9*	9.7	23.2	*33.8*
Subtotal, Mexican American	86.9	76.7	69.5	80.0	74.4	67.7
Hispanic, [1] foreign or mixed parentage	2.9	1.5	0.8	4.0	1.6	1.3
Other [2]	10.2	21.9	29.8	15.9	24.0	31.1
Total	100.0	100.0	100.0	100.0	100.0	100.0
(N)	(1,086)	(1,826)	(1,667)	(1,160)	(1,711)	(1,918)

Note.—Generationally endogamous cells are italicized.

[1] Excludes foreign stock from Mexico; includes foreign stock from Central and South America, the Philippines, and Spain.

[2] Includes natives of native parentage with Spanish surname with parents born outside the five southwestern states, natives of native parentage without Spanish surnames throughout the United States, and foreign stock outside of Mexico and other Hispanic countries.

The results for men and women by generation are presented in Table 1. They show the sex gradient to be as expected for a subpopulation occupying a low status. Women are more exogamous than men, with the respective over-all rates for individuals of 27 and 24 per cent. The generational gradient suggests that exogamy will probably increase in the future as relatively more Mexican Americans move out of immigrant status. The most exogamous are third-generation women (32 per cent), and the least exogamous are first-generation men (13 per cent). The generational gradient is steady (Table 1, "Subtotal" row). Sex differences are maintained within each generation, with women more exogamous than men. Similar findings were discovered in a recent two-generational analysis of Puerto Rican exogamy, and their interpretation there, as here, was made within a social-class context.

Most significantly, there is a pattern of endogamy within each generation as well as within the ethnic group. It is apparent that individuals of every generational status tend to marry those with the same generational background.

More important, the data indicate that marriage of second- and third-generation Mexican Americans are assimilationist. Both men and women are more likely to marry "Anglos" than to marry immigrants from Mexico. Among third-generation persons, the chances are actually higher that he or she will marry an Anglo than either a first- or a second-generation Mexican. Further evidence can be found related to this generalization. In Table 2, persons with foreign or mixed parentage have been sorted out into those with both parents and those with only one parent born in Mexico. Clearly, Mexican American men and women with both parents born in Mexico are more likely than those with mixed parentage to marry first- and second-generation spouses and less likely to marry third-generation spouses. By this indicator, the social distance between generations of Mexicans is greater than the social distance between some categories of Mexicans and Anglos. This apparently low degree of solidarity inside the ethnic group is not only contrary to much popular opinion but also to general sociological expectation about this group.

This three-generational gradient and the intra-Mexican variations may well exist in other ethnic groups, but to our knowledge it has not been previously demonstrated. It gives a hint to the processes that take place as assimilation of a subordinate population progresses. The data suggest, for example, that members of an ethnic group become less "attractive" to the native born as they appear to be more "ethnic." Conversely, they may become more "attractive" as they become more similar to members of the host society. As differentiations between them and members of the host society become fewer, exogamy may be facilitated.

B. *The influence of occupational status.*—Some of the sources of this tendency toward assimilation are suggested by the occupational gradient in Mexican American marriages. The only indicator of general social-class standing available on Los Angeles marriage licenses is the occupation of the bride and the occupation of the groom (parents' occupations are not reported). Because women's occupations are notoriously poor indicators of their social-class standing, we will here only examine the groom's occupation; that is, both brides and grooms are grouped according to occupational status of the groom. Thus, the kinds of generalizations we can draw from the two sets of data are more limited in the case of women than of men. In both instances, however, they are inconsistent with findings from earlier studies and, most saliently for our analysis, are also comparable with Fitzpatrick's data for Puerto Ricans.

Within these limitations, the analysis in general reaffirms the social-class context of exogamy (Table 3). Generally, the higher the socioeconomic status of the groom (or the new family of procreation) the greater the rate of exogamy. For Mexican American women, slightly more than half of those marrying high-status grooms married exogamously, with only 49 per cent marrying Mexican American men. Once again, as with generation, the gradient is remarkably steady. The most exogamous are women marrying high-status men,

Table 2

*Percentage of In- and Out-Group Marriages of Second-
Generation Mexican Americans by Nativity,
Los Angeles County, 1963*

Spouse	Second-Generation Mexican-American Grooms			Second-Generation Mexican-American Brides		
	Both parents born Mexico	Father only born Mexico	Mother only born Mexico	Both parents born Mexico	Father only born Mexico	Mother only born Mexico
Foreign born, Mexico	17.9	10.7	9.1	18.1	11.9	9.8
Foreign or mixed parentage, Mexico	36.5	31.5	34.0	38.6	34.2	36.6
Natives of native parentage	24.1	33.8	30.0	17.8	28.8	26.8
Subtotal, Mexican American	78.5	76.0	73.2	74.5	74.9	72.2
Hispanic foreign or mixed parentage	1.2	1.2	2.5	2.1	1.5	0.7
Other	20.3	22.8	24.4	23.4	23.6	26.1
Total	100.0	100.0	100.0	100.0	100.0	100.0
(N)	(885)	(588)	(353)	(811)	(605)	(295)

Note: For both categories (brides and grooms), X^2 significant past .001.

agreeing with Fitzpatrick's findings and probably his interpretation that "it is likely that . . . women are marrying up as
they marry out." The least exogamous are the women marrying low-status men.

Table 3

In-Group Marriages Among Mexican Americans
by Occupational Status of Groom

Occupation Group of Groom and Generation	Grooms		Brides	
	% in-group	N	% in-group	N
High[1]				
Mexican born	66.2	74	57.6	99
Mexican parents	63.1	187	49.3	207
Native of native parents	51.4	138	44.6	177
Total	59.6	399	49.3	483
Middle[2]				
Mexican born	87.5	353	75.3	413
Mexican parents	76.0	766	74.1	703
Native of native parents	75.6	870	69.0	1,039
Total	77.9	1,989	71.9	2,155
Low[3]				
Mexican born	88.7	626	87.3	612
Mexican parents	80.4	810	82.1	750
Native of native parents	65.6	593	71.3	624
Total	78.6	2,029	80.3	1,986
All[4]				
Mexican born	86.9	1,086	80.0	1,160
Mexican parents	76.7	1,826	74.4	1,711
Native of native parents	69.5	1,667	67.7	1,918
Total	76.4	4,579	73.1	4,789

[1] Includes professional, technical and kindred workers, managers, officials and proprietors (except farm).

[2] Includes clerical, sales and kindred workers, craftsmen, foremen and
kindred workers, and farm owners and managers.

[3] Includes operatives and kindred workers, non-household service workers, private household workers, laborers, and farm workers.

[4] All marriages include also those where occupation not reported, unemployed persons, students, and others with no occupation.

Within each occupational group, exogamy increases as
the person is further removed from immigrant status. This is
true for both brides and grooms. Within each generational

group, exogamy increases steadily with the socioeconomic status of the groom. This is true for each generation. Although the lowest rate of in-group marriage for men appears among the high-status third generation, the percentage of endogamy in the middle-status group far exceeds the endogamy of the lower status group.

In most cases, Mexican American women show a higher rate of outmarriage than do men. Generally, women of lower status levels have more restricted opportunities for forming social relationships outside the narrow limits of kinship and long-standing friendships.

The results tabulated in Table 3 show generally that both generation and occupation are relevant in Mexican American exogamy. To gain some insight into whether occupation or generation is more important in influencing endogamy, we begin by ranking the percentages in Table 3 in a new tabulation by generation and by occupation (Table 4). Then, if occupation is more important than generation in exogamy, the rank order will emphasize occupation (with the generation ordered within each occupation, as in col. 3). If generation is more relevant, it will emphasize generation (with the occupation ordered within each generation, as in col. 4). The results show that actual rankings conform much more closely to the hypothetical rank order emphasizing occupation (Table 4, cols. 1 and 2).

We note two departures from the hypothetical ranking among the men and one among the women. Interestingly, both Mexican American men and women in the low-status, third-generation group marry out more than would be hypothesized from the influence of social class (or occupational status alone). Possibly this group is more acculturated and comfortable with Anglos than occupation alone might suggest. Perhaps the effect of being native born of native-born parents counteracts the cultural isolation of a low-status blue-collar job. It might also be an age-associated pattern. Possibly, low-status third-generation persons marry earlier than middle-and higher-status persons in the same generation.

Table 4
Rank Order of Out-Group Marriage Rates by Sex, Occupation, and Generation

Rank, from Most to Least Outmarrying	Actual				Hypothetical			
	Rank, males (1)		Rank, females (2)		Rank if occupation more important than generation (3)		Rank if generation more important than occupation (4)	
	Occupation	Generation	Occupation	Generation	Occupation	Generation	Occupation	Generation
1	High	3	High	3	High	3	High	3
2	High	2	Middle	2	High	2	High	3
3	Low	3	High	1	High	1	Low	3
4	High	1	Middle	3	Middle	3	High	2
5	Middle	3	Low	3	Middle	2	Middle	2
6	Middle	2	Middle	2	Middle	1	Low	2
7	Low	2	Low	2	Low	3	High	1
8	Middle	1	Middle	1	Low	2	Middle	1
9	Low	1	Low	1	Low	1	Low	1

We do not feel these exceptions disturb the general conclusion that occupation is more significant than generation in explaining outmarriage for both Mexican American men and women. Since only the occupation of the groom is reported, it further supports the suggestion that women's exogamy is probably associated with their upward mobility. One complicating factor does exist. The conclusions previously reached are on the basis of three generations. The full impact of the third generation may not yet have appeared, and it is possible that when it does its thrust will be somewhat different than is presently shown. When we drop out the third generation completely and compare only two generations, we find that generational primacy does, in fact, assume considerable importance.

It is plain that within an ethnic population consisting largely of immigrants and their children, the ethnic culture and the kinship relations of the family are closely interwoven. This seems true whether one considers two generations or three, except that with the addition of a third generation, other kinds of social relationships and distinctions undoubtedly become more important. In the relatively open social system of Los Angeles, it is not surprising that occupational status is so significant.

C. *Age at marriage.*—Earlier research has shown that age of a man or woman at marriage is definitely patterned by ethnic and social-class subcultures. It is reasonable to expect that Mexican Americans in Los Angeles also show such patterns. The aggregate data, including all cases where neither party had been previously married, indicate that the median age is 22.0 for Mexican American grooms and 20.3 for brides (Table 5). This is slightly below comparable figures for the nation, although they have not been completely standardized. Nationally median age of bride at first marriage in 1963 was 20.4 for women and 22.8 for men. But the aggregate results conceal important generational differences.

First- and second-generation Mexican Americans tend to be notably older and third-generation spouses notably younger than the average American at time of marriage. This

Table 5

Median Ages of Grooms and Brides by Ethnicity
(Neither Party Previously Married)

Generation of Bride or Groom	Born in Mexico	Parents Born in Mexico	Third or More Generation	Not Mexican American
		Groom's median age		
Bride:				
First generation	25.9	26.1	22.0	23.3
Second generation	24.0	23.2	21.3	23.1
Third or more generation	21.8	21.2	20.8	21.8
Subtotal, Mexican American	24.9	22.3	21.1	N.A.
Subtotal, not Mexican American	22.4	22.0	21.0	N.A.
Over-all	24.7	22.2	21.1	N.A.
		Bride's median age		
Groom:				
First generation	23.7	22.1	19.4	19.8
Second generation	22.6	21.0	19.3	19.5
Third or more generation	20.7	19.8	19.1	19.0
Subtotal, Mexican American	22.4	20.6	19.2	N.A.
Subtotal, not Mexican American	21.7	21.5	19.9	N.A.
Over-all	22.3	20.8	19.4	N.A.

Note: Generationally endogamous cells are italicized.

gradient is not entirely unexpected in light of the variations in age composition of the first, second, and third generations. For example, in the Los Angeles SMSA, in 1960, only 13 per cent of the Spanish-surname population born in Mexico and over fifteen years of age was in the marriageable ages from fifteen to twenty-four. By comparison, individuals with native- or Mexican-born parents, respectively, accounted for 36 and 26 per cent of this marriageable age group.

Given the differences in age composition, we find that among persons of every generation, the more "Mexican" the spouse, the older the bride or groom. Without more study one might accept the notion that persons who marry spouses close to immigrant status are marrying into an older population and are themselves likely to be older than those who marry native-born Mexican Americans. Further examination of the grooms suggests that this is not entirely sufficient as an explanation.

Table 6 holds both age and generation constant for Mexican American grooms and examines the distribution of marriages by ethnicity and generation of brides. The data strongly suggest that in any particular generation of grooms, age has a stronger influence on mate selection by Mexican American men within the ethnic community than on the endogamy rate proper. In every one of the three generations, older Mexican American men tend to marry women close to immigrant status.

The Mexican American men who married Anglo women tended to be somewhat younger than the men who married first- and second-generation brides and older than those who took third-generation brides, although differences are minor. Among the brides who married Anglo men, the pattern is more mixed, although for neither brides nor grooms are there strong reasons to believe that the exogamous spouses are necessarily older (Table 5). (The explanation for these patterns might be cultural or demographic. Present data on this issue are not available.)

How can we explain why younger Mexican Americans are as likely to marry exogamously as are older persons? It is possible that the younger people are more antitraditionalist in their orientation than the older persons. One piece of data supports this contention. Preliminary results from field surveys show the prescriptive age of marriage for men to be rather high in this population. This would argue that the young are departing from the norms of the community. It is possible also that other studies which found the rate of exogamy to rise with age dealt with groups where the prescriptive age for marriage is low, where those who defer marriage until eco-nomically and socially established are antitraditionalist in their lives. One might also suggest that the opportunities for wide contacts and social mobility are much greater among the young. Our cross-sectional study captures persons in different age brackets. Thus, the twenty-one-year-old Mexican American

Table 6

Percentage of In- and Out-Group Marriages of Mexican Americans by Age of Grooms, Los Angeles County, 1963

Brides	Grooms, Foreign Born, Mexico			Grooms, Mexican Parentage			Grooms, Natives of Native Parentage		
	Less Than 25	25-34	Over 34	Less Than 25	25-34	Over 34	Less than 25	25-34	Over 34
Foreign born, Mexico	42.1 (49.7)	56.4 (63.1)	61.6 (71.0)	8.0 (10.3)	18.1 (24.3)	24.8 (32.4)	5.8 (8.2)	8.9 (12.9)	14.1 (26.7)
Foreign or mixed parentage, Mexico	23.0 (27.2)	24.8 (27.7)	19.8 (22.8)	30.5 (39.2)	37.7 (50.6)	40.7 (53.1)	23.6 (33.4)	25.8 (37.4)	20.0 (37.8)
Natives of native parentage	19.6 (23.0)	8.2 (9.2)	5.3 (6.1)	39.3 (50.5)	18.7 (25.1)	11.1 (14.5)	41.2 (58.4)	34.2 (49.6)	18.8 (35.5)
Subtotal, Inmarriage	84.7 (100.0)	89.4 (100.0)	86.7 (100.0)	77.8 (100.0)	74.5 (100.0)	76.6 (100.0)	70.6 (100.0)	68.9 (100.0)	52.9 (100.0)
Foreign or mixed stock:									
Hispanic	2.0	3.7	3.4	0.5	2.6	2.6	0.8	0.7	1.2
Other, Outmarriage	13.3	6.9	9.9	21.7	22.9	20.8	28.6	30.4	45.9
Total	100.0	100.0	100.0	100.0	100.0	100.0	100.0	100.0	100.0
(N)	(444)	(379)	(263)	(973)	(546)	(307)	(1,280)	(302)	(85)

Note: Percentages in parentheses are based on endogamous marriages only.

marrying an Anglo in 1963 may have had quite different experiences from the thirty-one-year-old person marrying a Mexican-born bride in the same year. Relationships with the larger Anglo society have changed considerably in the past decade.

IMPLICATIONS

At the outset, we stated that our paper had two purposes. The first was addressed to the probable future of a particular population—the Mexican Americans. We feel that our findings strongly suggest the assimilative potential of the population when external barriers are comparatively low, though this potential has been generally depreciated. We must not, of course, make the mistake of confusing a cross-sectional three-generational study with a longitudinal study; the internal differences in endogamy rates imply that the assimilative potential is related to nativity and rate of advancement in the group, and both of these may shift.

We also feel that this analysis strongly supports the responsiveness of Mexican Americans, along with other ethnic groups, to milieu—that is, to variations in both prejudice and opportunities, which themselves are associated.

More generally, these data can be interpreted as indicating underlying processes which occur in the breakdown of mechanical solidarity in an increasingly open system. Mexican Americans have been unusual in maintaining strong ethnic boundaries, in part because of many isolating mechanisms associated with their initial contact with Anglo populations. These mechanisms include the structural and emotional effects of two wars fought with neighboring Mexico within a hundred years, both of which impinged particularly heavily upon Texas, an area that still contains a large proportion of the nation's Mexican Americans. General "race" prejudice and severe educational and work segregation have been still other factors. The population is also quite segregated by religion. That is, Catholicism is the prevailing faith in a predominantly Protestant region. However, Catholic *practice* is far less equivocal in the Los Angeles area. Less than half of the marriages considered here, for example, were validated by Catholic ceremony. There is evidence that in other regards as well the religious practice of this population in the country falls far short of the Catholic norms. The population is also segregated by residence, both in rural and urban areas. In New Mexico, even more stringent historical and political circumstances have insured little contact with the surrounding Anglo population; the high endogamy found in Albuquerque is not surprising, despite the fact that the "Spanish" population is actually older than the relatively "new" white settlers from the East and North.

These kinds of isolating experiences were historically accompanied by considerable—almost exclusive—reliance on kin as principal sources of emotional and other support and also by considerable similarity in outlook and style of life. However, the extent of this isolation is generally declining—though only slightly in some parts of the Southwest, more substantially in others, like Los Angeles.

As isolation declines and as both upward and horizontal mobility become more common, there come to be many more varieties in style of life. Most important, primary-group relations decline in functional importance and they even cease to be maintained mechanically, that is, by style of life. Thus, the socializing and identity-maintaining structures of the ethnic group—and particularly the family—are structurally weakened. Intrafamily dissimilarity increases.

This kind of interpretation seems applicable in our case especially to the third-generation families living in the relatively open opportunity structure of the type found in Los Angeles, and helps explain their notable propensity toward assimilative marriage (whereas if ethnic loyalty were maintained, the generation of partner would have little relevance). Increased experience in the larger system—especially rewarding experience—decreases the saliency of the ethnic group as the prime source of identity, in turn weakening the control of the primary group over the social relations of its members. Ascriptive identity decreases in salience.

*Projecting or jutting beyond a line — to jump, leap

The particular history of this population warrants further exploration on this and other topics; the peculiar blend of minority and ethnic statuses provides an especially fertile ground for the development of hypotheses concerning the combined effects of a variety of social differences. This study, based on the severely limited data available in marriage licenses, appears to call for increased attention to the group not only as a social problem but as a sociological problem of interest.

III / CHANGE

The first two parts of this book spelled out who the Chicanos are and what problems they face in certain parts of the United States. Part III is entitled very simply "Change," for what is happening in the United States today with relation to Chicanos is too vast, too protean, too complex to permit more precise labeling. The change occurring is more than social change, political change, economic change, cultural change, educational change alone; it is all these and more, so we try to acknowledge the profundity of what is happening by using the simple yet powerful word *change*. For what is happening is the destruction of former attitudes, held by both Chicanos and Anglos, that Anglos were somehow privileged, more adequate, more favored by God, nature, government, and society.

Fernando Peñalosa writes of the different ways that change has come to the Chicano in Southern California. He notes such changes in employment, housing, family, and attitudes. Two of the changes are significant because of their long-range potential of fulfilling some of the aspirations of Chicanos. Peñalosa notes, first, that "the old conservative Mexico-oriented leadership has been giving way to a new leadership of college educated professionals who are thoroughly at home in the Anglo world, but who have retained their ethnic roots"; and, secondly, that "Mexican-Americans now have their own political organizations such as the Mexican-American Political Association (MAPA) and have emerged as a political force in their own right."

Nancie Gonzalez's description of activism in New Mexico is included here because it reveals that the Chicano Movement while serving as a catalyst to unify Chicanos also serves to divide them into factions which undoubtedly reduces their political effectiveness. Dr. Gonzalez begins her account with the *Alianza Federal de Mercedes* (Federal Alliance of Free States), founded by Reies Tijerina to return lands in New Mexico to the original hispano settlers, and continues through the Brown Berets, a militant organization formed to protect Chicanos from police harassment. The intent of her article is to describe Chicano political activism in rural New Mexico.

Additionally, however, Dr. Gonzalez provides insights into the kinds of, and reasons for, factionalism in the movement in New Mexico.

Dr. Gonzalez captures the essence of the meaning of factionalism in the Chicano movement when she writes:

> *New Mexico, with all its faults, with all its poverty, nevertheless comes closer to the pluralistic dream of society than does any other area in the nation. It is hoped that current events do not further polarize the positions with the Spanish-American ethnic groups to the point that some deny la raza altogether while others attempt to overthrow the entire system which has so far permitted and reinforced the Spanish traditions in the struggle for survival. At the same time, thousands of Hispanos have achieved positions in life which they appreciate and value—positions which they feel are dignified, free from harassment, and well remunerated. These individuals, understandably enough, resent what they see as racist militancy. Called* vendidos *(sellouts) themselves, many of them feel it is the militants who are "selling out"* la raza *by bringing the issue of ethnicity into what should be a war on poverty.*

The dilemma of factionalism, or pluralism, in the Chicano Movement need not have fatal consequences if both the militants and the moderates can learn to live together in some sort of "peaceful coexistence." The alternative, factional fights over ideological issues, can only serve to slow down progress; energies and leadership expended in such fights could be better spent in devising strategies to achieve objectives. It may be that when more Chicanos find themselves in positions where their responsibilities are heavy and their obligations far-reaching, the thrust of the movement will shift from ideological disputes to more efficient administration of policies devoted to attaining greater social justice.

The Changing Mexican-American in Southern California

Fernando Peñalosa

One of the hazards of any empirical science such as sociology is the constant temptation to reify what is essentially a statistical concept or a theoretical construct of the researcher. When such a model is essentially homologous with empirical reality, little theoretical or practical harm may come from reification. But when the model is essentially static, while the empirical reality with which the model is putatively homologous is in fact a process of dynamic change, either the theoretical or the practical consequences, or both, may be unfortunate. It may safely be asserted that the concept or construct "Mexican-American population" as ordinarily found in the sociological literature frequently manifests a significant gap with empirical reality.

The most often used, and undoubtedly the best, approximation to the parameters of this population relies on a count of the Spanish-surname population, particularly in the states of the Southwest. But while the term "Spanish-surname population" is operationally definable, the terms "Mexican

Fernando Peñalosa, "The Changing Mexican-American in Southern California," *Sociology and Social Research*, vol. 51, no. 4 (July 1967). Reprinted by permission of Sociology and Social Research, University of California, Los Angeles.

American population" or "Mexican-American community" are not so easily controlled. Existentially there is no Mexican-American community as such, nor is there such a "thing" as Mexican-American culture. The group is fragmentized socially, culturally, ideologically, and organizationally. It is characterized by extremely important social-class, regional, and rural-urban differences. Partially because of the great regional variations of this ethnic group, this paper will be concerned primarily with southern California, one of the areas of greatest concentration of this population in the Southwest.

Despite or perhaps because of its extreme fragmentation, there is significant evidence of increased self-consciousness of the group as it struggles through a crisis for self-identity. A perennial topic of discussion in Mexican organizations, as well as in talk given by Mexican-American leaders before Anglo groups is, "What shall we call ourselves?" In southern California the most prevalent term used is "Mexican-American." This term, however, has little currency outside of southern California, and even in the latter areas there is some dissatisfaction with the term. In recent years there has been an increase in use of the expression "Americans of Mexican descent" at the expense of the term "Mexican-American." Yet these terms are not in any strict sense synonymous, but realistically represent two quite different segments of the population under discussion. Persons of Mexican descent who were not at one time enculturated into the subculture of some Mexican-American neighborhood are best labelled "Americans of Mexican descent" rather than "Mexican-Americans." The former do not constitute an ethnic minority group as do the latter. Another recent trend is that the attempt to disguise Mexican ethnic origin by self-identification as "Spanish" appears to be on the wane.

At the present time, in southern California as in the Southwest as a whole, the Mexican-American population is increasing more rapidly than the white population as a whole and only slightly less rapidly than the Negro population. In southern California the Spanish surname population increased 92.3 per cent between 1950 and 1960, but more than 100 per cent in Los Angeles (100.5) and nearby Orange (122.0) counties. The result is that the Mexican-American continues to be the largest minority group in southern California. In 1960 there were 870,600 Mexican-Americans in the eight southern California counties. It is probably now well over 1,000,000. This population is 78.8 per cent native-born. The fact that immigrants from Mexico during 1955-60 accounted for 5.1 per cent of California's Spanish surname population five years and over in 1960 indicates that natural increase is not the only significant factor contributing to the population's growth. Since 78.0 per cent of the Mexican-Americans in southern California in 1960 were under the age of 35, this young population has a very high growth potential. Undoubtedly this fast growing segment of California's population will become numerically and proportionally even more important in the future.

The standard accounts of Mexican-Americans stress their relatively high degree of cultural conservatism. This population is partially indigenous to the region, since it was largely responsible for settling the Southwest before its acquisition by the United States from Mexico in 1848. The continuing waves of immigrants, largely rural lower-class in background, from Mexico have been of much larger dimensions than the flow of acculturated individuals into the mainstream of American life. Thus it has been that persons of Mexican descent have resided in southern California for almost two hundred years and many have largely retained their language and culture over this long span of time.

The primary reasons would seem to be the nearness of the country of emigration and the failure of the public school system to teach an adequate command of the English language and the other skills necessary for successful entry into the occupational world. As a result Mexican-Americans have had to compete economically with a continuous incoming supply of cheap Mexican national labor. The latest waves of the latter were those of the braceros and of the hundreds of thousands of "wetbacks" who have played their part in the continuing low average economic status of the Mexican-American population.

Despite great obstacles, this population as a whole is clearly moving further away from lower-class Mexican traditional culture and toward Anglo-American middle-class culture, so that both its cultural status and its social-class status are changing. It is true that immigrants in many ways reinforce the traditional patterns locally, but they are coming from a changing Mexico much more urbanized and industrialized than the Mexico known to the immigrant of two, three, or four decades ago. The latest waves of immigration have come from socioeconomically higher, more urbanized strata of Mexican society. Mexican-American migrants also come in important numbers from other states of the Southwest, particularly from Texas and New Mexico. The communities from which they have come are generally more traditionally oriented than southern California Mexican-American communities. On the other hand, in the latter, particularly the urban ones, intermarriage and normal social relations among the various subtypes of Mexican-Americans are promoting their merger into a more homogeneous population.

There have been no recent major published studies specifically concerning southern California Mexican-Americans, but the tacit assumption of general works or of studies of communities in other areas is that their conclusions apply with equal force to the former. Many reports have either concentrated or limited aspects of the group, or used source materials two or more decades old, or both.

The most competent documentations of traditional Mexican folk culture in both Mexico and in the United States often make the assumption that understanding this culture is somehow the key to understanding Mexican-American culture. The latter is frequently dealt with as if it were a variety of Mexican folk culture. The rejection of such an oversimplification does not imply, of course, that there is no value in understanding this "folk" or "preindustrial" culture with its close ties to the land, its different sense of time, its lack of emphasis on formal education, and a social structure based primarily on personal rather than impersonal relationships. At the same time, such concepts should not constitute a perceptual screen with which to view the current situation. It is important to note in this connection that in recent years Mexican-Americans in southern California have been categorized along with a number of other ethnic groups and social strata as "culturally deprived" or "economically disadvantaged." It is patent that the nature of the "cultural deprivation" or "economic disadvantage" of this ethnic group is primarily a handicap of class and not of culture, unless we specify lower-class culture. The middle-class Mexican immigrant and his descendants have not been ordinarily "culturally deprived" or "economically disadvantaged," unless they gravitate to a Mexican-American *barrio* with its particular culture. If they move into a predominantly Anglo neighborhood, as they usually do, their problems are normally no greater than those of middle class immigrants from other countries. Mexican middle class persons are more like American middle class persons in their general way of life and basic outlook than they are like lower class persons from their own country.

There is a reaction among educated Mexican-Americans and among some informed social scientists against the characterizations of Mexican-American culture to be found in authoritative books and articles on the subject. They feel that these sources tend to create stereotypes by which even well-trained and well-meaning Anglos will tend to perceive the group, not taking account of individual differences and achievements. Pride and sensitivity about the collective image remain important traits even among the most highly acculturated Mexican-Americans.

The type of characterization which is most unsatisfactory revolves about concepts of the Mexican-American population as largely engaged in migratory agricultural labor. Such broad generalizations as those quoted tend to blur the lines of distinction among the various social classes among Mexican-Americans. They further fail to differentiate clearly among a number of interrelated factors: the lower class, rural origins of the immigrants; the low average occupational status of Mexican-Americans at the present time; and the ways in which their present day problems are shared by the members of lower class groups, ethnic or otherwise. They further fail to take into consideration the broad rural-urban class, occupational, educational, and regional differences of the Mexican-American population. A homogeneity is postulated or inferred where none exists. Even if we confine our attention to one broad geographical area, such as southern California, and examine the culture and social structure of this population, the homogeneity fails to appear.

The Mexican-American subculture in its most common variant is probably best regarded and understood as a variant of American working-lower class culture. This culture is, of course, affected by all the limitations of lower status in a predominantly middle-class society. The group's way of life is further conditioned by the effects of the reaction of the group to discrimination. If we accept the concept of Mexican-American culture, at least in its southern California variety, as a variant of the United States working class subculture, but influenced to a lesser or stronger degree by traditional Mexican folk culture, it follows that these people should be regarded as partially Mexicanized Americans rather than as partially Americanized Mexicans. No one who has carefully observed the way of life of rural and of urban lower-class people in Mexico, which would represent the original roots of most Mexican-Americans, would make the mistake of considering them the reverse.

The forces of acculturation and assimilation working over a period of three or more generations have brought about the present situation. Most of the change has been slow and barely perceptible to many of the most-quoted authors in the field. Nevertheless, there was a major breakthrough during World War II of forces promoting change and the solution of problems confronting the Mexican-American community. At this time there was a great flow of people out of the *barrio* or Mexican-American neighborhood. Young Mexican-Americans took industrial jobs in increasing numbers, went off to war, traveled around the world, and were treated as individuals, some for the first time. During World War II Mexican-Americans volunteered in greater numbers and won more Congressional Medals of Honor per capita than any other ethnic group. Veterans especially returned to find themselves dissatisfied with the old ways, and many went to college under the provisions of the G.I. Bill. Occupational skills were upgraded because of wartime industrial experience, and because of the additional educational opportunities made available to younger members of the group.

Social change involves of course not only a realignment of individual perceptions, attitudes and actions, but also a reorganization of structural relationships within the community. It is important to note that the types of American communities, both rural and urban, into which Mexican immigrants and interstate migrants of yesterday and today have moved form . . . heterogeneous congeries. Some of the differences found from one Mexican-American community to another are undoubtedly due to the varying natures of the several Anglo-American matrices in which the Mexican-American communities are imbedded. The rate of sociocultural change therefore varies widely from one southern California community to another.

Before World War II the Mexican-American population in the Southwest was largely rural, but by 1950 it was two-thirds urban, and by 1960 it was four-fifths urban. In southern California this population was 83.7 per cent urban in 1960. With the tremendous rate of urbanization and metropolitanization of the region many communities that were rural towns or semiisolated suburbs have now become thoroughly urbanized, with a consequent further urbanization of the resident Mexican-American populations.

One significant phenomenon occurring in these newly urbanized areas has been an attenuation of formerly very rigid interethnic lines of stratification. The older studies characterized Mexican-Anglo relations in southern California as of a caste or semicaste nature, with virtually separate Anglo-American and Mexican-American castes in the communities studied. The World War II and postwar periods promoted occupational and geographical mobility to such an extent that rigid caste barriers against intermarriage and equality of employment and housing opportunities have all but disappeared, particularly in urban areas.

Changes in the employment pattern in the Mexican-American work force appear to lie at the very confluence of forces promoting changes in this population. Closely related to the fact of increasing urbanization has been the shift from rural to urban occupations and the shift from unskilled to skilled jobs. These shifts have affected primarily the younger generation. Just over a decade ago Broom and Shevky had phrased the problem of studying Mexican-American social differentiation as one of determining to what extent people had left migratory labor and become occupationally differentiated. But California as a whole no longer has a Mexican-American population which to any significant extent engages in migratory agricultural labor. Only 14.9 per cent of the Mexican-American labor force is engaged in agriculture, forestry, or fisheries, and only 12.2 per cent are employed as farm laborers or foremen. Mexican-American field hands were largely displaced during the World War II and postwar periods by the huge influx of contract laborers from Mexico, the *braceros.* Having been displaced from agriculture, Mexican-Americans are not likely to return to this type of employment in large numbers now that the *bracero* program has almost completely been suspended.

From a preponderance of unskilled employment, Mexican-Americans in California have since World War II been concentrated primarily in blue-collar work of a semiskilled or skilled nature (46.3 per cent) as compared to the total number of unskilled (farm laborers and foremen, other laborers, and private household workers: 23.4 per cent). A significant proportion for the first time are now found also in entrepreneurial, professional, and other white collar occupations (22.2 per cent). Especially important has been the entry of Mexican-Americans into types of professional employment where they are in a position to assist in the efforts to solve the manifold problems confronting Mexican-Americans in southern California urban centers. Because to assert that Mexican-Americans have largely left behind the problems associated with migratory agricultural labor is not to say that they have no problems. It is rather that now their problems have become those of an underpriviliged urban minority group.

The most serious problem undoubtedly lies within the area of education. In this connection it is important to recognize that Mexican-American children are not necessarily any more "culturally deprived" than are children of other low-income families. School authorities in southern California generally consider "bilingualism" as a handicap. Some teachers and administrators consider it as virtually tantamount to mental retardation. This is, of course, a misreading of the true meaning of bilingualism, which is equal fluency in two languages. The problem is obviously a lack of command of English, and not the ability to speak Spanish. Yet all poor and underprivileged people speak poorly and with an accent because they have not enough contact with the majority. True bilingualism, a potential asset in an increasingly international world, is actually discouraged, or at least is not fostered, by the public schools.

Educational progress of the group as a whole has been relatively slow. Between the last two censuses of 1950 and 1960 the average number of years of schooling of the Mexican-American population in California increased by a little over one year (from 7.6 and 8.0 to 8.9 and 9.2 for males and females respectively). It is only in long range perspective that any impressive educational progress can be seen, e.g., the percentage of Mexican-Americans in Los Angeles who were completing junior college in 1957 was as large as the percentage of those completing the eighth grade in 1927.

Another focus for change among southern California Mexican Americans lies in family structure. In urban areas of southern California at least, the traditional extended family group including siblings and their children is no longer found to any significant extent. The *compadrazgo* or ritual coparenthood relation no longer has any significance as a fictive kinship relation. Related to the increased emphasis or individualism is the move away from traditional Mexican values and toward the Anglo-American values of achievement, activity, efficiency, and emphasis on the future.

The breakdown of traditional Mexican family structure appears to be related to a relatively high incidence of juvenile delinquency for the group. At the same time, Mexican-Americans delinquency is on the downgrade because many of the neighborhoods which contributed to such conditions are slowly disappearing as a result of urban renewal and freeway construction. As a proportion of total state commitments, Mexican-Americans delinquents dropped from 25 per cent in 1959 to 17 per cent in 1965.

Housing discrimination has eased considerably in southern California urban areas and Mexican-Americans can now purchase or rent housing in many desirable areas formerly closed to them. This is not to deny that widespread discrimination still exists. It is ironic, therefore, that analysis of voting results in precincts with high proportions of Spanish surname individuals showed that in the November 1964 state election Mexican-Americans voted heavily in favor of the controversial Proposition 14. The latter, when passed, (although recently ruled unconstitutional by the California Supreme Court) put a provision into the state constitution outlawing antidiscrimination legislation in the housing field. Mexican-Americans apparently failed to realize that the measuse was directed against them as well as against the Negro. Their political leaders had simply assumed that Mexican-Americans would vote against a measure which was self-evidently against their own interests. They had failed to reckon with the Mexican-American fear of Negro competition for housing, and the latent hostility between the two groups in some residential areas.

Some Mexican-American neighborhoods have disappeared through forced urban renewal, that is, without the consent of the persons displaced. Some Mexican-Americans have come to refer cynically to urban renewal as "Mexican removal," since for the families concerned no problems are solved by urban renewal. In a number of southern California communities in the past two or three years, Mexican-American leaders (notably in Pico-Rivera in 1964) have been able to muster enough political power, with the assistance of sympathetic outsiders, to prevent urban renewal programs from uprooting them from their homes to higher priced housing elsewhere. It is now unlikely that a situation, such as that of Chavez Ravine, will be repeated. The latter was taken over several years ago by the city of Los Angeles for a housing project, but sold for $1.00 to the Los Angeles Dodgers for a baseball stadium. The highly publicized forcible removal of several Mexican-American families from the ravine left an indelible impression on the public, Mexican and Anglo alike.

Anglo professionals tend to perceive Mexican-American problems as connected with various forms of social disorganization. Mexican-Americans, on the other hand, perceive their problems primarily in terms of the blocking of their aspirations. While biculturalism and bilingualism are viewed by most Anglos as problems, they are not so viewed by most Mexican-Americans. On the other hand, these two characteristics do in fact lead to problems in a society ostensibly committed to cultural pluralism but in reality sustaining the melting pot ideology. There have always been cleavages and factionalism in Mexican-American communities, but never before has the issue of whether to assimilate or not to assimilate been so clearly placed before Mexican-American public opinion.

The major goal now presented to the Mexican-American community by its leaders is no longer simply the abolition of discrimination as it was in the nineteen-thirties and nineteen-forties, but rather of allowing the Mexican-American to make the best use of his abilities including the opportunity to capitalize on his bilingualism. Formerly the community was drained of talent as trained, professional people left the ethnic enclave and became integrated into the dominant society. Now they are finding that by moving professionally back into the *barrio* and working on Mexican-American problems they can advance their own careers and become recognized as community leaders. The community is therefore no longer losing its potential leadership as it once did. The old conservative Mexico-oriented leadership has been giving way to a new leadership of college educated professionals who are thoroughly at home in the Anglo world, but who have retained their ethnic roots.

Current changes appear to indicate a metamorphosis of the group from a lower ethnic caste to a minority group resembling a European immigrant group of a generation or two ago such as, for example, the Italian-Americans in New York, Boston, or San Francisco. Thus, for the first time since the 1850's Mexicans in southern California were appointed to public policy-making positions during the recent administration of Governor Edmund G. Brown. These political appointees in state and local government have been in a position to help open up employment opportunities to other Mexican-Americans and have also provided for better communication between various state agencies and the people. Similarly, Mexican-Americans now have their own political organizations such as The Mexican-American Political Association (MAPA) and have emerged as a political force in their own right. At election time the Anglo-American power structure has become increasingly cognizant of this new political force. Mexican-Americans for their part have learned that if they want such benefits as streets paved and kept in good repair, street lighting, adequate schools, Mexican-Americans on teaching staffs and on the police force, they have to make their power felt at the polls. As a result, a significant number of officials have been elected. There are at latest count 15 mayors, 56 city councilmen and 20 school board members of Mexican-American origin throughout the state, the great majority in southern California.

Another indication of increasing Mexican-American political strength was the recent defeat of the *bracero* program, for which Mexican-Americans are taking a great deal of the credit. Their leaders had long fought this program which they felt had undermined efforts to establish minimum wages, adequate housing, and schooling for farm workers and their families.

On the national level, one result of the 1960 and 1964 campaigns was that numerous political patronage opportunities were opened up to professional Mexican-Americans in the Peace Corps, the Alliance for Progress, AID, and in the War on Poverty. Mexican-American leaders are increasingly becoming concerned not only by what they can do for their own ethnic group but also for their country as a whole. They are especially eager to utilize their unique abilities and skills in promoting United States goals in Latin America, to which area they will no doubt continue to be sent in increasing numbers. Southern California, where the largest urban concentration of Mexican-Americans in the country is found, has produced and no doubt will continue to produce more than its share of such leaders, as this population as a whole moves even closer to the mainstream of American life.

The Continuing Scene: Activism in New Mexico, 1966-69

Nancie L. Gonzalez

. . . A minority within the minority group of Hispanos has managed to make its voice heard in a variety of ways, and although some may fear the militancy of the new movements, others will welcome them as past-due harbingers of change.

Activism itself is not particularly new in New Mexico or anywhere else, if one means by this the attempts of some members of a depressed or underprivileged sector (or their sympathizers) to improve their status. Romano (1968) has emphasized this fact in a highly critical essay on works by Anglos on Spanish-American culture. Some of the older activist organizations in New Mexico among Spanish-Americans include *La Mano Negra, Las Gorras Blancas*, LULAC (League of United Latin American Citizens), the G. I. Forum, the American Legion, Veterans of Foreign Wars, and others mentioned in the preceding chapters. The first four of these organizations were founded specifically by Spanish-Americans in order to fight for better conditions for their group. The first two used extra-legal means, while the others worked within established

Nancie L. Gonzalez, "The Continuing Scene: Activism in New Mexico, 1966-1969," in *The Spanish Americans of New Mexico: A Heritage of Pride* (Albuquerque: The University of New Mexico Press, 1969), pp. 179-196. Copyright The University of New Mexico Press.

channels. . . . The veterans' organizations in New Mexico also worked actively for similar causes, and have been said by some (Holmes 1967) to have been instrumental in illustrating the political power of the Hispanos as a group. Aside from these there have always been activists within the various church groups and even within the structure of welfare, as seen in the Life With Pride organization. . . .

The list could be extended considerably, but today when activism is mentioned it is not generally groups such as these which are meant. Indeed, all those mentioned, with the exception of *La Mano Negra* and *Las Gorras Blancas*, would most likely be considered by the newer activists as being hopelessly embroiled in and controlled by the Establishment and therefore incapable of improving the lot of those they claim to serve. Others might argue that these same groups in fact are out of touch with the lower-class elements of their particular minority or ethnic group and are for these reasons unable to accomplish the goal of improving the lot of those lowest on the social scale.

THE ALIANZA

In tracing the development of the more militant activist organizations in New Mexico at the present time, one must once again return to a consideration of the Alianza. . . . It may truly be said that this organization was the first movement with civil rights implications to attract attention within the state of New Mexico. Before this there had been other groups such as the Mexican-American Political Association (MAPA) and others which had managed to make a small dent in areas such as Colorado, Texas, and California but which went largely unnoticed here. The plight of the migrant workers—particularly the grape pickers under Cesar Chavez—was considered to have only local (Californian) implications, and the kinship of their *Causa* with that of the Spanish-speaking people in New Mexico was apparently not at first appreciated by most New Mexicans. The 1966 Delano Proclamation and its cry of "*huelga*" (strike) found sympathizers here, but there was no immediate action linking this with conditions in New Mexico.

After the incidents in June 1967 at Tierra Amarilla, the Alianza attracted the attention of the whole country. The national news media such as *Newsweek* carried stories of this "wild west show," as it was often presented, and an incredulous public was made to realize the fact that the poor farmers of Spanish descent in northern New Mexico had serious problems and needed to be heard.

However, the initial reaction, largely stimulated by the sensational aspects of the events which were highly dramatized in the press, was that law and order had broken down in New Mexico (if indeed they had ever existed) and that New Mexicans were witnessing a return to the simpler but more brutal code of the frontier. In a sense, there was an element of this involved; however, contrary to what most people thought, the Alianza saw itself as a citizens' group called upon to correct an injustice which the regularly constituted law enforcement bodies could not handle, in part because they themselves were involved in bringing about the infringement of rights. Some members of the Alianza had been arrested and imprisoned for unlawful assembly after they had been forbidden by the state's attorney to gather. Their brethren then attempted to free them and at the same time make a citizen's arrest of the responsible party. The rest is history, but it is important to repeat that a jury found Reies Tijerina, the leader, not guilty of the state's three most serious charges stemming from this incident.

At first there seems to have been no direct connection between the Alianza and other activist organizations in existence outside the state of New Mexico. However, after Tierra Amarilla many of these groups made offers of assistance in order to bring the Alianza into the ranks of the Spanish-American and other radical civil rights movements.

Many of the people deeply involved in the Alianza took part in the Poor People's March on Washington in 1967, and here again national publicity was achieved. By this time many persons from outside the state had come to work with the Alianza and it appears that there were some attempts at reorganization or restructuring of the group at this time. There seem to have been efforts to model it after more radical civil rights movements elsewhere, but these efforts did not have complete success.

In addition to the Alianza, several other new activist-type organizations have appeared only recently on the New Mexican scene; they will be described very briefly, including what seem to this author to be the interrelationships among them and offering an interpretation of the relationships between this new activism and the rest of the New Mexican sociocultural system. Among the groups which will be considered are the Alianza itself, the Brown Berets, the United-Mexican American Students (UMAS), and two youth groups called *Los Caballeros de Nueva España* and *Los Comancheros del Norte.* Finally, the development of an underground Chicano press, represented by eighteen newspapers which have recently popped up all over the Southwest,[1] will be examined.

In the analysis of the Alianza as a nativistic, revivalistic cult movement . . . the author noted that many of the demands of the group were unrealistic and impractical and that survival might depend upon the group's willingness to modify some of its claims and doctrine and, at the same time, align itself more closely with other civil rights movements in the nation. As Frances Swadesh (1968) and Joseph Love (1969) have shown recently, the Alianza to an increasing extent has taken on many of the characteristics of true civil rights movements. Along with Love, but contrary to Swadesh, the author feels that the Alianza is still better understood as a nativistic cult than as a civil rights movement, in spite of the fact that it has tended to move in the latter direction over the past two years.

Tijerina, the leader of the Alianza, remains a charismatic figure and has become a symbol of the plight of the underdog Spanish-American in New Mexico. Yet he steadfastly refuses to modify many elements in his doctrine and his behavior which might bring his cult more fully in line with the broader New Left movements. He has been strongly criticized by non-Hispano spokesmen of the radical New Left, precisely on the basis of the charismatic and cultlike flavor of the movement (Kennedy 1968). As such, the Alianza remains something unique within New Mexico and among the Spanish-speaking everywhere. It is still largely rural in its membership; it is still almost exclusively dependent upon its leader for guidance and formation of doctrine; and it frequently comes into philosophical collision with representatives of other American minority groups such as Blacks, Jews, and White radicals. It is noteworthy that Cesar Chavez and his grape pickers union have not been particularly brotherly. Relations are cordial but not overly close between the two leaders. Chavez heads a union and a civil rights movement, not a revivalistic or nativistic cult.

It is perhaps significant to note the differences in the terminology used by the Alianza and the Californian and Texas activist movements. The Alianza stresses the mestizo blood of its members and places great value on being brown, a result of having sprung from a union between Indian and Spanish. In this respect, the activist movements share the ideology of the Mexican-American who also prides himself on being a mestizo. However, the term Mexican-American, which is so broadly accepted outside the state of New Mexico, is still not used by the Alianza itself. The Alianza prefers the term *"Indo-Hispano,"* and although the members frequently refer to themselves as *Mexicanos*, there is still no real identification with the term "Mexican-American."

The insistence upon use of *Indo-Hispano* has the effect of clouding the issue of Spanish theft of land belonging to the American Indians. This issue is one of the really weak spots in the peculiar logic of the Alianza. When Indians question the right of the Hispano to the lands as granted by the King of Spain, the answer, usually considered inadequate by Indian observers, is that the Alianza represents the interests of both Indians and the descendants of the early Hispano settlers. In fact, it is true that they represent the mixed-blood descendants of the Hispanicized Indians, but hardly of the Indians who have retained their ethnic identity and purity of race.

In the fall of 1968 the Alianza made its first venture into organized politics in the state of New Mexico. Tijerina ran for governor as a candidate of the Peoples Constitutionalist Party (the Alianza party) until his name was removed from the ballot at a very late point in the campaign on the grounds that he had been convicted of several charges in regard to the 1966 sit-in in the Echo Amphitheater incident. Since his case had been appealed before the District Circuit Court it was decided, after some dispute, that he really was not eligible to run for office. Therefore, the man chosen to run as his lieutenant governor (interestingly enough, an Indian, Jose Alfredo Maestas) ran in his stead. Only 1,540 votes were secured for the positions of governor and lieutenant governor.

The voting record probably reflects several related facts—first, the generally short campaign period, since the Alianza determined to run candidates at a fairly late date; second, the possibility that some votes were improperly counted (this possibility always exists in New Mexico, and there were many rumors to this effect in the fall of 1968); third, the probable decline in organization membership (recognized by Tijerina himself, who felt that by running he might be able to reawaken fervor among some of his former adherents); fourth, the very real and certain fact that Tijerina is a charismatic leader whose followers are not all likely to vote for a substitute even though endorsed by the leader himself. Other candidates of the Peoples Constitutionalist Party had varying success in gathering votes, although none won an office. Those who obtained the highest number of votes were well-known names in the community, often for reasons other than their association with the Alianza.

In assessing the present position of the Alianza the author would predict that it will continue to make itself heard and may have some success in stimulating social change. The fact that it is already having some impact is shown by the bombings of the Alianza headquarters and of the homes and property of its officers. There have been at the time of this writing four such bombings, the latest occurring on March 15, 1969. So far no one has been injured, and the bombings have been, in a sense, tokens of the resentment and fear that the Alianza awakens among some sectors of the New Mexican population. Another kind of evidence that the Alianza may be having some effect is the recent suggestion by Representative Gonzales from Texas that Congress investigate the land claims issue.

THE BROWN BERETS

This group, modeled after the black berets of the Black Panther movement, has only recently appeared in New Mexico. It seems likely that the local organization sprang from contacts made by some New Mexicans in Washington for the Poor People's March. The Brown Beret idea apparently originated in California, and now there are local chapters in many southwestern cities. Unlike the Alianza, it is not only urban-based but has a much broader coverage. It includes primarily young people, which also sets it apart from the Alianza in which older persons predominate.

In Albuquerque the Brown Berets first burst upon the scene with demands for police reform following the killing of a young Spanish-speaking man by a police officer in the summer of 1968. It is reported that at the present time the organization has reached fifteen of the lower-class Spanish-American *barrios* in Albuquerque and that each of these is represented by three individuals whose names are kept secret for their personal protection. One of their spokesmen, whose name has been frequently in the local news in relation to Mexican-American civil rights, has also been associated with the Alianza, even though he has never been a member. During the recent school board election this spokesman ran as a candidate of the Peoples Constitutionalist Party. He and his running partner lost, although another person of Spanish surname garnered more votes than any other candidate in history.

The Brown Berets reject individuals such as the latter who cooperate with the Establishment. This includes persons who work for the Office of Economic Opportunity, Model Cities, and other governmental or governmentally funded agencies. Such persons are referred to as *vendidos* (sell-outs), *Tio*

Tomases, Espanglos, Lulacks, and, most recently, "Oreo Cookies" (brown on the outside and white on the inside).

This terminology reflects the increasing polarization among persons of Spanish heritage in New Mexico, as well as elsewhere. The group seems to be dividing along the politically defined lines of extreme Right on the one hand and extreme Left on the other. These differences are certainly linked to increasing radicalism in a broader political sense in the United States as a whole. There are clear linkages on the Right with the John Birch Society and other such groups. Similarly, there are linkages on the Left with non-Hispano groups such as the Students for a Democratic Society (SDS), the Third World Liberation Front, and others. The increasing differences between the poles is also symbolized by the terms Chicano and Hispano. Neither is a new term, but their more subtle meanings have changed.

Chicano has always had a bit of defiance in it and has also been used, at least in New Mexico, to indicate a clever person, one with the ability to outwit the unsuspecting Anglo. There has also been a certain amount of derogation in its usage, even by the Spanish themselves. However, it has only been recently that it has also come to include a sense of militancy. Today the youthful Spanish-Americans are using Chicano more and more, and as it becomes more fashionable it also becomes less derogatory.

On the other hand, the term Hispano is still preferred by many, especially the older persons and the less militant. In view of these linguistic distinctions, in the succeeding pages the term Chicano will be used when referring to the newer activist movements or ideology, and Hispano will be retained for the older type of activity, including what may be referred to as the Establishment "activism."

However, at this point some note should be made of the increasing usage of the term "Mexican-American" in New Mexico. Although, as has been pointed out several times, this term has for many years been resented by the local Spanish-speaking community, in the past two years there has been an increasing pride in making this self-identification—again largely among the more youthful militant activists. The author attributes this new usage to the greater linkages between local and Texan and Californian groups. It should be emphasized, however, that those who use the term "Mexican-American" are still probably a minority in New Mexico, and most of the persons preferring this term live in or south of Albuquerque.

There is some evidence that this newer terminology is becoming fashionable even among some middle-class Hispanos. One informant told of a recent incident at a LULAC meeting where the members were asking each other what term they preferred to use for themselves. The informant stated that most of the people replied "Mexican-American." This would hardly have been the case two years ago and would still not likely be true in the northern areas. Bodine (1968) has made this point in reference to Taos where he recently did field work.

The newer activism is found among youths ranging from high school through college and among the younger elements who are not necessarily highly educated at all. Thus, there is a group known as *Los Caballeros de Nueva España* (The Gentlemen of New Spain) which was formed in Albuquerque in the fall of 1968. They welcome members between the ages of 10 and 24, but most of them appear to be high school students or dropouts. The group claims to have about 150 members, and they are primarily interested in furthering educational policies which will be more beneficial for children of Spanish heritage.

OTHER GROUPS

Another group of youth, but with a rural rather than an urban base, is called *Los Comancheros del Norte.* This group appears to be centered in Tierra Amarilla, with members from the entire northern New Mexican area. It is important to note that both the Comancheros and the Caballeros have stated principles and goals which support the Alianza. In referring to themselves they use, at least in print, the term Indo-Hispano which is a self-conscious term used only by the Alianza.

In addition to an interest in improving the educational system, both of these groups emphasize the return of the land-grants and specifically mention the Alianza in this regard. Neither group expresses the militancy of the Brown Berets, although it is possible that they might become more militant in the future. One young Chicano was quoted in the newspaper, *El Grito del Norte* (January 11, 1969), as follows:

> *Let's not fight among ourselves. Let's get organized and fight the gringo who controls everything. Let's not fight in the bars, let's not hit our wives. Let's not have one barrio fighting the other. Let's organize, vatos!*

At the University of New Mexico a branch of the United Mexican-American Students (UMAS) was formed late in 1968. Like so many other organizations, this one's structure does not conform to the usual organizational form. As one young member said, "Whenever two or three Chicanos are gathered together we have a meeting." The group has so far restricted itself to protesting the Anglo students' domination of a spring campus event known as "Fiesta." The group claims that the Fiesta activities in past years have tended to emphasize the "cowboy" aspect of New Mexican culture to the exclusion of its Mexican or Spanish heritage. They wish to have included *Mariachis*, Mexican-type *Charro* events, Spanish or Mexican food at the barbecues, etc.

Although this kind of activity would seem to be merely the playful antics of college students, most observers feel that this again is only a symbol of general discontent of UMAS members and that their activities will become more serious in the future. The group declines to give names of its members, and it is at this time almost impossible to find out how many there may be. They claim a potential strength of 1,500, but this seems a little high. At meetings during the spring of 1969 on the campus of the University of New Mexico they sometimes drew up to 200, but some of these were sympathizers or curiosity seekers and not potential members.

UMAS is sufficiently well organized to publish a mimeographed bulletin entitled *Plumas de Umas* (Pens of the United Mexican-American Students), written partly in Spanish and partly in English. One of their goals is to create a Mexican-American Studies program at the University of New Mexico, preferably under the control of Chicanos. In line with this, they are beginning to agitate for the hiring of more Chicano professors. (There were thirty-nine professors, instructors, and graduate assistants of Spanish surname at the University of New Mexico in the spring of 1969, but most of these were considered "oreo cookies" by the Chicano students.)

UMAS has probable linkages with the Denver Crusade for Justice, which sponsored what it called the "Chicano Youth Liberation Conference" in March of 1969. Delegates from New Mexico as well as from other southwestern states attended this meeting and exchanged views and techniques which will undoubtedly give a still greater homogeneity to the activities of these youth groups throughout the Southwest.

In summarizing these budding Chicano organizations, it should be noted that each one serves a somewhat different segment of the total deprived population, and although there is no overall formal organization among them there are nevertheless clear linkages through the network of individual contacts. Thus some members of UMAS may also be Brown Berets, and all look to the Alianza and its activities as somehow being symbolic of their cause as well. On the other hand, the Alianza itself seems more closely tied in with the two high school youth groups mentioned previously and may even have been instrumental in their formation. At the same time, as the individual young members of the high school groups grow up they will probably unite with the Brown Berets or UMAS, or both.

The goals of these groups are not easy to define specifically, although in general they are concerned with the lack of power of the Spanish-surname or Spanish-speaking segment of the population in this country. They feel that organized agencies in the past have not been successful in relieving the plight of the poor, and they now preach more revolutionary tactics in achieving a better way of life. Certainly there have been many instances of appalling injustice for persons of Spanish surname in New Mexico, as elsewhere. But since here most of the persons in the lowest social classes are of this ethnic group, it is sometimes tempting to suggest that they are in this position because they have been discriminated against. The author would reverse this and argue that they are discriminated against because they are in the lower class, but that being of Spanish-American origin is related to the fact that they are in the lower class. In trying to account for this, the position is sometimes advanced that they are genetically inferior and therefore doomed to perpetual poverty and low status. This is clearly a bigoted, uninformed viewpoint. On the other hand, the suggestion that these people are in this position because they have been and are being discriminated against also seems to the author to derive from an uninformed point of view.

The problem has to do with social structure and the values supporting it rather than with personal relationships, in this writer's opinion. What is meant by this is that the dominant society is structured in such a way that certain kinds of behavior are better rewarded than others. The author would thoroughly agree with the opinion that the lower-class Spanish-American's lack of ability in his second language, English, has often hindered his progress in achieving material well-being. This is most often a result of his inability to compete in schools at the lower level, and his feeling of inferiority when he recognizes that he is not being rewarded as are his Anglo schoolmates. Although there are undoubtedly some teachers who dislike or even despise their Spanish-American wards for their differences, there are also many who feel anguished by what they perceive to be a lower level of performance among these children. They are unable to advance these students according to the same set of criteria as those they use for the Anglo children, and having no other guidelines they fail the Spanish-speaking child.[2] This position is now quite well recognized by educators in general, and it is becoming a particular issue in the Southwest. The Southwestern Cooperative Educational Laboratory, Inc. (SWCEL), a private, nonprofit educational, research and development facility, is currently conducting research and constructing programs to deal with the problem of bilingualism and teaching English as a second language in New Mexico public schools.[3]

Given this lower level of performance in grade school, the system continues to work against the individual with this background. But at this point these individuals share more with the poverty-stricken across the nation than they do with the majority of the Hispanos in New Mexico. That is, when it comes to getting jobs, the less well educated are the ones who suffer. Without jobs, material well-being is difficult or impossible. The structure of welfare is one which prevents starvation, but welfare does nothing to improve the individual's feeling of dignity and worth. Once on welfare the individual has, in effect, "two strikes" against him socially, and it is very difficult for him to go on to anything else.

One informant, himself an Hispano with a Master's degree from the University of New Mexico, told of interviewing an eight-year-old boy—a dropout from the second grade. He asked the boy what he thought he might do when he grew up. The child replied, "Well, there's always welfare." Welfare as a way of life can clearly become a pattern which is passed on from generation to generation, and it is one of the most damning indictments against the welfare system that this should be so.

However, the alternative to poverty and low status is not necessarily complete assimilation or "anglicization," as many of the Chicanos seem to believe. There are thousands of persons of Spanish heritage in New Mexico today who live comfortably, who are able to move in any social circle they desire without fear of prejudice or discrimination, and who at the same time have preserved their sense of identity with *la raza.* Many of these speak Spanish poorly or not at all, but this is in part a function of our educational system and not necessarily because they themselves have desired to give up all that is Spanish in their background. Furthermore, many of these middle-class Hispanos retain some of the values of the traditional culture in relation to such things as family structure, religion, and everything else which forms part of the Spanish-American mystique. Social scientists have not yet investigated thoroughly and do not understand the process of acculturation, either in terms of sociocultural systems or in terms of an individual's adaptations to systems other than the one he first learns. Whatever occurs, it is not a matter of clearcut and total change in way of life and world view. One must pose further questions, such as What are the criteria by which acculturation may be evaluated? Which factors operate as independent variables and which co-vary as interdependent units?

The concept of pluralism is one with which many people are concerned today. The position that several cultures may coexist within the same society—equal in terms of material welfare, self-determination, and role in government, but each retaining its individuality and self-pride—is for some a dream and for others a very possible reality.

New Mexico, with all its faults, with all its poverty, nevertheless comes closer to the pluralistic dream of society than does any other area in the nation. It is to be hoped that current events do not further polarize the positions within the Spanish-American ethnic group to the point that some deny *la raza* altogether while others attempt to overthrow the entire system which has so far permitted and reinforced the Spanish traditions in the struggle for survival. At the same time, thousands of Hispanos have achieved positions in life which they appreciate and value—positions which they feel are dignified, free from harassment, and well remunerated. These individuals, understandably enough, resent what they see as racist militancy. Called *vendidos* themselves, many of them feel it is the militants who are "selling out" *la raza* by bringing the issue of ethnicity into what should be a war on poverty.

New Mexico needs to revamp some of its worst features. This will be difficult, because New Mexico is a part of the structure of the nation itself and as such is subject to the same pressures as are the other states. But the unique history and the pride of heritage found here among the Hispano people could be the raw materials for a true pluralism in the future—a pluralism which encompasses not just one ethnic minority but all variations on the theme of Hispanic America, as well as those non-Spanish groups which have also been involved in building the unique society of New Mexico.

1. Members, Chicano Press Association: Carta Editorial, P.O. Box 54624, Terminal Annex, Los Angeles, Calif. 90054; El Chicano, San Bernardino, Calif.; Chicano Student Movement, P.O. Box 31322, Los Angeles, Calif. 90031; Compass, 1209 Egypt St., Houston, Texas 77009; El Gallo, 1265 Cherokee St., Denver, Colo. 80204; El Grito del norte, Route 2, Box 5, Española, N.M.; La Hormiga, 1560 34th Ave., Oakland, Calif. 94601; Inferno, 321 Frio City Road, San Antonio, Texas 78207; Inside Eastside, P.O. Box 63273, Los Angeles, Calif. 90063; Lado, 1306 N. Western Ave., Chicago, Ill. 60622; El Machete, 206 Oakland Ave., San Jose, Calif. 95116; El Malcriado, P.O. Box 130, Delano, Calif. 63215; El Paisano, UFWOC Box 155, Tolleson, Ariz. 85353; El Papel, P.O. Box 7167, Albuquerque, N.M. 87104; La Raza, 2445 Gates St., Los Angeles, Calif. 90031; La Verdad, 3717 University Ave., San Diego, Calif. 92105; La Voz, 2820 Whittier Blvd., Los Angeles, Calif.; La Voz Mexicana, P.O. Box 101, Wautoma, Wis. 54982. Source: *La RAZA Yearbook,* September 1968, p. 60.
2. A. M. Padilla and K. K. Long, graduate students of psychology at the University of New Mexico, carried out a study in which they ". . . sought to identify factors which could be used to differentiate successful from unsuccessful students of Spanish-American backgrounds.
   "The unsuccessful population consisted of students who had failed to complete a four year course of studies at the University of New Mexico. Successful students were defined as those who had completed studies for an advanced degree. A 101-item questionnaire was completed by students from both populations (N=50). Items related to: family history, early and later school adjustment, interpersonal relations, and vocational attitudes. Analyses indicated that both groups did not differ significantly on items relating to family history (e.g., number of siblings, father's educational level, etc.); however, successful students were shown to be both highly competitive and more achievement-motivated than the unsuccessful students. In addition, successful students were better able to adjust to university regulations" (personal communication). The results of this study will be published in the future.
3. The focus of SWCEL in general is the improvement of early educational opportunities for culturally divergent children of the Southwest. Its principal source of funds is the U.S. Office of Education, although it also welcomes donations from private sources. The Lab began operations in June, 1966, under the direction of Dr. Paul Petty, then Dean of the School of Education, University of New Mexico.

IV / LA RAZA
AND POLITICAL ACTIVITY

Identifying, describing, and analyzing the Chicano is an intriguing problem that has occupied the attention of many people for many years. The concern with the question is to discover the elements which make Chicanos what they are, the belief being that if we know who Chicanos are, then we can relate to them with greater understanding.

The difficulty is that we have no commonly accepted indices for defining a people's substance, a people's "nature." The selections offered below present differing conceptions of who Chicanos are. The term *la raza* cannot be defined solely in a dictionary sense for it means more than the "united people" or "united race." For a Chicano, being a member of *la raza* is being a member of an indentifiable group that is bound together by common language, shared hardships, shared fears, common self-doubts, and a life lived at the lower end of the social and economic scales in the United States. So the first ingredient of being a member of *la raza* is to have lived a life in which one's hardships can be attributed to being not only poor and uneducated but also being victimized by members of another "race," the white race, which has used the handicaps of the Chicano against him and thus "kept him in his place."

But there is another dimension to being a member of *la raza.* It is even more difficult to define because it is based on emotion. The emotion can be one of pure joy or happiness induced by any number of events: the birth of a son, the return of a brother, the gathering of the family, the harvest of an abundant crop, or the celebration of a holy day. It is the occasion for much music, many tears, and unrestrained laughter. Or the emotion can be one of extreme sorrow due to the death of a family member, the eviction of the family, the immigration of part of the family, or the discovery of a serious illness in a loved one. This occasion brings forth an abysmal gloom which cannot be alleviated by tears, prayer, or entreaty.

As a result of such unhappiness a member of *la raza* may do things which are inexplicable to most Anglos. If he considers himself demeaned in any way, perhaps he will resign from his job. His sense of honor seems exaggerated to those who ask, "What does he have to be so proud of?" The point is that usually he *has nothing but pride*—but that is enough. With it no man can put him down; without it no position, no job, no wealth, can make him a man in his eyes and in the eyes of *la raza*. And so he throws away a good career because his worth, his honor, his manhood have been questioned.

One could go on. Membership in *la raza* permits one to *chingarse*. There is no satisfactory translation of the verb for it has overtones which suggest sex as well as shortcoming. The closest approximation in English would translate to "foul up." But it is only an approximation for the English verb. "Foul up" means to find oneself in a position where one's actions have produced results not commensurate with intentions and so the product is a mishap which no one anticipated or wanted. Conversely, *chingarse* means that one knowingly, willingly, and deliberately embarks on a course of action that will lead, inevitably, to a conclusion that is not desirable in itself but is acceptable if the journey is worth the price. For instance, when a man with a proclivity for drink knowingly cashes his paycheck in a bar and decides to stay and have a drink with the boys, he knows his wife will be unbearable to live with if he doesn't hurry home, sober and paid. But he is willing to *chingarse* with her because the drinks are cool, the boys congenial, the music heart-rendering, and the waitresses inviting. He has succeeded in courting disaster, but it won't be forthcoming for awhile and the trip is certainly a pleasant one—now. Somehow, if one is a member of "*la raza*," he expects to *chingarse* from time to time. What is the use of being of *la raza* if one didn't?

William Madsen offers a somewhat staid and scholarly view of *la raza* in the first reading of Part IV. Madsen's interpretation of *la raza* is conventional in that it enumerates the differences in life style between Chicanos and Anglos and posits those differences as explanations for membership in *la raza.*

Armando M. Rodriguez argues that membership in *la raza* is conferred by common language (Spanish) and common culture. He suggests that the differences in language and culture have created prejudices and discriminations against *la raza* which have acted to bind them together. He concludes by pointing to the same humanity shared by Chicano and Anglo and pleads that it become the basis for increased opportunity for the minority group in the future.

We are not concluding that militancy is the remedy to racial unrest in the United States today. We are merely stating that an evaluation of the past permits us to see that militancy has paid off more for Chicanos than has moderation. To say that increased payoffs to Chicanos have resulted from their militancy could be construed as an indictment of militancy since the use of force is implied in the achievement of social goals. But if such an interpretation is reached then the companion question must be "Why does the United States political and governmental system respond more effectively to militancy than to moderation?" We raise the question not to answer it but rather to lend a measure of balance to the issue of militancy versus moderation in American government and politics as it relates to minority group movements.

Unbeknownst to many Anglos is the fact that Chicanos have been organized politically in the United States for over two generations. The first organizations were designed to work through the existing political systems to achieve their goals. When the passage of time revealed the bankruptcy of this approach toward social justice, more militant Chicano organizations sprang into existence.

Alfredo Cuéllar reviews in excellent detail the history of organized Mexican-American political activity in the Southwest. He detects four distinct stages of organized political activities involving Chicanos: the conflict and apolitics stage; (2) the politics of adaptation stage; (3) the politicization of Mexican-Americans stage; and, finally (4) the Chicano Movement.

Clearly, the thrust of Cuéllar's argument is that Chicanos in the United States have gone through various political stages and mediums in trying to achieve social justice. He suggests, more implicitly than explicitly, that working through "the establishment" has yielded relatively modest political harvests to the Chicanos, and thus they have been driven to employ ever more forceful, more militant means to achieve their goals.

World View
William Madsen

The Mexican-American thinks of himself as both a citizen of the United States and a member of *La Raza* (The Race). This term refers to all Latin-Americans who are united by cultural and spiritual bonds derived from God. The spiritual aspect is perhaps more important than the cultural. The Latin recognizes regional variations in behavior and realizes that custom changes. The spirit of the Spanish-speaking people, however, is taken to be divine and infinite. As one Latin expressed it, "We are bound together by the common destiny of our souls."

In Mexico, the concept of *La Raza* carries the idea of a splendid and glorious destiny. Mexicans see their greatest national strength in the spiritual vigor of *La Raza*. In Texas, the history of discrimination and economic subordination has modified the concept of the ultimate destiny of *La Raza*. Many Spanish-speaking Texans would say that God had originally planned a glorious future for the Mexican-American but it probably will never be attained. The failure of *La Raza*, he would continue, is due to the sins of individual Latins. Some believe that *La Raza* is held back by the sins of all Mexican-Americans, "The only ones among us who are surely free from sin are the little children." Other Latins think that only the worst sinners are holding back *La Raza*, "We could meet with God's favor again if the drunks and thieves would reform. We all suffer because of the sins of a few." I once asked a Latin if he thought the Anglos were in any way responsible for holding back the Mexican-Americans from their God-given destiny. "Of course not," he replied, "If we lived by God's commands we would be so strong that no one could block us. Of course, the Anglos take advantage of our weaknesses but it is we who make ourselves weak, not the Anglos."

The Mexican-American does not suffer undue anxiety because of his propensity to sin. Instead of blaming himself for his error, he frequently attributes it to adverse circumstances. The Latin does not think he missed the bus because he arrived too late. He blames the bus for leaving before he arrived. It is believed that everybody is subject to temptation under certain circumstances. Many succumb due to human weakness, which is a universal rather than an individual failing. Thus, Juan did not get drunk because he voluntarily drank too much. He got drunk because too much liquor was served at the party. The most common temptations that lead men astray are the opportunities to amass money or power. The main weakness of women is their inability to withstand sexual temptation. The safest course for the individual lies in avoiding exposure to a position where temptation is too great. In any case, the people of La Raza always suffer. Resisting temptation or succumbing to it can both be painful experiences. "Because we suffer in this world, we shall certainly be blessed with joy in the next," a laborer said.

In all aspects of existence, the Latin sees a balance of opposites. Pain is balanced by pleasure, life by death, creation by destruction, illness by health, and desire by denial. God maintains this balance by seeing that no extreme exists without a counterbalance. Pain must follow pleasure and a hangover must follow a drunk. God's ledger sheet is held to be exact and without error. Through creation and destruction, He maintains the balance of the world. He does not give life without death nor pleasure without pain. "One has to suffer to deserve," said Maria. It is a comforting philosophy for a subordinated group.

Suffering is also made acceptable by a strong belief in fatalism. It is generally believed that the good or bad fortune

The belief that all events are predetermined by fate...

of the individual is predestined and every occurrence in human existence comes to pass because it was fated to do so. Fatalistic philosophy produces an attitude of resignation, which often convinces the Anglo that the Latin lacks drive and determination. What the Anglo tries to control, the Mexican-American tries to accept. Misfortune is something the Anglo tries to overcome and the Latin views as fate.

The Latin world view contains unpondered conflicts in the concepts of Divine will, individual will, and fatalism. Sometimes, events are explained as the result of the impersonal mechanism of fate, "What will be, will be." Certain individuals maintain that human fate is correlated in a mechanical way with the position of the heavenly bodies at the moment of birth. Others who accept the possibility of astrological divination point out that the course of the stars and planets is controlled by God. Most Latins believe that fate is a mechanism of God's will. Although the fate of the individual is decided before birth, God has the power to alter it. Through prayer, sacrifice, and even bartering, one can induce God to modify one's fate. The paramount nature of Divine will is reflected in the saying *Haga uno lo que haga, todo es lo que Dios quiere* (Do what one will, everything is as God wishes).

Unlike the Anglo world view where man emerges as the dominant force except on Sunday, the Latin view conceives of God as all-powerful and man as but a part of nature that is subject to His will. God enters all aspects of the Mexican-American's daily life and His name is used with familiarity. The name Jesús is still given to boys in the most conservative Latin homes. The Latin cannot understand why the Anglo considers this name amusing or *sacrilegious when it is intended to show honor and respect to the Lord. The Mexican-American relationship with God was described in these words, "We see God in the beauty around us. He is in the water, the mountains, and the smallest of the plants. We live with God while the Anglos lock Him into Heaven."

It is sometimes said that the Latin works with God and the Anglo works against Him. The Mexican-American takes satisfaction in raising plants. He regards their growth and

The misuse, desecration, or profanation of anything regarded as sacred.

flowering as proof of God's will and beauty, while his own role is merely that of an attendant. One Mexican-American expressed his horror at Anglo attempts to create new botanical hybrids, "God gave us the plants to tend and admire and use for food. He did not intend for us to create our own. We should take things as they are given. Only God is the Creator." Another Latin fears the results of the probing of outer space, "We go too far," he said. "Now we are entering God's domain. We will arouse his wrath."

The Mexican-American world view was eloquently expressed by Don Luis. "We are not very important in the universe. We are here because God sent us and we must leave when God calls us. God has given us a good way to live and we should try to see the beauty of His commands. We will often fail for many are weak but we should try. There is much suffering but we should accept it for it comes from God. Life is sad but beautiful."

FOCAL VALUES

Acceptance and appreciation of things as they are constitute primary values of *La Raza.* Because God, rather than man, is viewed as controlling events, the Latin lacks the future orientation of the Anglo and his passion for planning ahead. Many Mexican-Americans would consider it presumptive to try to plan for tomorrow because human beings are merely servants of God and it is He who plans the future. The Latin lives for today instead of creating a blueprint for the future. He is dedicated to living the moment to its fullest in the roles assigned to him by God.

The most important role of the individual is his familial role and the family is the most valued institution in Mexican-American society. The individual owes his primary loyalties to the family, which is also the source of most affective relations. Gregorio said, "I owe everything to my family. Were it not for my parents' love for each other, I would never have been born. They raised me and taught me all I know. They have protected me and in my parents' home I know I will always find love and understanding. When one has a family, one is never alone nor without help in time of need. God created the family and one way to show respect to Him is to respect one's parents." The worst sin a Latin can conceive is to violate his obligations to his parents and siblings. Within the family, respect rests primarily upon the basis of age. The oldest male is head of the household and rules it. The old command the young and the males command the females. Latin society rests firmly on a foundation of family solidarity and the concept of male superiority.

The ideal male role is primarily defined by the concept of *machismo* or manliness. Every Mexican-American male tries to make his life a living validation of the assumption that the man is stronger, more reliable, and more intelligent than the female. He strives to achieve the respect of his society by acting like a "real man" in every situation. Perhaps the most common anxiety found in male Latin society is the fear of failure in the role of manly behavior. Next to devotion to the family, the male's "manliness" outweighs all other aspects of prestige. As one Latin male explained, "To us a man is a man because he acts like a man. And he is respected for this. It does not matter if he is short or tall, ugly or handsome, rich or poor. These things are unimportant. When he stands on his own feet as he should, then he is looked up to."

Machismo demands a high degree of individuality outside the family circle. It might appear that family obligations would conflict with a young man's need to be an individual and to stand alone. Actually, no conflict exists. The Latin male always represents his famliy and he must represent it with honor and devotion. In the outside world, he must tolerate no overt offense to his family whose honor he will fight to defend. As a representative of his family, he seeks to maintain its public image by becoming indebted to no one, acknowledging no obligations that might conflict with his familial role, and striving to achieve societal respect for himself as a man. Ideally, the Latin male acknowledges only the authority of his father and God. In case of conflict between these two sources of authority, he should side with his father. No proper father, however, would act counter to God's will for such behavior would make him less of a man.

The value of *machismo* governs male behavior in almost every facet of social life but wields its greatest influence in connection with the concept of honor. The conduct of a male in any social situation must support his public image as a person of honor and integrity. A situation that might compromise his image as a man of dignity is avoided. A Latin clerk commented, "Unless I am sure that I command the respect of the other guys in a gathering, I would rather not stick around. Only a fool would associate with those who look down on him."

Honor and respect are closely associated with lack of indebtedness or obligation to those outside the family circle. For this reason, the Latin male is reluctant to ask for a loan or a favor. When he feels that circumstances require him to seek help from others, he tries to settle his accounts as quickly as possible. Anglo merchants and professional men are well aware of Mexican-American reliability in paying accounts. The Anglo who has done a favor for a Mexican-American friend has witnessed his earnestness in repaying the favor. "You are not whole and entire when you are indebted to another," Raul said. The more conservative Latins are reluctant to seek help from institutions because acceptance of charity is felt to be humiliating. It reflects on the head of the household who has failed to provide and thereby weakened the strength and solidarity of the family.

The obligations and loyalty involved in affiliation with formal organizations are regarded as a threat to the self-reliance of the individual and the self-sufficiency of his family. Unions, civic action organizations, and mutual aid societies consistently meet with failure in their attempts to recruit and hold membership from the male population of Latin folk society.

The concept of male honor requires the Latin to avoid being proven wrong. To take a stand on an issue and then retreat is regarded as degrading. Therefore, the Latin avoids openly stating an opinion unless he is ready to stand by it and defend it. When the Latin backs down from a stated opinion, he loses respect in the community. It is far better to avoid commitment on any issue than to risk being proven wrong. Involvement in controversial issues is regarded as foolhardy.

The manly Latin must repay an insult to himself or his family in order to defend the honor with which God endowed him. Revenge is usually achieved by direct physical attack, which may not be immediate but must be inevitable. The offended Latin may seem to ignore a minor insult at the moment but he does not forget it. A more serious offense may be met with a threat of future retaliation such as, "You will pay for this," or "We'll meet again." An open threat of this type must be carried out in order to maintain the *machismo* of the insulted individual. The act of revenge may take place months later and often occurs after an evening of drinking. The offender may be beaten, stabbed, or occasionally mutilated. Retribution settles the account but never restores normal relationships. The avenger has regained his honor but he does not forgive his enemy. The Anglo practice of shaking hands after a row is regarded as weak and unmanly.

Weakness is looked down on in all spheres of male activity. A man should be mentally and physically strong. Cripples are pitied but never regarded as manly unless their physical disability is compensated for by other strengths. Weakness in drinking ability is always humiliating. The true man drinks and drinks frequently and in quantity. Inability to maintain dignity when drinking is absolute proof of weakness as is the refusal to drink.

A favorite sport of the younger generation is testing the *machismo* of their fellows in a drinking situation. In this game, it is implicitly understood that hidden accusations and taunts are not serious. They are forgotten on leaving the bar unless some individual has gone too far or is too sensitive. An inebriated male is frequently egged on to make a stand that he cannot defend. His argument is then crushed with a well-turned phrase that is considered a triumph and a moment for hilarity.

Words and phrases with double meanings are used to insult the masculinity of one's drinking companions. Such verbal dueling may be developed into a fine art. The champions are those who can disguise their attacks with words of flattery so that the victim feels complimented rather than insulted. The possibility of taking serious offense limits verbal dueling to groups of very close friends. When the same disguised taunts are directed toward an enemy, a fight may result if the hidden meaning of the verbal thrust is recognized.

Male virility is better proven by direct action than by triumphs in verbal dueling. The Latin male does not take his sex life lightly. He regards the female sex as a desirable quantity that exists to be conquered, and he is the conqueror. He is proud of the seductions he chalks up and does not hesitate to point them out to his companions. Seduction is the best proof of manliness. He regards prostitution as a pleasurable institution but rarely one in which he can prove his *machismo* except in an endurance contest. The only thing he proves by hiring a prostitute is his financial ability. This procedure does not call for the intelligence, strategy, and knowledge needed to seduce a reluctant female. The true man must demonstrate not only his physical prowess but also his power to lure women into sexual adventures.

PRESCRIBED BEHAVIOR

The Latin thinks of a true man as being proud, self-reliant, and virile. He is jokingly compared to a rooster. Ramón observed, "The better man is the one who can drink more, defend himself best, have more sex relations, and have more sons borne by his wife. If unmarried, the better man is the one who has the most girl friends; if married, the one who deceives his wife most."

The Latin woman plays the perfect counterpart to the Latin male. Where he is strong, she is weak. Where he is aggressive, she is submissive. While he is condescending toward her she is respectful toward him. A woman is expected to always display those subdued qualities of womanhood that *woman look upto man — strength*

make a man feel the need to protect her. A Mexican-American wife asked, "How can I expect a man for a husband unless I demonstrate my dependence on his strength?"

While the male feels compelled to demonstrate his sexual power with as many women as possible, the Latin woman must guard her purity above all else. A respected woman has had sexual experiences only with her husband. A loose woman is an object of jest and ridicule. Protecting the purity of a woman is no easy task in a community filled with males stalking their prey. Because women are regarded as weak, suggestible, and less intelligent than males, the purity of a female must be defended first by her parents and then after marriage by her husband.

feelings of the women

The Latin wife is expected to show her husband absolute respect and obedience. For a wife to question her husband's orders or decisions is to doubt his intelligence—an unforgiveable sin. She does not resent her subordinate role nor envy the independence of Anglo women. Her role fulfillment is seen in helping her husband to achieve his goals as he sees fit. The Latin wife must never express sorrow or anger at her husband's *extramarital activities. It is understood that his sexual adventures will not threaten or weaken his devotion to his family. The Mexican-American wife who irritates her husband may be beaten. She should accept this punishment as deserved. Some wives assert that they are grateful for punishment at the hands of their husbands for such concern with shortcomings indicates profound love.

Husband and wife share the joint obligation of teaching their children how to conduct themselves with dignity and honor in any social situation. In addition to serving as models, parents are supposed to instruct their children within the home and expose them to experiences outside the home that will prepare them for adult life. An "educated" person is one who has been well trained as a social being. Informal education within the family is viewed as more important than formal schooling.

The educated persons displays polish and courtesy (*urbanidad*) in his social relationships. He knows how to avoid

women accept extramarital activities by husbands and beaten are more important than "formal education"

"Educated" means an academic education

* *adulterous*

offending others and how to defend himself. He knows all the rules of Latin etiquette and the techniques for politely maintaining social distance outside the home. He respects his elders and conducts himself so as to receive the respect due him. In social interaction, he is expected to maintain a proper relationship with neighbors, friends, and acquaintances. Proper relations between members of *La Raza* involve ritual and respect patterns that are alien to the Anglo. Latin social relationships are highly formalized and life itself is seen as dramatic and ceremonial.

PROSCRIBED BEHAVIOR

X

A person lacking urbanity may be characterized as inexperienced, for shortcomings are best blamed on circumstances. A discourtesy may be excused if the offender can be described as young and inexperienced. If this description does not fit, the impropriety may be interpreted as an insult or an offense. A child or young adult who violates tradition through ignorance rather than malice is called *tonto* (dumb or foolish). The implication is that the individual's shortcomings are due to lack of experience and will be overcome with maturity. The term is also applied to Anglos.

A proper relationship between experienced persons must preserve the dignity and individuality of each. Above all, one must not give offense to a friend or acquaintance. Polite social distance precluding direct involvement in the affairs of others is mandatory. Direct questioning of another's motives or methods may be taken as insulting, particularly if it is directed at an elder.

Direct criticism is also considered offensive. It is wrong to criticize the subjective beliefs of another person and even more inexcusable to try to change them. As long as a Latin conforms to the rules of proper conduct, he is entitled to his own beliefs. One may resent another's actions but not another's opinions or interpretations. This view is expressed in the Mexican-American saying, *Cada cabeza es un mundo* (Each head is a world unto itself). A person may think as he pleases but he should not try to impose his ideas on anybody else. These concepts of propriety are a major factor in the hostility felt toward missionaries and public health workers who are trying to change Mexican-American beliefs. A distinguished Latin citizen voiced his opinion on what he called "brain-washing." "Americans have abandoned geographic imperialism but to them mental imperialism is a wide open field."

To question the beliefs of another is to belittle him (*hacerlo menos*). A person also feels belittled when someone questions his accomplishments or compares them with greater successes achieved by others. When Memo mentioned the double he hit in a baseball game, he was offended that Pepe called attention to a home-run hit by José. The new mother of a baby girl was crushed when a friend asked her if she had seen Concha's baby boy, the third son in the family.

The most common way of belittling or abasing others is to attain greater social or material success than one's friends. To do so is dangerous for it may arouse the emotion of envy in others. It is considered prudent to conceal personal gains or advancement. Mexican-Americans value inconspicuous consumption as highly as Anglos value the conspicuous display of wealth.

Latins regard envy as a destructive emotion and admit that it is a major barrier to the material advancement of *La Raza*. Envy is felt to be such a powerful emotion that it is difficult or impossible to suppress. Sometimes, envy is so potent that it endangers the health of the person experiencing it. Envy also results in malice and hostility toward the person or family envied. A Mexican-American repairman explained:

> *My people cannot stand to see another rise above them. When I rented my own little store, my best friends became jealous. When I painted my house, my neighbors thought I was trying to shame them. And after I purchased my new car several people stopped speaking to me. Every one tries to pull the one above him down to his own level. If you try to get ahead, you make enemies. If*

*you don't get ahead you are criticized for laziness or
stupidity. My people are hard to live with.*

Envy may be aroused by success in almost any kind of
activity. Josefina experienced envy when her neighbor bought
new window curtains. Margarita felt envy and jealousy when
her best friend married a highly desirable bachelor. Pedro
resented Memo's success with the girls. A schoolboy experienced envy and anger when a classmate got a new bicycle.
Envy occurs most commonly among neighbors, fellow workers, classmates, and other circles of daily contact. It is most
strongly felt when an equal has made sudden gains and risen
to a higher position. The tendency then is to try to equalize the
position by pulling the successful individual down. While the
Anglos try to keep up with the Joneses, the Latins try to keep
the Garcias down to their own level. "We spend more time
deprecating the success of others than in trying to improve
ourselves," Pablo said.

LEVELING MECHANISMS

One leveling mechanism is gossip spread by the
envious person about the individual who has gotten ahead of
his neighbors. Gossip is considered improper behavior and
frequent gossiping outside of the family circle can lower a
person's prestige. Nevertheless, gossip is common. Criticism
of another person is generally aired only in the family circle or
in private, to a close friend. Because friendships overlap, the
gossip spreads through the community in a remarkably short
time and damages the prestige of the person involved. The
person who starts the gossip takes pains to conceal his identity
from the victim who would certainly seek revenge.

Ridicule is another leveling mechanism. It is used
when only slight envy is felt. The ridiculing is done directly by
a group of close friends so the victim will not pin the blame
on any one of them. Such ridicule is usually gentle and often
successful in removing the offensive behavior that aroused the
envy. Pedro, a poor crop picker, saved his money to buy a fine

suit at a department store. The day after the purchase he wore it to a cantina to drink with his friends. His magnificence made a sharp contrast with their drab and soiled work clothes. Immediately the joking began. "Pedro has come into money," Juan called, "the drinks are on him." Pepito asked if Pedro planned to run for mayor. Each jibe produced laughter but the general behavior indicated it was all in fun. Nevertheless, Pedro had an uncomfortable evening. The next night he came to the cantina in his work clothes. A few days later he quietly informed Pepito that he had given the new suit to his wife's brother who was getting married. No one believed his story but Pedro now looks and acts like his fellows in the bar.

Direct action may be taken to halt the advancement of the person envied. Two brothers who enlarged their cantina into a small night club were boycotted by their former friends. Several times the screens on the windows were slashed and the window frames broken. One night a truck "accidentally" rammed the wall of the establishment and the large crack had to be repaired at considerable expense. "We are doing a good business but our customers are strangers, not friends," one of the brothers said.

Witchcraft is the most feared leveling weapon of the envious. Failure in any undertaking may be attributed to witchcraft designed to reduce the victim to the level of his neighbors. Consuelo was unable to hold the well-paid job she had obtained in a large Anglo store because of her sudden and persistent headaches. She felt sure that somewhere a witch was tormenting the head of a doll made in her image.

Because a successful individual expects to be envied, he may imagine more hostility directed against him than actually exists. As a defense, he may begin gossiping about those whom he suspects of working against him. The defensive behavior of the upwardly mobile individual often creates as big a barrier as envy between him and his old friends.

The Mexican-American fears not only the envy of others but also their greed, dishonesty, and treachery. Early in life, he learns that he lives in a threatening and hostile universe. The motives of those outside the family are open to suspicion. The other fellow may be planning to belittle him or rob him. This cultural fixation enhances the value of social distance and further explains the reluctance to join organizations such as labor unions. The Mexican-American is taught to keep his defenses high. To drop them for a moment might give someone the opportunity to deprive him of what is rightfully his. He suspects both Anglos and Latins but believes that members of *La Raza* are most likely to yield to the temptation to do him in. He sees both his strengths and his weaknesses as part of his heritage from *La Raza* whose vision of a glorious destiny is blocked by wrongdoing.

"We are a people turned against ourselves," Roberto said. "The greatness God intended for us will never be ours for we are too busy devouring each other."

This author is a real neck racist M... T...

Bilingual
Education-Profile '70
Armando M. Rodriguez

For nearly three years I have traveled back and forth across our country as a representative of our national government, spurring both governmental and private agencies to direct some of their resources to the Spanish-speaking population. In doing so I have found our people—Puerto Ricans, Cubans, and Mexican-Americans—to be regarded in some communities as non-existent, in others with fear, in others with respect, and in others with suspicion. I also found that this population is referred to as Spanish-Americans, Latinos, Hispanos, Spanish-Speaking Americans, Spanish-Surnamed Americans, Americans of Spanish or Mexican Descent, Los Batos Locos and a number of other names I choose not to repeat here tonight. But whatever we are called, we are La Raza, a name that unites us linguistically and culturally.

I have also found out that there are approximately 10 million of us, that more than 80% of us live in urban communities like Chicago, and that more than 70% of us are in the three states of New York, Texas and California. I also found that the states of Michigan, Illinois, Indiana, New Jersey, Ohio, Wisconsin and Iowa are the fastest area for settlement of Spanish speakers in the country outside of New York, Texas and California. I also found that the Spanish speaking

Armando M. Rodriguez, "Bilingual Education—Profile '70," in *Congressional Record*, 91st Cong., 2nd sess., February 26, 1970.

American population is the youngest in the country with more than 50% under age 20. I found that our educational attainment—based on 1960 census figures—is the lowest in the country for any distinctive ethnic or racial group (in Texas it barely reaches the 5th year of school); that the dropout rate of the Spanish speakers is the highest in the country, exceeding 50% in some of the high schools in New York, Chicago, Los Angeles and San Antonio. That more than 80% of the youngsters from Mexican American families starting school in Texas do not finish. That in California less than 1% of the students enrolled in the seven campuses of the University of California are Spanish-Surname—how many of those are Puerto Rican or Mexican American, we do not know. This is the higher education situation in a state where 14% of the public school enrollment is Spanish-Surnamed. A shocking statistic is that the Mexican-American enrollment at California State College in Los Angeles, located in the heart of East Los Angeles, a barrio of more than 400,000 Mexican Americans, dropped almost 50% last year. These are some frightening statistics that tell a little about the second largest minority in our country.

Who is La Raza when you strip away the educational and economic chains that bind him? For the most part, he is still an alien, unknown in his own land. This is true even in the Southwest, where the cultural heritage is a living reminder of the part that Spain and Mexico played in forming the character of this nation. The Mexican is pictured on the one hand as the peon, who, hat in hand, holds the reins for John Wayne in the movies, or is the Frito Bandito on T.V. On the other hand, he is the glamorous *hidalgo*, the ambassador of good will for the city of San Diego and a participant in the Rose Bowl Parade. Between the fanciful extremes of the peon and the hidalgo is La Raza. Probably the most telling observation ever to be printed about us came from the pages of *Newsweek* (May 23, 1966): "We're the best kept secret in America."

I would like to say here today that the secret is now out. We are fast becoming America's most promising human catalyst for the creation of a democratic society where cultural heritage and language assets are prime instruments in the acceptance of human diversity as major national goal. I refute that television report in April of last year that identified La Raza as "The Invisible Minority." If the producers could sense what I feel and see in my travels, La Raza would be identified as the "dynamic and responsible minority." The old image that the Puerto Rican or the Mexican American is neither Puerto Rican, Mexican nor American: he is suspended between two cultures, neither of which claims him, is rapidly disappearing. Tomorrow's Puerto Rican and Mexican American —those forceful, creative, bold youngsters under 25 will be the American citizens who successfully retain and cherish their cultural heritage and simultaneously participate fully in the larger cultural environment of our society. And I suggest that the frontier of this movement will be found in the urban areas of our cities throughout this country. Who is the Puerto Rican or the Mexican American? He is that unique individual who has suffered from cultural isolation, language rejection, economic and educational inequalities, but who has now begun to take those instruments of oppression and turn them into instruments of change. Bilingual and bicultural education in our public schools will be a reality very shortly. The national moral and legal commitment of our federal government for educational programs that reflect the culture and language of the students will be a common part of curriculums throughout the country. And to a great extent this sweeping movement must be credited to the patience and perseverance of our youth —cultural qualities that for so many years was termed, "passivity."

It is this sweeping movement, vigorously enunciated by the Youth Movement, that will destroy an environment now existing that says to us and particularly the youngster in school, that the only Americanism is that which permeates the textbooks with little or no reference to positive historical accomplishments unless achieved by the Anglo. Mexican American and Puerto Rican children can and will do well scholastically, but only in schools, including colleges, that not only emphasize the Anglo way of life, but also fosters pride in the Mexican American and Puerto Rican for his origin, history, culture, and bilingual background.

A high school girl from the barrio in East Los Angeles said: "We look for others like ourselves in these history books, for something to be proud of for being a Mexican, and all we see in books, magazines, films, and TV shows are stereotypes of a dark, dirty, smelly man with a tequila bottle in one hand, a dripping taco in the other, a serape wrapped around him, and a big sombrero."

This, my friends, is not the hispano here or anywhere in the country. I ask that all of you here join me in a fight to eradicate such stereotypes from every aspect of our media. The negative images of La Raza in advertising on TV is one of the most destructive forces now existing for the creation of a society where cultural and human diversity is an imperative thread in the strength of the total fabric. This fight must be won before freedom for all of us can be realized. I would like to quote from three different sources which reveal the deep feeling of pride, dignity and concern so important for all of us, not because it is good or true but because these feelings exist especially among our youth who fight for self-dignity and positive image recognition.

"Who am I?" asks a young Mexican American high school student. "I am a product of myself. I am a product of you and my ancestors. We came to California long before the Pilgrims landed at Plymouth Rock. We settled California the Southwestern part of the United States including the states of Arizona, New Mexico, Colorado and Texas. We built the missions, we cultivated the ranches. We were at the Alamo in Texas, both inside and outside. You know we owned California —that is, until gold was found here. Who am I? I'm a human being. I have the same hopes that you do, the same fears, the same drives, same desires, same concerns, same abilities; and I want the same chance that you have to be an individual. Who am I? In reality I am who you want me to be."

This same concern for dignity and respect is found in the poetry of Alberto Alurista:

Mis ojos hinchados
   flooded with lagrimas
de bronce
melting on the cheek bones
of my concern
   razgos indigenos
the scars of history on my face
   and the veins of my body
that aches
   vomito sangre
y lloro libertad
   I do not ask for freedom
I am freedom

And this freedom means education. And this freedom means a bigger share in the economic and political pot.

Perspective on Politics

Alfredo Cuéllar

The political development of Mexican Americans can be traced through roughly four periods of political activity that begin with the American conquest of the Southwest.

Such a survey must begin with conflict. Though the first three generations of American rule (from the late 1840s until about 1920, the first phase of political development for Mexican Americans) can be termed "apolitical," it is a period that covers widely disparate activities. Through the first generation (until perhaps the mid-1870s) there was widespread violence and disorder accompanying the consolidation of the conquest. In the following 50 years throughout most of the Southwest Mexican Americans were politically submerged. Neither the violence of the first generation nor the quiescence of the second and third can be considered "normal" American political participation. Force and its aftermath of suppression were the rule.

There were two exceptions to the dominant apolitical pattern. Organized political activity was very much present in New Mexico. Here the political system, even during the long period of territorial government, reflected the demographic and social weight of a large Spanish-speaking population. In southern California, moreover, a wealthy land-owning group of Mexicans retained substantial, although declining, political power until the late 1880s and the coming of the railroads.

Alfredo Cuéllar, "Perspective on Politics" in Joan W. Moore with Alfredo Cuéllar, *Mexican Americans*, ©1970. Reprinted by permission of Prentice-Hall, Inc., Englewood Cliffs, New Jersey.

In the second period, what may be considered conventional political activity began, born in a context of violence and suppression. This period (beginning roughly in the 1920s) was a time of adaptation and accommodation, reflecting the changing position of Mexican Americans in the social structure of communities in the Southwest. A small Mexican American middle class began to gain some strength and tried to come to terms politically with a still hostile and still threatening social environment.

This period of accommodation was typified by the efforts of the new Mexican American groups to prepare and to "guide" the lower-class and newly arrived immigrant Mexican Americans to "become Americans." Notably, they did *not* press for full political participation. As we shall see, it was also during this period that at least some of the negative ideological assumptions about Mexicans held by the majority were reflected in their political activity.

The third period, beginning in the 1940s, saw increased political activity. Although the results fell far short of full participation in American political life, this period was characterized by a more aggressive style and more organization. During this time, so to speak, the Mexican Americans began to "play the game" according to Anglo political rules. The new idea of progress became associated with exercising the franchise and attempting to gain both elective and appointive office. The political achievements of Mexican Americans in New Mexico exemplified political progress. There, they had kept a political voice through the change from Mexican to U.S. rule: there were Mexicans in the state legislature and in Congress. Most areas, however, fell short of the accomplishment in New Mexico, especially south Texas, where political exclusion and manipulation were the heritage of violence and suppression. This exclusion and manipulation continued in many communities to be enforced by the local Anglo power structure.

The new aggressiveness that appeared after World War II was largely a phenomenon of urban life and reflected again the changing situation of Mexican Americans. They were becoming more urbanized, and more were middle class; they were increasingly American-born. World War II itself was one of the most important forces for change: hundreds of thousands of Mexican Americans served in the armed forces and gained radically new experiences, being sent outside their five-state *"barrio"* and given opportunities to develop a drastically changed view of American society.

In recent years a fourth type of political activity is becoming important. For convenience, it may be called the radicalization of Mexican American political activity. This new style is exemplified in the growth of the *Chicano* movement. Although this movement assumes different forms in various parts of the Southwest and although its acceptance is far from uniform, it is a very different concept of political activity. It questions and challenges not only the assumptions of other generations of Mexican American political leaders but some of the most basic assumptions of American politics as well.

These four phases are roughly sequential, as noted in this outline, but they also overlap a good deal. Violence continues to suppress Mexican American political activity in many communities and to foster an apolitical attitude. In other areas there is a tentative and fearful kind of accommodation politics. Conventional political activity is slowly bringing a quite new political visibility to the Mexican Americans, which is particularly evident in Washington with the recent creation of the Interagency Committee on Mexican American Affairs. Radical politics is also becoming institutionalized in some parts of the Southwest. Despite this confusing and complex overlapping and coexistence, we will discuss each type of political activity separately.

CONFLICT AND APOLITICS

Conflict between Mexicans and Anglo Americans characterized the American Southwest for the better part of the nineteenth century.[1] Let us recall some of the history of the region with specific reference to its political consequences. . . . The first sizeable number of Anglos who entered this region settled in Texas in 1821 under the leadership of Stephen Austin. Alarmed by their rapid increase in numbers and their failure to accept Mexican law and custom, the Mexican government shut off further Anglo immigration in 1830. The end result was the Texas Revolution of 1835-1836, just 15 years after the first legal immigration began. In spite of the Texas declaration of independence from Mexico, there were then 10 years of sporadic warfare, culminating in open warfare between the United States and Mexico in 1846 after the annexation of Texas by the United States.

The Treaty of Guadalupe Hidalgo ended the declared war, but it did not end the fighting between Mexicans and Anglos. Even in New Mexico, acquired "bloodlessly," an abortive rebellion followed the American occupation. In Texas, the next generation lived through an almost endless series of clashes, which reached the status of international warfare again in the late 1850s. Mexico's defeat and the humiliating invasion she suffered cost her nearly a third of her territory. For years afterward elements in Mexico dreamed of reconquest. On the American side the new territories were vast and remote from the central forces of government. The feeble hold that the United States had on the Southwest, the recurrent fears of Indian rebellion, and the divisive forces unleashed by the Civil War were all reflected in American fears of reconquest. Today, with the United States stretching from sea to sea, we rarely question the inevitability of this pattern. But a hundred-odd years ago, this "Manifest Destiny" had something of the character of a crusade, a national mission to be accomplished despite the acknowledged existence of great obstacles. In this climate of opinion, defeating Mexico was a very special victory, and holding these territories a special cause.

Anglos used force to gain control, and Mexicans retaliated with force. Texas, the scene of virtually all of this activity and the home of most Mexicans resident in the United States, saw hostilities between substantial armies and a nearly constant state of guerilla warfare. Many Mexicans, perhaps the most dissident, chose to return to Mexico. From the Texas point of view, many of those who remained were ready as always to join any successful marauder from across the border.

Of these, the most successful was Juan Cortina, who first invaded Texas in 1859 in a series of skirmishes known now as the Cortina Wars. These long "wars" illustrate many of the important themes in Texas-Mexican-American history, showing the comparative lack of distinction between "Mexican" and "Mexican American." They illustrate the racial nature of the conflicts, and they also show that these early decades of conflict were inextricably linked with some larger American problems, most notably the Civil War. . . .

It should be reiterated that the shift in land use entailed a shift in ownership. Often, political promises were made and broken; legal contracts were made and broken; legal protection for Mexicans—landowners and others—was promised and withheld. As Webb concludes in his history of the Texas Rangers, "The humble Mexicans doubted a government that would not protect their person and the higher classes distrusted one that would not safeguard their property. Here, indeed, was the rich soil in which to plant the seed of revolution and race war."[2]

Juan Cortina's expeditions began as a personal vendetta in Brownsville, Texas against an Anglo sheriff who used unnecessary force in arresting one of Cortina's former ranchhands. Cortina soon extended his campaign to a call for the general emancipation of Mexicans from American rule. He exhorted Mexicans to rise against their oppressors, to claim their lands and to drive out the *gringos.* Mexicans on both sides of the Rio Grande flocked to his camp. His army engaged troops in Texas in numerous battles, although eventually he and his army were forced to retreat into Mexico.

A few years later, after the Civil War, Cortina "helped" U.S. federal troops in the skirmishes and military occupation that preceded Reconstruction, an act that confirmed his unpopularity among Texas Anglos. Cortina went on to become brigadier general in the Mexican army and later, governor of the border state of Tamaulipas in northern Mexico. But as late as the middle 1870s he was still leading raids into Texas.

Hundreds of other leaders led groups ranging from the pseudo-military to the simple bandit (though Mexicans often viewed such bandits as *guerilleros* fighting for their people). In California, "outlaws" such as Tiburcio Vásquez and Joaquín Murieta (the latter so romanticized that it is difficult to separate fact from fancy) and in Texas, Juan Flores Salinas, were variously remembered by Anglos anxious for law and order and by Mexicans unwilling to recognize the legitimacy of the American regime. A monument to Salinas was erected in 1875 and carries the inscription: *que combatiendo murió por su patria* ("who died fighting for his country").

The end of the Civil War, however, released troops for the "pacification" of the southwestern Indians, and the railroads could bring in hordes of Easterners looking for land and a new frontier. The era of overt violence between Anglo and Mexican American came to an end and was followed by a long period of quiet. With the beginning of revolution in Mexico in 1910 came the beginning of large-scale immigration. This process rekindled the historical distrust of Mexican Americans, especially now that their numbers were being rapidly increased by refugees from Mexico. It was therefore not surprising that this process would have a depressive effect on political participation among Mexican Americans at this time.

There seemed always to be incidents to keep the Americans fearful. In 1915, for example, a Mexican agent was arrested in a Texas border city with a detailed "Plan de San Diego, Texas," for an insurrection in the Southwest in which "all Anglos over the age of 16 would be put to death." Bandit activities in Texas were being carried out to finance the revolutionary plans of the Flores Magon brothers, who were then operating out of Los Angeles in an effort to begin yet another revolution in Mexico. I.W.W. and anarchist activities among the Mexicans added to the anxiety. Then, in 1916 General Pancho Villa climaxed a number of border raids with an attack on Columbus, New Mexico. The United States retaliated with the Punitive Expedition of General John Pershing into northern Mexico. This comic-opera rerun of the tragic war with

Mexico 70 years earlier increased distrust and resentment toward the Mexican American population. Then came the famous Zimmerman Note of 1917, which appeared to confirm all suspicions: the Germans offered to unite Mexico and Japan with Germany for a war against the United States to restore the Southwest to Mexico and give the Far West to Japan. Mexico showed no interest in the scheme, but it touched a sensitive nerve in the United States. As usual, the Mexican Americans in the Southwest were caught in the middle.

Given the background of distrust and violent suppression it is not surprising that the style of the first important Mexican American political groups should have been very circumspect. They could not have been anything but accommodationist.

THE POLITICS OF ADAPTATION

The politics of accommodation can be traced from the 1920s with the appearance of several new political organizations. A good example was the *Orden Hijos de America* (Order of the Sons of America), founded in San Antonio in 1921.[3] The founding members came almost entirely from the newly emerging middle class. Apparently, though, a few refugees from the Mexican Revolution were also involved. More important, both the social and the economic position of these founding members were precarious, and one can note in their announced objectives important concessions to the Anglo definition of the proper role for Mexicans in politics. For example, the goals of the OSA did *not* include demands for equality, either between Mexican Americans themselves or in terms of the dominant majority. Thus, only "citizens of the U.S. of Mexican or Spanish extraction, either native or naturalized" were eligible to join.[4] This exclusion by citizenship was meant—and acted—as an exclusionary mechanism. The implication was that Mexican Americans were more trustworthy to Anglos than Mexican nationals, and also more deserving of the benefits of American life.

This can be understood partly as a reaction to the Anglo conception of Mexicans as an undifferentiated group of low status, regardless of social achievement or citizenship. Hence, all were equally to be distrusted. As an organization of upwardly mobile individuals (albeit of modest achievements) OSA was concerned to show the dominant Anglo majority that they were different from other, "trouble-making" Mexicans. Of course citizenship would have been functionally useful if the *Orden* had been a truly political group, but the symbolic meaning of the requirement is indicated by another regulation. The organization declared itself "to assume no partisan stand, but rather to confine itself to training members for citizenship."

Obviously, "training members for citizenship" is not a strong political position, although presumably this included some activities aimed at increasing political participation, such as by voting. In general, though, this adaptive position could be interpreted as a reflection of the great social and economic vulnerability of Mexican Americans during the 1920s. Validation and recognition meant being as noncontroversial as possible—and preferably with declarations of loyalty to the United States of America.

OSA functioned for nearly ten years. By that time some splintering had begun to occur in the group and its chapters, and on February 17, 1929, several Mexican American groups, among them the OSA itself, the Order of Knights of America, and the League of Latin American Citizens, met in Corpus Christi, Texas. Out of this meeting a new organization emerged to meet the need for harmony and to present a unified front to the Anglo American community. The theme of unity was embodied in the name of the new organization: the League of United Latin-American Citizens, or LULAC. Once again, membership was restricted to citizens of Mexican or Spanish extraction, one of the group's aims being "to develop within the members of our race the best, purest and most perfect type of a true and loyal citizen of the United States of America."[5]

This obvious sensitivity to Anglo opinion was intensified by the debate in Congress and in the press at the time concerning the rising tide of Mexican immigration. This affirmation of loyalty and citizenship may therefore be interpreted as one further example of a protective device used by middle-class Mexican Americans vis-à-vis the Anglo society.

Thus in 1929, to protect themselves from social and economic sanctions, the willingness of Mexican Americans to assert even minimum political demands was tempered at all times and in all expressions by a desire to reaffirm citizenship and loyalty to the United States. It is not surprising that there was at this time no pressure for Mexican civil rights, particularly if it might have involved any kind of open demonstrations. (As a matter of fact, Article 1 of the LULAC's by-laws contains one item that states, "We shall oppose any radical and violent demonstration which may tend to create conflicts and disturb the peace and tranquility of our country.") Once again, a statement designed to appease, to reassure those Anglos who feared the worst. And it also served as a warning to Mexicans who might conceivably entertain such radical notions.

Notable by its omission among 25 articles is any demand for any form of cultural pluralism, despite the willingness of some members to preserve a semblance of their ethnic identity.

Throughout, the aims and purposes of the new organization reflected its middle-class orientation, a conformity to the standards of Texas Anglo society, and above all, an emphasis on adapting to American society, instead of emphasis on aggressive political participation, and much less on any kind of political participation based on a separate ethnic identity.

Such circumspection must, as we have noted earlier, be judged in the context of the political milieu of Texas in the 1920s. Both Mexicans and Negroes "know their place." Although Mexicans did vote in Texas, in some counties the votes were under the control of an Anglo political boss.[6] In other counties Mexicans seldom voted because of the poll tax and other such limitations. The influence of the Anglo *patron* may be seen in the following letter written by one such boss, who felt it necessary to scold his "Mexican-Texas friends" for forming such a group as LULAC:

> *I have been and still consider myself as your Leader or Superior Chief . . . I have always sheltered in my soul the most pure tenderness for the Mexican-Texas race and have watched over your interests to the best of my ability and knowledge. . . . Therefore I disapprove the political activity of groups which have no other object than to organize Mexican-Texas voters into political groups for guidance by other leaders. . . . I have been able to maintain the Democratic Party in power with the aid of my Mexican-Texas friends, and in all the time that has passed we have had no need for clubs or political organizations.*[7]

Between hostility and economic vulnerability Mexican Americans were making the best of a difficult situation, which was very slow to change. LULAC gained power among the middle class and ultimately became a spokesman for those Mexican Americans who had achieved a measure of economic and social advancement. In Texas it is still an important political group. Other organizations (as well as branch chapters of LULAC) appeared throughout the Southwest, and many were modeled after LULAC. All of them skirted the question of aggressive political action with considerable skill. Accommodation was the style in the 1920s and 1930s; it may very well have been the only possible style. Since World War II LULAC has taken a much more aggressive stance, a change preceded by a number of changes in the structure of the Mexican American population.

THE POLITICIZATION OF MEXICAN-AMERICANS

The politicization of Mexican American communities in the Southwest dates only from the years following World War II. For the most part politicization was prefaced by deep social changes among the Mexican American population, discussed elsewhere in this book. In sum, they brought Mexicans into new and partly unforeseen contact with American society, particularly in urban areas. The word "urbanization" hardly conveys their impact. A demand for labor brought hundreds of thousands of Mexicans into cities from rural areas, and at the same time many hundreds of thousands of young Mexican American men found themselves in uniform—and racially invisible to Anglos from other areas of the United States and to other peoples in foreign lands. At the same time, however, their families began to find that the urban areas of the Southwest, like rural ones, were highly discriminatory (this was the time of the "zoot suit riots" in Los Angeles and San Diego, California[8]). (In the rural areas, however, the social fabric that supported and justified discrimination was hardly changed.)

In the cities the urban migrants could find only poor housing, the lowest unskilled employment, and restricted access to schools and other public facilities. As before, few Mexican Americans took part in political activity, although the tradition of political accommodations now seemed outmoded. So did the political organizations built to formalize this relationship to the larger community. A middle class had begun to increase rather rapidly as a result of wartime prosperity, and it was increasingly dissatisfied. Against this background a group of articulate former servicemen (helped substantially by the educational and training benefits of the G.I. Bill of Rights) began to press for changes in the community. In Los Angeles a more open environment facilitated a new alliance with labor elements, Anglo civil leaders, and religious leaders.

One outcome of this alliance was the California-based Community Service Organization (CSO). In Los Angeles the CSO tried to develop indigenous leaders to organize community activity around local issues, using the techniques of larger-scale grassroots community organization. In this manner the Community Service Organization mobilized large segments of the Mexican American community into activities directed against restricted housing, police brutality, segregated schools, inequitable justice, and discriminatory employment, all problems endemic in the Mexican American areas of southern California as much as in other parts of the Southwest. In this process CSO became an important and meaning-ful post-World War II political phenomenon in the Mexican American community.

In general CSO pressed for full and equal rights for Mexican Americans. The new emphasis was the extra appeal for active and increased participation by as many elements of the community as possible. Therefore, in contrast to previous organizations, CSO tended to be more egalitarian. Under the influence of an outside catalyst (Saul Alinsky's Industrial Areas Foundation) it became a group that no longer served as the vehicle of a relatively few and successful Mexican Americans. Although the leadership tended to be new middle class, on the whole it made an effort to recruit members of the working class and other lower-class elements, including new arrivals from Mexico. CSO also had some non-Mexican members, although they were comparatively few.

This idea of an alliance of equals from various strata, of Mexican American society became important. In contrast to the paternalism of previous organizations such as LULAC, there was little concern with the assimilation of lower-class elements into the mainstream of American life. Nor, for that matter, did CSO show any interest in "Mexican culture." The guiding idea of CSO was to cope with concrete and immediate social, economic, and political problems.

The founders of CSO assumed that American institu-tions were basically responsive to the needs and demands of the Mexican American population. There were no questions about the legitimacy of these institutions; it was always as-sumed that proper community organization and action would force Anglo institutions to respond to the needs of Mexican Americans. Accordingly, getting Mexicans to exercise the right to vote became a prime CSO objective. Members organ-ized large-scale nonpartisan community drives to register voters. In Los Angeles these registration drives rather sig-nificantly increased the number of Spanish-surname voters. The immediate results were electoral victories by Mexican American candidates, there and in nearby communities. Furthermore, CSO pressure on public housing authorities, on the Fair Employment Practices Commission (FEPC), and against police brutality also yielded results. Housing authorities eased discriminatory practices, Mexican American representation was included in the FEPC, and the police department agreed "to go easy on Mexicans" on the Los Angeles East Side.

At the time members considered CSO tactics radical and militant, and throughout the 1950s the CSO remained a politically powerful organization that emphasized direct, grassroots community action. Numerous CSO chapters were organized throughout the state of California, each duplicating the Alinsky approach to community organization.

In recent years CSO has declined as a potent community organization, in part because of the withdrawal of financial support from the Industrial Areas Foundation, and in part because it lost some of its most energetic members. For example, the single most well-known former member of CSO, César Chávez, split with the urban-centered CSO to organize a union of farm workers. Also contributing to the decline of CSO was the rise of competing organizations of Mexican Americans.

Other organizations in the Southwest reflect the aggressive political style growing after World War II. In Texas, there is the important American G.I. Forum. The G.I. Forum was founded by a south Texas physician, Dr. Hector Garcia; the immediate cause of its formation was the refusal of a funeral home in Three Rivers, Texas, to bury a Mexican American war veteran in 1948. The incident attracted national attention, and the idea of the G.I. Forum spread rapidly not only in Texas but also throughout the Southwest, to several midwestern states, and to Washington, D.C. Although the Forum is concerned with nonpartisan civic action, it has moved increasingly toward more direct and aggressive political activities. In Texas, where its main strength lies, the G.I. Forum launched intensive "Get out the vote" and "Pay your poll tax" drives in the 1950s. Subsequently, it has continued voter registration drives since the repeal of the Texas poll tax. On a number of other issues, the Forum continues to act as a spokesman against the problems that beset the Mexican American community in Texas.

If the CSO and the American G.I. Forum reflect the goals of the immediate postwar years, two political groups founded in the late 1950s show a shift in both the political goals and the resources available in the community. In California the Mexican American Political Association (MAPA), founded in 1958, and in Texas the Political Association of Spanish-speaking Organizations (PASSO) were organized essentially as groups pressuring the political system at the party level. These were not primarily attempts to organize the Mexican American poor to register and vote; they were efforts to use growing middle-class strength to win concessions for Mexican Americans from the Anglo-dominated political parties. Essentially the goal of both associations was simply to get Mexican Americans into political office, either as nominees for elective office in the regular parties or as appointees of elected Anglo officials. Thus the best-publicized effort of either group was the successful deposition of the Anglo political structure in Crystal City, Texas, in the early 1960s. In this venture, PASSO joined with some non-Mexican groups, notably the Teamsters and the Catholic Bishops' Committee for the Spanish Speaking. (Although the victory in Crystal City was short-lived, it was as significant to Texas Mexicans as the more recent victory of a Negro mayor in Mississippi was to the black community.)

Both MAPA and PASSO gain strength by virtue of their statewide connections, which are particularly important in the outlying rural areas where repression has been a norm. Statewide ties give courage and support to local efforts. (At this writing one of the strongest MAPA chapters in California is the chapter in the Coachella valley, a citrus- and date-growing area not far from Palm Springs. The local chairman, a vociferous spokesman for Mexican American laborers, is constantly subject to harassment. He is also constantly in demand outside the immediate area. The intervention of outside elements in a local and rather repressive situation has reduced isolation and repression. As in Crystal City, one of MAPA's victories has been the election of Mexican American officials in the grower-dominated town of Coachella.)

Although both MAPA and PASSO are still largely confined to California and Texas, respectively, there are branches and organizational efforts in other states. The two associations once considered amalgamation into a regional group; but, incredibly, the effort failed because the two groups could not agree on a common name. Texas Mexicans could not afford the then too overt ethnic pride suggested by "Mexican American," and the California group would not accept the euphemism "Spanish-speaking." At these discussions, one disgusted delegate finally proposed "CACA" (a Spanish equivalent of the English "doo-doo") to represent the "Confederated Alliance of *Chicano* Associations." Interestingly, only in such an intensely in-group situation could the name *Chicano* be suggested. At the time this word could not be used for a serious political discussion.

THE *CHICANO* MOVEMENT

Throughout this chapter we have suggested that Mexican American political activity has often been related to social structural factors. Because much of this political activity was possible only after certain structural changes in Mexican American life, there were seldom any real alternatives beyond simple reaction to Anglo pressure. The importance of the *Chicano* movement as an alternative to pressures from the majority society can hardly be overemphasized. It is a distinctively novel development in the Mexican American community. The *Chicano* movement developed in southern California no earlier than 1966, and it is already a sharp new force in the political expression of Mexican Americans throughout the southwest.

The *Chicano* ideology includes a broad definition of political activity. Ironically, such thinking was possible only for a new generation of urbanized and "Anglicized" (that is, assimilated) young Mexican Americans, who were much less burdened by social and class restrictions than their elders and whose education had exposed them to new ideas.

The exact beginnings of the movement are obscure. There is some evidence that the *Chicano* movement grew out of a group of conferences held at Loyola University in Los Angeles in the summer of 1966. As originally conceived by its Catholic sponsors, the conferences were to create fairly innocuous youth organization for the middle-class Mexican students attending various colleges throughout California. Very quickly the movement grew beyond the intent or control of its sponsors (Loyola has never been very noted for its interest in Mexican American education) and it drew in yet others, not students and not middle class, who were attracted by the ideology of *chicanismo*. Thus it cannot be understood as a movement limited to the young, to students, or even to urban areas. It must also be understood as including the followers of Reies Tijerina in northern New Mexico and César Chávez' embattled union of striking farm workers in central California. In 1969 Rodolfo (Corky) González was the principal leader and inspiration of the *Chicano* movement in Denver although his interests were mainly in urban civic action. Moreover, "Corky" has organized regional youth conferences and his influence spreads far beyond the local area. No one leader has yet emerged in southern California or in Texas.

As this wide range of activity shows, the *Chicano* movement is extremely heterogeneous, and its elements have different aims and purposes. In this way the movement cuts across social class, regional, and generational lines. Its aims range from traditional forms of social protest to increasingly more radical goals that appear as a sign of an emerging nationalism. It is a social movement, in that it can be described as "pluralistic behavior functioning as an organized mass effort directed toward a change of established folkways or institutions."[9] The dynamic force of the movement is its ideology— *chicanismo*.

The new ideology is advanced as a challenge to the dominant Anglo beliefs concerning Mexicans as well as to the beliefs of Mexican Americans themselves. Although we have emphasized that students are by no means the only element of the *Chicano* movement, we will reconstruct *chicanismo* primarily as it has been developed among students. Actually, this is only one of several ideological strands but it is the most consistently developed, thus the best illustration of the change from protest to nationalism and a synthesis of the ideology of *chicanismo.*

The first student form of the *Chicano* movement coincided with the development of new student organizations in California universities and colleges in 1966 and 1967. Some of these groups were the United Mexican American Students (UMAS), the Mexican American Student Association (MASA), Mexican American Student Confederation (MASC), and Movimiento Estudiantil Chicano de Aztlán (MECHA). More recently the Mexican American Youth Organization (MAYO) has appeared, with particular strength in Texas. (MAYO is also the name adopted by the new organizations of *Chicanos* in California prisons.) These student groups were first concerned with a rather narrow range of problems in the field of education, particularly those concerned with increasing the number of Mexican American students in college. To the extent that these student groups were active in the Mexican American community, they were involved with various forms of protest against specific and long-standing grievances, such as police brutality and inferior educational facilities, although other forms of community activity also involved political campaigns.

Chicano student groups thus have never repudiated ordinary forms of political activity, although for them such forms as voting constitute only one political alternative. Actually, given the wide range of problems facing the Mexican American community, *Chicanos* view conventional forms of political activity as perhaps the least effective. Instead, they favor forms of confrontation as the most effective means to gain access for the traditionally excluded *Chicano*, even though it has, on occasion, led to violence. In general, this conception of politics contrasts sharply with the ideas of more conservative Mexican American leaders, most of whom adhere to very limited and "safe" politics with an emphasis on voting and "working within the system" to gain political leverage. This is not to say that *Chicanos* reject working for social change within the system; as a matter of fact, much recent activity has focused on bringing about change in the universities and colleges as well as in the public school systems. Nevertheless, whereas the moderates seek to bring major change in American society through nonviolent means, the more militant speak of the need for "revolutionary activity," though they often leave the details and direction of this revolution unspecified. While they admire the life style and aspirations of revolutionary leaders like Ché Guevara, they have thus far made no systematic theoretical connection between the *Chicano* movement and the general literature on revolution. The theoretical underpinnings of the *Chicano* movement thus often lack a strong direction.

And yet, the advent of the *Chicano* movement does represent a revolutionary phenomenon among Mexican Americans. As we shall see, most of the change from traditional forms lies in (or is reflected in) the ideology of *chicanismo.* Basically eclectic, *chicanismo* draws inspiration from outside the United States and outside the Mexican American experience. The Cuban Revolution, for example, exerts some influence, as do the career and ideals of Ché Guevara. For instance, the Brown Berets (a *Chicano* youth group) affect the life style of this revolutionary. Black Power also offers something of a model. Most recenty, *Chicanos* have resurrected the Mexican revolutionary tradition.

Basically, however, *chicanismo* focuses on the life experience of the Mexican in the United States. It challenges the belief system of the majority society at the same time that it attempts to reconstruct a new image for Mexican Americans themselves. *Chicanos* assume that along with American Indians and black Americans, Mexicans live in the United States as a conquered people. This idea allows *chicanismo* to explain the evolution of the *Chicano* as essentially conflictual. In each conflictual relationship with Anglos, the Mexicans lost out and were thus forced to live in the poverty and degradation attendant upon those with the status of a conquered people. This is no better illustrated than by the Mexicans' loss of communal and private property. As a result, they had no choice but to work the land for a *patrón* (usually an Anglo, but sometimes a Mexican, who exploited his own people). When the Mexican was thrown off the land, he was forced to become an unattached wage-earner, often a migrant farm worker; or he might migrate to a city, where the exploitation continued. In any event, *chicanismo* emphasizes that the Mexican was transformed into a rootless economic commodity, forced either to depend on migrant farm work or to sell his labor in the urban centers, where his fate depended upon the vicissitudes of the economy. Ironically, indispensable as Mexican labor was for the economic development of the Southwest, the Mexican got little recognition for his contribution and even less benefit from it.

Chicanos therefore see the economic expansion of the Southwest as essentially a dehumanizing process. They also point out that during periods of economic depression in the United States, when the Mexican became "superfluous" and "expensive," Anglo society had no qualms about attempting to eliminate Mexicans from the United States, as in the repatriations of the 1930s. . . . The repatriations are viewed as a conscious attempt to eliminate the *Chicano* from American society.

The thrust of *chicanismo* is not only economic, but also cultural. In many ways, the exploitation and suppression of his culture is what most angers the *Chicano*, who views the attempt to deracinate Mexican culture in the Southwest as the reason why Mexican Americans are disoriented about their culture and often attempt to deny it. The *Chicano* points out that the Anglo himself often views Mexicans with a great degree of ambivalence. Anglos sometimes take over aspects of "Spanish" (which is really Mexican) culture and at the same time deny it to the Mexican himself. In this fashion Mexicans were denied the development of a more autonomous cultural life, especially as it touches upon Spanish language use, the arts, and so on. (This was done in spite of the agreements made in the signing of the Treaty of Guadalupe Hidalgo. Early drafts of the treaty contained Mexican government efforts to make formal recognition of language rights for Mexicans who chose to remain in the United States after the Mexican War. These provisions were not approved by the U.S. Senate.)

Worse yet, the ideology goes on, the cultural suppression continues to the present day, reinforced by Anglo institutions, particularly the schools. The extreme position (although by no means infrequent) is represented by the fact that Mexican American students in the public schools are corporally punished for using Spanish, their native language. Under these circumstances, it is understandable that the Mexican American student remains ignorant and often ashamed of his past. When the Mexican is mentioned in textbooks, it is in a romanticized and stereotypically Anglicized version of "Spanish culture" that may be congenial to Anglos but is remote and irrelevant to the Mexican American. The *Chicano* considers this type of whitewashed "Spanish" culture particularly galling because he feels that while Anglos may selectively choose certain motifs from Mexican culture, the person behind the culture, the Mexican himself, is given neither recognition nor respect.

Chicanismo also focuses on race, and in some ways this emphasis constitutes one of the most controversial aspects of *chicanismo.* It is argued that Anglo racism denies the Mexican his ethnicity by making him ashamed of his "Mexicanness." Mexican ancestry, instead of being a source of pride, becomes a symbol of shame and inferiority. As a consequence, Mexicans spend their lives apologizing or denying their ancestry, to the point that many dislike and resent being called "Mexican," preferring "Spanish American," "Latin," "Latin American," and similar euphemisms. For these reasons, the term *"Chicano"* is now insisted upon by activists as a symbol of the new assertiveness.

Advocates of *chicanismo* therefore hope to reconstruct the Mexican Americans' concept of themselves by appeals to pride of a common history, culture and "race." *Chicanismo* attempts to redefine the Mexicans' identity on the basis not of class, generation, or area of residence but on a unique and shared experience in the United States. This means that appeals for political action, economic progress, and reorientation of cultural identity are cast in terms of the common history, culture, and ethnic background of *la raza.*

Chicano ideologues insist that social advance based on material achievement is, in the final analysis, less important than social advance based on *la raza*; they reject what they call the myth of American individualism. The *Chicano* movement feels that it cannot afford the luxury of individualism; if Mexicans are to confront the problems of their group realistically they must begin to act along collective lines. Hence, the stirrings of a new spirit of what *chicanismo* terms "cultural nationalism" among the Mexican Americans of the Southwest.

Chicanismo has led not only to increased participation in community activities, but also to a heightened and often intense interest in cultural life. *Chicano* poets, playwrights, journalists, and writers of all varieties have suddenly appeared. There are *Chicano* theater groups in several large cities (often known as the *teatro urbano*) and one nationally known and well-traveled group from Delano, California (*El teatro campesino*), which tells the story not only of the striking California farm-workers but of *Chicanos* in general. Newspapers and magazines also reflect this desire to disseminate the idea of *chicanismo.* Throughout the Southwest numerous *Chicano* "underground" newspapers and magazines publishing literary materials have emerged. There is even a *Chicano* Press Association, a regional association representing *Chicano* publications from Texas to California. Furthermore, because of the strong base in colleges and universities, a serious and generally successful drive to develop "ethnic studies" programs has appeared, especially in California. As part of the drive to spread the idea of *chicanismo* in education, *Chicanos* place an emphasis on Mexican contributions to American society, thus giving *Chicano* college students a new conception of their past and present.

Chicano student groups share an orientation similar to that of black students, and on occasion they cooperate and support each other on similar demands. (There is more mutual support between black and brown students than between their counterparts at the community level.) The alliance between black and brown students, however, has not been close, harmonious, or continuous. *Chicano* student organizations have not yet been significantly involved with Anglo radical student groups, although these groups sometimes claim their support or claim that they are working for the benefit of *Chicanos.*

THE ECHO OF *CHICANISMO*

How much has this student manifestation of the *Chicano* movement affected the larger Mexican community? At this writing the ideological reverberations have been considerable, particularly among the young people of college age and including also those in the secondary schools. We must not forget that the Mexican American population is very young. Some counterparts of *Chicano* college militancy have appeared throughout the Southwest in high schools as, for example, among students in Denver, Los Angeles, San Francisco, and many smaller cities.

The demands have often been modest, in most instances no more than for increased counselling services for Mexican American students and other changes in the methods and content of instruction. In some Texas cities and in Denver, Colorado, the student militants further demanded the end of punishment for using Spanish on the school grounds. In most cases the school boards have acceded to this particular demand. But the reaction of the Anglo community has often been fierce. In Los Angeles a school "walk-out" by Mexican American students in 1968 resulted in the arrest of 13 alleged leaders for criminal conspiracy. In Denver a sharp reaction by the police resulted in the injury of 17 persons and the arrest of 40. In other areas in the Southwest there have been similar, if less publicized, responses to *Chicano* militancy.

Neither the Anglo reaction nor the rapid spread of *chicanismo* should be taken to mean that a full-blown social movement is in progress among Mexican Americans. In many areas, on the contrary, established Mexican American leaders have dissociated themselves from the *Chicanos.* For instance, a school walkout by Mexican students in Kingsville, Texas brought an angry denunciation from a Mexican American Congressman from Texas and other community leaders. At the same time, the *Chicano* movement poses a very difficult dilemma for most older Mexican Americans. They sympathize with the goals of *chicanismo,* yet they fear that the radical means used to pursue these ends will undermine their own hard-earned social and economic gains. The Anglo community expects a denunciation of what it considers to be irresponsible acts of these young people. But for the older leaders to oppose the *Chicano* protest might be a slow form of personal political suicide as well as acting to exacerbate divisiveness in the Mexican American community.

In California, *Chicano* student groups have grown rapidly; they have acquired the power to pass on Mexican American faculty appointments in many high schools and colleges. Typically such faculty members are avidly sought to assist with the new ethnic studies programs and centers. Ultimately, though, *Chicano* students are faced by responsibility to the community. These students are aware that the popularity of *chicanismo* among Mexican American students means a major opportunity for the development of an entire new generation of young professionals to carry these ideas back to the Mexican American community.

Beyond the universities there have been other sources of support, some of them quite substantial. Grants and direct organizing assistance have come from American Protestant denominations, notably the National Council of Churches. In 1968 a substantial ($630,000) grant from the Ford Foundation to the Southwest Council of La Raza (headquarters in Phoenix) helped the organization of a number of militant *Chicano* groups. The Southwest Council of La Raza considers itself permanent and accepts money for *"barrio* development" from not only the Ford Foundation but churches, labor groups, and other interested organizations. Both the announced ideals of the council and its membership assure commitment to the ideals of *chicanismo.*

The *Chicano* movement began as a protest. Only later did its dynamics carry it toward an increasing cultural nationalism. The first steps toward social change did not go beyond demands for equality of opportunity for Mexican Americans, which are still being made (by the less militant in the movement). Until recently no Mexican American had tried to define the problems of the community in any terms except those of assimilation. It is precisely these ideas of assimilation and social "adjustment" that the *Chicano* militant rejects. As a new alternative, *chicanismo* represents a conception of an autonomous and self-determining social life for Mexican Americans.

It is interesting that it was not until the 1960s that the *Chicano* leaders emerged to question some of the oldest and most fundamental assumptions of Mexicans in American society. This protest probably would not have been possible in a period of general social calm and stability. That the *Chicano* protest emerged when it did is perhaps due in large part to the emergence of other social groups that also began to question basic notions about American society. But if these other groups feel a sense of alienation in American society, the *Chicano's* alienation is doubly acute. It is not only from American society that he feels alienated; he also feels left out of the mainstream of Mexican history and, simultaneously, he feels a sense of guilt for having "deserted" the homeland. It is this sense of being in two cultures yet belonging to neither (*ni aquí ni allá*) that is the source of his most profound alienation and now, anger. It is against this background that the *Chicano* is attempting with a deep sense of urgency to reconstruct his history, his culture, his sense of identity.

In practical terms the result is increasing radicalization, with which comes a new set of problems. Cultural nationalism has emerged, bringing with it questions that must be answered if the *Chicano* movement is to become a potent force for all Mexican Americans in their diverse circumstances throughout the Southwest and other parts of the United States.

1. The historical material in this chapter is drawn heavily from the historical source materials cited in Chapters Two and Three, and also on Walter Prescott Webb, *The Texas Rangers: A Century of Frontier Defense* (Boston: Houghton Mifflin Co., 1935), and on Ralph Guzmán, "The Political Socialization of the Mexican American People" (unpublished manuscript, 1967).
2. Webb, *Texas Rangers*, p. 176.
3. This section draws heavily on Guzmán, "Political Socialization." See also Miguel D. Tirado, "Mexican American Community Political Organization" (unpublished manuscript in files of Ralph Guzmán, University of California Santa Cruz, 1969), and Robert A. Cuéllar, "A Social and Political History of the Mexican-American Population of Texas, 1929-1963" (unpublished Master's thesis, North Texas State University, Denton, Texas, 1969).
4. Article III, constitution of OSA, cited by O. Douglas Weeks, "The League of United Latin-American Citizens," *The Southwestern Political and Social Science Quarterly*, X (December 1929), p. 260, cited in Tirado, "Mexican American Political Organization," p. 5.
5. Weeks, "League," p. 260, cited in Guzmán, "Political Socialization," p. 355.
6. Mexican American voting was "managed," in V.O. Key's term. For a specific discussion of Texas Mexican American politics see his *Southern Politics* (New York: Vintage edition, Alfred A. Knopf, Inc., 1949), pp. 271-76. Key also puts the Texas pattern into the general Southern political context.
7. Letter published in the *Hidalgo County Independent*, Edinburg, Texas, March 8, 1929, cited in Weeks, "League," pp. 275-76, cited in Guzmán, "Political Socialization," p. 160.
8. The zoot suit riots were a series of racial incidents in Los Angeles during the summer of 1943—later called "race riots"between U.S servicemen and Mexican American youth (also called "pachuco riots"). These battles, the humiliation of Mexican Americans, ensuing mass arrests of Mexicans (*not* of the servicemen who were later shown to have provoked them) had a deep impact on the Mexican American community. It resulted immediately in a sharp increase in Anglo discrimination of all kinds against Mexicans and laid the ground for a deep anger and bitterness among the Mexican American community which had been largely impotent to deal with the situation. McWilliams gives an account of the riots in *North from Mexico*.
9. As defined in Abel, in *Why Hitler Came to Power*, as cited in Martin Oppenheimer, *The Urban Guerilla* Chicago: Quadrangle Books, 1969), p. 19.

V/CHICANO LITERATURE AND SCHOLARSHIP

The new type of Chicano literature is excellently illustrated by Armando Rendon in his book *The Chicano Manifesto* from which "The People of Aztlán" is taken. In this selection Rendon describes what he believes to be the unique characteristics of Chicanos and their culture. From those characteristics he constructs a profile of the "new Chicano" who he feels is destined to bring to a high level of culture all Mexican-Americans residing in the United States. This new culture will be founded upon the proud acknowledgment of the uniqueness of the Chicano's history, racial heterogeneity, and future destiny.

Most of the characteristics of Chicano literature are present in this article by Rendon: an almost mystical appeal for Chicanos to unite because destiny has marked them as a special people, a hypernationalism based upon racial identification, an uncritical denunciation of all that is Anglo, and finally a proclamation that all will be better for Chicanos when the movement replaces those in power with the "Brown" who are currently out of power.

This type of literature has a strong attraction for the young since it is based upon the truth of prejudice and discrimination experienced by all Chicanos sometime in their lives. Since each Chicano has experienced prejudice, and perhaps discrimination, he is willing to accept the proposition that all Anglo institutions are racist. He does not expect reforms that will eliminate the prejudice and discrimination of the institutions themselves. He believes that reform can come only from his efforts and from a complete rearranging of the governing structures of society—and perhaps of society itself. Additionally the young believe it possible to govern by slogan, i.e., "Brown Power" and thus find that particular appeal most attractive.

Mexican-Americans, who are proud of their heritage but who acknowledge that the Anglo society, while far from perfect, has tried to respond to their suggestions for reform and has not been uniformly racist, find it impossible to defend their position and their own reputations against the oversimplified, but powerful, charge that Anglo racism is to blame for their condition. The "single-factor" cause of the Chicano condition, i.e., Anglo racism, is attractive because it substitutes hatred for complexity, rhetoric for reason, and slogans for programs. Perhaps, however, this kind of effort is needed to create pride among the Mexican-Americans who can then use it to begin participating in their own civic affairs for the first time in their lives.

"Poverty in the Valley of Plenty" by Ernesto Galarza has been included for two reasons: first, it introduces the reader to Dr. Ernesto Galarza, the Dean of Mexican-American intellectual-activists, who has devoted his life to securing better conditions of every sort for his fellow Chicanos as well as for the underprivileged generally; and, secondly, because Dr. Galarza has documented, in painstaking detail, the dispute between the grape growers in California and the labor union seeking to represent the grape-pickers.

The account presented by Dr. Galarza is important in several respects. First, Galarza documents what the dispute between the principals was about. Secondly, he illustrates how the "system," in this case a congressional investigating committee, almost automatically appears to favor the status quo supporters and thus perforce obliges those wishing to change the status quo to prove beyond a reasonable doubt that the changes sought will create a more desirable, a more productive, a more stable post-status quo than that existing in the status quo. To realize how unreasonable the aforementioned obligation is one need only reflect on how easy or difficult it is to substantiate such arguments—keeping in mind that only future developments can answer the question. Finally, Galarza describes how Richard M. Nixon, today the President of the United States, then a young congressman seeking a Senate seat, used the hearings as a vehicle to gain the political support of the grape growers in California. The significance of the position Nixon took in the hearings offers one reason why Chicanos today are reluctant to accept him as *their* President.

In the California grape dispute, *as Galarza documents*, Nixon, by no stretch of the imagination, could be judged to be pro or even neutral toward Chicano interests; he was quite clearly hostile to those interests.

The People of Aztlán

Armando Rendon

We are the people of Aztlán, true descendants of the Fifth Sun, el Quinto Sol.

In the early morning light of a day thousands of years old now, my forebears set out from Aztlán, a region of deserts, mountains, rivers, and forests, to seek a new home. Where they came from originally is hidden in the sands and river-beds and only hinted at by the cast of eye and skin which we, their sons, now bear.

Driven by drought, or enemies, or by the vision of a new motherland, my people began walking toward the south in the hope of founding a new world. Among the earliest of my ancestors were the Nahúas, from whom sprang the most advanced and sophisticated peoples of the North American continent. They made their own wandering journey to Aná-huac, as the region of the Valley of Mexico was then known. From about the time that the Christ Passion was unfolding on the other side of the world, and for perhaps a thousand years afterward, a way of life and thought was evolving which the man-god Quetzalcoatl had forged and which the Nahúas, the Toltecs, the Chichimecas, and then the Aztecs nurtured through the centuries.

The Toltecs forged Teotihuacán, the City of the Gods and the center of the Nahuatl religion. Their influence continued for fifteen hundred years, until the arrival of Hernando

Reprinted with permission of The Macmillan Company from *Chicano Manifesto* by Armando B. Rendon. Copyright 1971 by Armando B. Rendon.

[margin handwritten notes: "Tenochtitlán - 1325" "Cactus upon a rock"]

Cortez, the final inroad of a searching people that was to spell the end of a great, involuted civilization.

The Chichimeca, nomadic tribes who, tradition tells us came from the North, from Aztlán, or what is now the southwestern part of the United States, began moving down by ancient trails into the Valley of Mexico in about the eleventh century A.D. The Aztecs, who derive their name from Aztlán, were the last significant group to arrive in Anáhuac. Those that survived this exodus came among shallow marshes by a lake and in 1325 founded the city of Tenochtitlán. It was there in the marsh waters that they saw a sign, an eagle grasping a serpent in its claw as it perched upon a cactus sprouting from a rock. "Tenochtitlán means cactus upon a stone."

[margin handwritten notes: "SUNS" "5°SOL"]

Quetzalcoatl gave birth in his people to the Fifth Sun. Four Suns prefigured the coming of el Quinto Sol, which was to destroy and subsume the rest. The Fifth Sun was the epoch of the Aztec civilization. Huitzilopochtli, who led the Aztecs out of Aztlán, personifies this Fifth Sun, but Quetzalcoatl (historically identified with Topiltzin, the last Toltec king, who reigned in the late tenth century) is the creator of the epoch and its spirit. Earth, air, fire, and water preceded the fifth epoch; the Fifth Sun was movement, progress, life vibrant. The people of the Fifth Sun developed a complex system of religion in a region that was to be New Spain, Mexico, and much of present Central America. They developed an elaborate symbolic language to depict their beliefs. To convey the concept of the Fifth Sun a basic pattern was used of five circles, one circle at each of four corners, with the fifth in the center. An intricate refinement is seen in a circular network of human features incorporating the five-circle mode; the great Aztec calendar stone is a huge representation of this principle. (Laurette Séjourné in her book *Burning Water* provides an invaluable description and interpretation of the religion and language of our ancient forebears.)

Discovering the spiritual sensitivity and depth of the people of the Fifth Sun, the Chicano begins to fathom what must be one of the most psychologically important elements

PAZ

in the make-up of the Mexican. Octavio Paz, the Mexican poet and former ambassador to India, comments in *The Labyrinth of Solitude* that the Aztec religion was notable for its generally being a "superimposition" on older beliefs (the Nahuatl religion was so infused with various primitive ideas and superstitions that the Aztec version suggested a predisposition to Catholicism and its ally, Spanish rule). Paz says unequivocally, "The Mexican is a religious being and his experience of the divine is completely genuine. . . . Nothing has been able to destroy the filial relationship of our people with the divine."

The spiritual experience of the Chicano, in turn, is profound. From the standpoint of the people of Ollin Tonatiuh, the Nahuatl name for the Fifth Sun, the Chicano's religious experience embodies all of nature. The epic of the Four Suns begins with the Sun of Night or Earth, depicted by a tiger, a period that by itself is sterile; then the Sun of Air, or God of Wind, pure spirit whose indwellers became monkeys; the Sun of Rain or Fire, in which only birds survive; and finally the Sun of Water, friendly only to fish.

The Fifth Sun is born out of man's sacrifice. At its center is the spirit; its mode is movement. It is the unity, cohesion, synthesis of all that has come before, bound into the human soul. Thus, the Fifth Sun is the very foundation of life, of spirituality, not in the restricted sense of an organized religion but in the nature of a common bond among all soul creatures. We can speak, therefore, of a union with the cosmos, of a cosmic sense of spirit, of an alma Chicana (a Chicano soul). The concept of La Raza Unida is a further reassertion and profession of that principle of a cosmic Chicano existence. We can think of ourselves as a community of the future and of the past seeking its destiny in the present.

My people have come in fulfillment of a cosmic cycle from ancient Aztlán, the seed ground of the great civilizations of Anáhuac, to modern Aztlán, characterized by the progeny of our Indian, Mexican, and Spanish ancestors. We have rediscovered Aztlán in ourselves. This knowledge provides the dynamic principle upon which to build a deep unity and

Carnalismo

brotherhood among Chicanos. Ties much more profound than even language, birthplace, or culture bind us together—Aztlán represents that unifying force of our nonmaterial heritage. This is not meant to revive long-dead religions, but rather to resurrect still-living principles of brotherhood (carnalismo), of spiritual union, which we have come so close to losing.

A statement composed in March 1969 in Denver, Colorado, during a Chicano youth conference sponsored by the Crusade for Justice, elaborated for the first time the concept of Aztlán. Notably, a young Chicano writer and poet, Alberto Alurista, proposed Aztlán as the fundamental theme, and thus inspired a new awareness of self-concept and intent among Chicanos. In brief, the Spiritual Plan of Aztlán . . . asserts:

> In the spirit of a new people . . . we, the Chicanos, inhabitants and civilizers of the northern land of Aztlán, from whence came our forefathers, reclaiming the land of their birth and consecrating the determination of our people of the sun, declare that the call of our blood is our power, our responsibility, and our inevitable destiny. . . .
>
> With our heart in our hand and our hands in the soil, we declare the independence of our mestizo Nation. We are a bronze people with a bronze culture. Before the world, before all of North America, before all our brothers in the Bronze Continent, we are a Nation. We are a union of free pueblos. We are Aztlán.

Alberto Alurista

References to Aztlán as the place of origin of the Mexican Indian peoples are negligible in North American chronicles. Two of the most easily attainable texts by historians in the United States are William H. Prescott's *History of the Conquest of Mexico* (1843) and Alvin M. Josephy, Jr.'s *The Indian Heritage of America* (1968). Prescott, in reviewing the various histories, compiled for the most part by priest-scholars, noted that "The ingenuity of the chronicler was taxed to find out analogies between the Aztec and Scripture histories, both old and new. The emigration from Aztlán to

Anahuac was typical of the Jewish exodus." This suggests the legend that the American peoples were derived from one of the lost tribes of Israel. Commenting on another possible source, Prescott wrote:

> The theory of an Asiatic origin for Aztec civilization derives stronger confirmation from the light of tradition, which, shining steadily from the far North-west, pierces through the dark shadows that history and mythology have alike thrown around the antiquities of the country. Traditions of a Western, or North-western origin were found among the more barbarous tribes, and by the Mexicans were preserved both orally and in their heiroglyphical maps, where the different stages of their migration are carefully noted. But who at this day shall read them? They are admitted to agree, however, in representing the populous North as the prolific hive of the American races. In this quarter were placed their Aztlán and their Huehuetlapállan, the bright adobes of their ancestors. . . .

In a footnote, he said of the maps: "But as they are all within the boundaries of New Spain, indeed, south of the Rio Gila, they throw little light, of course, on the vexed question of the primitive adobes of the Aztecs."

It so happens that the Rio Gila flows from southwestern New Mexico, starting a few miles west of where the Rio Grande cuts through the center of New Mexico before it forms a border between Texas and Mexico. From there, the Gila connects with the Colorado River at the junction of California, Nevada, Arizona and Sonora, Mexico, just above the Gulf of California—a convergence of rivers and cultures as significant for the Americas as the confluence of the Tigris and Euphrates in Mesopotamia! Yet Prescott would have us seek a more distant source.

In a comprehensive study of the Indians of the Americas, Josephy recounts the arrival of the Mexica, a Nahuatl-speaking tribe, "weak and relatively primitive," in the Lake Texcoco area in the early thirteenth century, and their settling on the site of today's Mexico City. The historian says that the Mexica took the name Aztec from Aztlán, whence they had come, "somewhere vaguely to the Northwest and may even have been in the present-day United States Southwest."

An analysis and compendium by Mexican historians of the ancient native peoples, *Mexico a Través de los Siglos* (1939), relates, according to its editors, "the pilgrimage of the Mexicans from the time they left Aztlán until they founded the City of Mexico." The first of the three volumes in this work presents a detailed account of the Nahuatl religion and of Nahuatl origins, and notes specifically that the region encompassing Nevada, Utah, New Mexico, Arizona, California, and the Mexican States of Sinaloa and Sonora contain artifacts and remains of living facilities closely related to those of the Aztecs in the Valley of Mexico. That region is also given the name Chicomoztoc, literally, las siete cuevas (seven caves), later to become the fabled and much-sought seven cities of Cibola. Huehuetlapállan was the most important of these population centers. But the Mexican scholars clearly identify Aztec and Mexican origins with the southwestern United States. However, aside from the two United States sources cited, further reference to Aztlán is difficult to find in Anglo history; it is obviously of no consequence except to the Chicano. We still know very little about our ancient origins.

The Chicano is unique in America. He is a descendant of the Fifth Sun, bound to the land of Aztlán by his blood, sweat, and flesh, and heir to gifts of language and culture from Spanish conquistadores. But in him, too, is another dimension.

Some observers have said of the Mexican American that he is an in-between, neither Mexican nor American. The truth is that the Mexican American is a fusion of three cultures: a mezcla of Mexican Indian, Spanish, and the North American—yes, even the Anglo-dominated society is his to absorb into himself.

Too many Mexican Americans have invested solely in the Anglo world, cannot see the value in their multiculture, and do not have the courage to reclaim it and fight for it. I refer not to the culture that the gringo has allowed us to retain, of taco chains and fiesta days, but to the culture, which is the indomitable wellspring of our mestizo character, the fusion of Mexican Indian, Spanish, and now even Anglo. In the Southwest, the Chicano, who is the blending of these three elements, personalities, and psychologies, has come to a time of self-assertion. The word Chicano is offered not merely as a term of differentiation (some would say separation or racism) but also as a term of identification with that distinct melding of bloods and cultures. The term Chicano is anything but racist, because it declares the assimilation of bloods and heritage that makes the Chicano a truly multicultured person.

Chicanismo offers a new or renewed adaptation to a reality of life for the Mexican American. Segregated, maligned, despised, subjugated, destroyed for what he is, and barred from becoming what he would be, the Mexican American turns toward a new path. Unleashing the frustrations and emotions of many generations of lifetimes, reviving suppressed memories, and casting off the weighing terrors, he resurrects himself as a Chicano. He can face the onslaught of cultural racism perpetrated by the Anglo, which he has only endured up to now, with new power, new insight, new optimism—if not for himself, at least for his family and the Chicanos that are to come.

By admitting to being Chicano, to bring this new person, we lose nothing, we gain a great deal. Any Mexican American afraid to join with the Chicano cause can only be afraid for himself and afraid of the gringo. The black has faced this truth and found that he must make his way as a black or as nothing, certainly not as the white man's "nigger." We can no longer be the Anglo's "Pancho."

The Federal bureaucrat who shies away from being too Chicano or plays down the cause should get out of government and stop being window dressing; he is harming the people he could especially serve por no tener tripas.* The Mexican American businessman or professional who disclaims his Chicano roots and will have nothing to do with la causa because it might hurt sales or cut down the size of his Anglo clientele has sold out to the gringo dollar long ago and now betrays the very people who probably put him where he is. The people in the barrio who criticize and decry the Chicano revolt because "it's not how we do things" have forgotten two histories, and they lie to themselves if they believe that the gringo will eventually relent and give them or their children an education, a job, a decent home, or a future.

Any Mexican American who can celebrate the Fourth of July and el diez y seis de septiembre must realize that revolt, action for change, is not a thing of the past. The Chicano revolt is a marriage of awareness and necessity that must be consummated over and over if justice is to be done. The Chicano revolt embodies old values that have been suppressed over generations. It goes a step beyond the black revolution in that Chicanos assert that they have a personal and a group point of view which the dominant "culture," made up of blacks and whites, must accept now or suffer the consequences. The Chicano insists that the Anglo respect his language and grant it equal value in any educational system where Chicano students are dominant. The Chicano insists that his culture, his way of life, and that *he* as a person be taken into account when housing is built, when industry offers jobs, when political parties caucus.

There has been a two-way infusion of Anglo-Saxon and African elements within the dominant "culture" to the extent that the color of one's skin, unfortunately for both sides, is the sole measure of acceptance or rejection of one's fellow man in American society. If it were not for color there would be little to distinguish black from white. Black people display a cultural perspective and philosophy little different from what the Anglo desires and demands. We Chicanos see the Negro as a black Anglo. But we Chicanos, as we must

* (Editor's note: The expression "por no tener tripas" means "for lack of courage.")

admit sooner or later, are different from the Anglo and the black in more ways than merely color. Our people range widely from light-skinned güeros to dark-skinned Indios. Certainly, we have our share of black blood from the Negroes who escaped into Mexico, a free country, from the southern slave states, and even Arab-Semitic traces from the Moors. The güeros remain Chicano by force of cultural attraction; they would rather be Chicano than Anglo, although they could easily pass as a white gringo.

But besides color, the Chicano may be discriminated against because of his Spanish surname, which he may change; or by his Spanish accent, which he may hide by calling himself "Spanish"; or by the effects of past discrimination, which restrict the kinds of jobs or social encounters he will seek; or even by the family structure which, if strong enough, could effectively thwart the desire to break away from the Chicano community. Add to this list of barriers, dark, "swarthy," or "Indian" skin, and economic and social stability may be an impossible objective. Yet there are still too many Mexican Americans who not only refuse to accept who and what they are, but reject the fact that however comfortable and secure they may be in their present situation, they evolved out of days of discrimination. Nor should they be blind to the jeopardy in which they remain, because they will always be different from the gringo.

The impact of discrimination on the Mexican American has been somewhat obscured by our lack of numbers, our generally passive resistance in past years, our dependence on the white man's justice, even our own blind acceptance of the white man's way as *the* way. Time and again I have questioned Chicanos about the discrimination they have experienced. Invariably, every one who began the conversation with the approach that he had never been discriminated against soon reversed his view. Racism, cultural discrimination, has affected every Chicano. Any of us who at some time has denied his heritage by changing his name or birthplace or by purifying his English of any accent, any who has been forced to leave his home alone or with his family for lack of opportunity, and has felt shame in his language, accent, or skin color, or in the food he eats—that Chicano has tasted the Anglo's kiss of death.

The Anglo-American society is a bastard issued from the promiscuous concubinage of several hundreds of ethnic and racial peoples who have cast their cultural identities into the American melting pot. While it may have been easy and necessary for some ethnic, non-Anglo-Saxon people to do it, it is not necessary—nor easy—for Mexican Americans to throw away their birthrights. The need is exactly the opposite. We Chicanos, the people of el Quinto Sol, must realize Aztlan in ourselves, individually and as a group. We are part of the land, but we need not seek a geographic center for our Aztlan; it lies within ourselves, and it is boundless, immeasurable, and limited only by our lack of vision, by our lack of courage, by our hesitancy to grasp the truth of our being.

We are Aztlán and Aztlán is us.

Our ancestors also foresaw that after the Fifth Sun another epoch would ensue, but what form it would take they did not know or say. We Chicanos face the same unknown future. We do not know where the Chicano revolt will lead. It must lead somewhere. Will Chicanos have a say in what eventually happens? Was the Aztecs' Sixth Sun the coming of Cortez, of the white man, and the advent of his destruction? Is this also to be the Chicano's Sixth Sun— destruction at the hands of the white man, the Anglo, the gringo?

Poverty in
the Valley of Plenty
Ernesto Galarza

In the spring of 1948 the Hollywood Film Council (A.F. of L.) made a contribution to . . . striking farm workers. It produced and distributed a twenty-minute sound motion picture entitled *Poverty in the Valley of Plenty.*

Poverty was a sober documentary, simply pictured and narrated. Its location, the Valley of the Doleful, was only a hundred miles from the Valley of the Dolls; its tone, immeasurably far from the sex operas of Sunset strip. Among those who were considered to record the narration was the future governor of California, Ronald Reagan, then president of the Screen Actors Guild, sports announcer and actor.[25]* The final choice was Harry W. Flannery, whose diction on the sound track carried with compressed vibration the story of the Oakie migration to DiGiorgio country. The Council was acting in the tradition set forth by Justice Jackson, in *Thomas v. Collins*, that "labor is free to turn its publicity on any labor oppression, substandard wages, employer unfairness and objectionable working conditions." These and other themes were being dramatized by the Kern County strike, and the Council proceeded to record them on film.

*The original footnote numbers are retained here.

Ernesto Galarza, "Poverty in the Valley of Plenty," in *Spiders in the House and Workers in the Field* (Notre Dame, Indiana: University of Notre Dame Press, 1970), pp. 30-56. Reprinted by permission of the publisher.

The documentary consisted of 57 scenes. It opened with panoramic shots of the southern San Joaquin Valley and the sunny poverty of Arvin, Weedpatch and other communities that surrounded the DiGiorgio Farms. Many of the shacks and hovels were homes of the DiGiorgio workers.

In the first 37 scenes the camera panned "the gorgeous sight" of the San Joaquin with close-ups of campsites "where the landscaping," Flannery narrated, "is done with junk." In this sequence the purpose was to set the stage for the last twenty scenes of the strike itself. The stress was on the industry and the corporation farmer, on agribusiness. Shooting near Arvin the camera crew picked up what Flannery described as "the homes of the farm workers." "These workers, toiling in a great industry," he went on, "are deprived of the rights and opportunities which are granted to all other industrial workers. . . . This cold-water shower . . . is used by twenty-five or thirty families." To wash their clothes, "women have to heat the water on an open fire." It would be ten years before the State of California would grant farm workers compulsory workmen's accident compensation, so Flannery could say: "There is no law requiring a farm corporation to carry compensation insurance for their employees." The narrator gave the setting the broad sweep of the southern Valley: "Beneath this divine canopy of cleanliness and purity . . . nine or ten people live in a one-room shack." The script also touched the raw nerve of the industry—the employment of Wetbacks. "Immigrant workers are smuggled across the Mexican border by headhunters employed by large farm interests. . . . Tools and equipment," Flannery went on acidly, "would be housed in a nice, clean, waterproof shed." He added the bitter reminder that "it was here that John Steinbeck got his inspiration and material for his book, The *Grapes of Wrath.*"

Beginning with scene 37 the pictures and narration centered on the strike proper. There were the picket lines, the Union meeting, Jimmy Price speaking, the distribution of groceries brought from afar by labor caravans. Here and there on the sound track there were direct references to Joseph DiGiorgio and the DiGiorgio Corporation; he was "clever, shrewd . . . the largest grape, plum and pear grower in the world . . . the richest and most powerful of the corporation farmers." His Corporation "symbolizes bargaining on a big scale."

The allusions to Mr. Joseph and the DiGiorgio Fruit Corporation woven into the first 37 scenes proved the undoing of the film. They did not draw a sufficiently sharp line between the generalizations about the industry and the specific statements on the strike. This line, as the lawsuits proved, could be bent either way. It was to be given a name years later by the Corporation's attorneys, the firm of Brobeck, Phleger and Harrison of San Francisco. The name, taken from the legal rules on defamation, was Inducement, Innuendo and Colloquium. It was on this line that Brobeck was to fight through not one but twenty summers.

To better gauge the tactical use and the damaging power of inducement, innuendo and colloquium . . . it is necessary to point out that the agri-businessmen, the Kern County Special Citizens Committee, felt vehemently that they themselves were the targets of the film. It was about them, they knew, that Flannery talking when he said: "Farming is a big business; it has laws of its own, or I should say, the lack of laws to protect and benefit the greater number of people." This was a general charge against agribusiness, and so the Special Citizens understood it. The articulate public opinion of the area was incensed over the alleged falsehoods of the film. It was Robert DiGiorgio himself who made this plain when he testified: "The statements and representations in the film are grossly misleading, false and defamatory and discredit DiGiorgio Fruit Corporation *and all of the farmers of Kern County in the eyes of the public.*"[26] The italics are added to fix the point around which inducement, innuendo and colloquium were to churn in legal arguments. The emphasis which has been added to Robert's words was not, of course, intended by him. In later contexts, he no doubt realized how close he had come to fumbling with his most effective allies, inducement, innuendo and colloquium.

Poverty in the Valley of Plenty was sponsored jointly with the Hollywood Film Council by the Screen Actors Guild, the American Federation of Musicians, the California State Federation of Labor, the Los Angeles Central Labor Council and other affiliates of the A.F. of L. Prints were sold and screened throughout the country. It helped materially in raising some $87,000 in strike funds. Members of a subcommittee of the House Committee on Education and Labor saw it in Washington, on 16 March 1949. H. L. Mitchell, in presenting the film to the subcommittee, indicated the wide scope of its theme: "The DiGiorgio strike and the conditions under which agricultural workers live throughout the country."[27] A television station in Los Angeles broadcast it soon after the prints were released in March 1948.

As an organizing device, when shown to farm laborers the film was effective. As a fuse for the deep hostilities of the Special Citizens, it was much more so. The film closed with Flannery's words: "These people have only one remaining hope to right the many injustices that have been inflicted upon them. That is to organize." To prevent such organization was the sole assignment of the Associated Farmers, for whom Joseph DiGiorgio raised funds.

But Flannery had gone further. He stirred sleeping passions by referring to the *Grapes of Wrath*, the suppression of which had once been attempted by Wofford B. Camp and Harold Pomeroy, secretary of the Farmers. Camp was the writer of the preface to *A Community Aroused.* "Poverty in the Valley of Plenty" was recalling passages in Steinbeck's classic that spoke familiarly to the tenants of Arvin, Lamont, Corcoran, Farmersville and a hundred other rural communities. It was the voice of Tom Joad repeating: "I been thinking a hell of a lot, thinkin' about our own people livin' like pigs, an' the good rich earth layin' fallow, or maybe a fellow with a million acres, while a hundred thousand good farmers is starvin'." And of Ma Joad, answering: "Tommy, don't you go fightin' them alone. They say there's a hundred thousand of us shoved out. If we was all to get mad the same way, Tommy, they wouldn't hunt nobody down."

But before the hundred thousand Joads could "get mad the same way," the eleven Special Citizens did. "Poverty in the Valley of Plenty" was their first target, and against it the Corporation filed the first of the nine actions for defamation, entitled

Complaint for Libel—the First /   No. 559 852
In the Superior Court of the State of California
in and for the County of Los Angeles
DiGiorgio Fruit Corporation, a Corporation,
Plaintiff,
v.
Paramount Television Productions
Filed 16 May 1949

The film had been broadcast over station KTLA in Los Angeles by arrangement between the Hollywood Film Council and Paramount Television Productions. The showing took place in May 1948. It was the television premier for *Poverty.* Thereafter the film was booked for exhibition in union halls, college campuses, churches, luncheon clubs, conventions and farm labor gatherings throughout the country.

The Corporation never had mixed feelings about the Union film. To the DiGiorgios it was a package of <u>unmitigated</u> libels deliberately put together to destroy their business and tarnish their reputation. Nevertheless, for a full year they made no effort to challenge *Poverty.* The reasons for this delay can only be surmised. A suit for defamation by sound motion pictures presented novel legal problems. An injunction to prevent showing of the motion picture was considered and rejected. Some of the sympathetic exhibitors were potential defendants the DiGiorgio Fruit Corporation would not be anxious to sue, among them Fordham University, Robert DiGiorgio's *alma mater.* The Corporation had to complete its own detailed analysis of the contents of the film and to weigh carefully the collateral risks and advantages of a libel suit, including the publicity value of such a move.

A few days before the statute of limitations had run out the DiGiorgios made up their minds. The first target was

✗ absolute

Paramount Productions. The complaint asked for $100,000 in special and $100,000 in punitive damages.

The Corporation demanded that certain corrections in the script be broadcast over KTLA. The station met these demands but the suit was not dropped. It remained inactive for exactly twelve months during which the Corporation's attorneys refined their strategy and bided their time. They had in hand, potentially, as many lawsuits as there had been exhibitors. The place, date and names of the next defendants were sensitive matters of strategy.

Although the filing of a lawsuit is in theory a respectful appearance before Justice and her court, this one was to be different. It was to be announced under the most advantageous political auspices. From what quarter they would come was indicated by the

RUMBLINGS IN THE HOUSE

In March 1949 a subcommittee of the House Committee on Education and Labor, under the chairmanship of Representative Augustus Kelly, held hearings in Washington on House Resolution 2032, a bill to repeal the Labor Management Relations Act of 1947. On the sixteenth H. L. Mitchell showed *Poverty* to the subcommittee.

Mitchell's appearance was a plunge into the roiled waters of the 81st Congress. The 80th, with 243 Republicans in control of the House, had passed the 1947 Act. Fred A. Hartley was installed as chairman of the Committee on Education and Labor. All but five of the committee members were unfriendly to organized labor.[28] Hartley's bill, House Resolution 3020, with the support of the Republican forces in the Senate under Senator Taft, became law over the President's veto. It was the major controversy pending before the House when the Democrats took control, with 262 members against 171 Republicans. The chairmanship of the House Committee on Education and Labor passed to Congressman Lesinski, its membership divided between sixteen Democrats and nine Republicans. Among them were names headed for the neon lights of American politics—John F. Kennedy, Adam Clayton Powell, Thruston B. Morton and Richard M. Nixon.

Lesinski's nominal majority of seven Democrats was misleading. The Dixiecrat coalition in the House worked in the committee to reduce that majority to a narrow balance between thirteen regular Democrats, three swingers and nine Republicans.[29] The three could tip the balance on any given vote of either the full committee or any of its subcommittees. Lesinski, like all committee chairmen, held the reins tightly on his slim majority. So did the chairmen of the satellite subcommittees, composed of three Democrats and two Republicans.

Mitchell's film showing was only one of a series of incidents which kept the issue of farm labor before the House during both the 80th and 81st Congresses.

On 22 March 1948 Congressman Alfred J. Elliott of California staged a full-scale attack on the farm labor Union and the strike. From the records of the House Un-American Activities Committee he retrieved some references to Mitchell as a former leader of the Southern Tenant Farmer's Union. Elliott presented the House with documentation to prove that the DiGiorgio workers were overwhelmingly opposed to unionization. This was the petition bearing over one thousand names, including that of the superintendent of the Farms. Elliott told the House: "Here is a case where communistic activities are connected with a program of picketing the DiGiorgio Farms." He concluded with a demand: "In all fairness to the State of California and the DiGiorgio Farms . . . I ask that a committee from the Committee on Un-American Activities, or a committee from the Committee on Education and Labor, go to California and make a thorough investigation to see what we can do to stop this picketing . . . because this type of picketing harassment is Un-American. I hope the House will back me up in asking for an investigation and correct this situation once and for all."[30]

On March 30 Chairman Hartley announced that his committee would indeed investigate the strike. Mitchell promptly agreed to co-operate, even though an investigation, goaded by Elliott's unabashed demands to stop the strike, might be heavily biased.[31]

Hartley did not move, however, and the Republican defeat that ousted him from the chairmanship left the decision up to Lesinski. The Republicans from California would not let the matter rest. Congressman Phillips spoke to the House on 24 June 1949, asserting that "there is no strike on the DiGiorgio ranch with picketing by people who ever worked for Mr. DiGiorgio." He referred to the film that Mitchell had shown on March 16 of the previous year.[32]

Congressman Cleveland M. Bailey from West Virginia, whose political base was the United Mine Workers of his district, and the author of a resolution to repeal the Taft-Hartley law, answered Phillips. "I can assure the gentleman," he said, "that this Congress will have the facts on that situation in California if we have to send a subcommittee out there. . ." There would be action, Bailey promised, "in accordance with the information that the committee reports." In the course of his remarks Bailey concealed his bias no more than did Elliott. The DiGiorgio Corporation, he added, was already fastening its tentacles upon the fruit and vegetable markets of the world. It was an attempt, he charged, "bordering on the edge of becoming a monopoly" which Congress would have to defeat before it destroyed the American farmer.[33] For background to these debates on the floor of the House, Congressman Thomas H. Werdel, representing DiGiorgio's district, from time to time inserted in the Appendix of the House *Record* Extensions of Remarks highly favorable to the Corporation.

Thus matters stood when early in October Chairman Lesinski decided to act on Elliott's demand. He did so in a complicated manner that was to lead to important confusions.

The House had approved Resolution 4115, which authorized Lesinski's committee to hold nationwide hearings on the effects of Federal projects on public schools where civilian and military personnel were concentrated. Bailey was appointed chairman of Subcommittee Number 1 to conduct these hearings; but to avoid duplication of travel and expenses, he was also instructed to hold hearings in Bakersfield on the DiGiorgio strike. The authority under which this secondary assignment was given, however, was not delegated by the House under Resolution 4115 but under another House Resolution, Number 75. House Resolution 75 dealt with the general authority of Lesinski's committee to conduct thorough studies and investigations relating to matters coming within the jurisdiction of the committee. Lesinski made it clear that the Bailey subcommittee was to be primarily responsible for the educational problems of Federally impacted areas, as they were called. Another subcommittee, chaired by Congressman Burke, was to be primarily responsible for hearings and the report on labor-management relations. Bailey, rather than Burke, was assigned to the DiGiorgio strike simply because that was the way the travel schedules of the two subcommittees worked out.

Bailey set the strike hearings for November 12 and 13, 1949. Advance notice of several weeks was given both to the Union and to the Corporation. The scene, now shifting from Washington to Kern County, was prepared for the second

Complaint for Libel—the Second /   No. 566 888
In the Superior Court of the State of California
in and for the County of Los Angeles
DiGiorgio Fruit Corporation, a Corporation,
Plaintiff,
v.
Harry W. Flannery, National Farm Labor Union,
Hollywood
Film Council, Los Angeles Central Labor
Council, et al.
Filed 8 November 1949.

The long delay in filing this suit was to pay large dividends, but it must have strained the patience of the DiGiorgios. To Robert the film was from the outset "a scandalous, libelous, scurrilous movie." Insofar as Mr. Joseph was concerned, it was something on the order of the *scandalum magnatum* of the thirteenth century of English law-defamation of magnates of the realm. The months, the years, were passing, and the lone picket still remained at the gates of the Farms, causing damage to the business, trade and repute of the Corporation.

The film, alleged Brobeck, Phleger and Harrison in complaint number two, was a libel which violated Section 45 of the Code of Civil Procedure of California, namely, "a false and unprivileged publication by writing, printing, picture, effigy or other fixed representation to the eye, which exposes any person to hatred, contempt, ridicule or obloquy, or which causes him to be shunned or avoided, or which has a tendency to injure him in his occupation." The libel was a tort, that part of the common law which deals with twisted conduct that violates another's rights to keep his mind at peace and his body in one piece. Libel, from *libellus*, "little book," is defamation set down in writing as defined in Section 45, to differentiate it from spoken defamation or slander. . . .

Brobeck, Phleger and Harrison's complaint on behalf of DiGiorgio cited showings of the film in Washington, D.C.; Berkeley, California; New York City; Los Angeles, "and numerous other places throughout the United States." It prayed the court for a million dollars in general and a million in punitive damages. It set forth at least fifteen specific charges of libelous untruths about the Corporation, to wit: that it was unfair to its employees; that it denied them rights and opportunities granted to all other industrial workers; that it refused its employees accident insurance protection; that it robbed its employees of normal American rights; reduced them to the status of serfs; provided them with rude habitations unfit for human use; exacted $26 a month rent for hovels; forced nine and ten people to live in one shack; compelled them to heat water over open fires; payed them eleven hours wages for twelve hours of work; denied them compensation for loss of limb; refused them workmen's compensation for physical injury; denied them adequate medical care; deprived their children of decent educational opportunities; and that the Corporation participated in smuggling Mexican nationals into the United States through intermediaries called head hunters.

All these, the complaint alleged, were tortious and immoral actions directly attributed in the film's pictures and sound track to the Corporation. The length of the list of allegations and their variety were in themselves something of a precedent in libel suits. Even so, it was not to be understood as a complete list. This was because of the nature of the medium—a sound motion picture. The DiGiorgio attorneys inserted paragraph VII in the complaint, which read:

Because the words, sounds and pictures are contained on a motion picture film and sound track, and are inextricably connected and interdependent for their meaning and effect, it is impossible to set them out in this complaint.[34]

The legal strategy behind this language was a bold one. Section 45 of the Civil Code rested on the traditional cases of libel, which for five hundred years or more had dealt with words printed or otherwise inscribed. The general rule as to defamation in this form was that "the complaint must set out the particular defamatory words as published."[35] Where the pleader must, from the nature of the case, resort to a verbal description of the defamatory matter "as where movements, postures, or pictures are used," a modification of the rule was to be allowed.

Poverty was a statement in visual images, not in "writings." These images could not be set forth in a written complaint. The words that accompanied the images were spoken. If both were defamatory there was libel in the images and slander in the words. Did the images make the spoken words libelous, or did the spoken words make the images slanderous? A test of the rule was in the making. In 1963 some legal opinions were still holding that "the great weight of authority supports the view that in the absence of any statutory provision to the contrary, a libelous statement must be reproduced verbatim."[36]

These doubts were not reflected in paragraph VII of the complaint. On the contrary, it advanced a legal theory to the effect that in a libel using the medium of a motion picture with sound track, it was not possible to reproduce easily in the complaint either (a) the pictures or (b) the verbal sounds or (c) the words signified by those sounds. The medium by its very nature combined these elements into an inextricable mix from which neither words nor sounds nor pictures were any longer separable. It was a bold rush into the nebulous and Di Giorgio's lawyers carried it off with complete success.

The traditional rule about specific setting forth of words, to which Brobeck paid such scant attention, was intended to give defendants clear notice of the exact language they were supposed to defend themselves against, or to justify. Gilbert and Nissen, the attorneys for Flannery and the unions, made an effort to protect their clients in this quarter. They filed a demurrer on the ground that the usual rule of pleading in libel must be followed. Superior Court Judge McKesson ruled on the demurrer on 9 January 1950, holding that because of the difficulties involved DiGiorgio's attorneys need not describe the allegedly libelous scenes in greater detail. An appeal from this ruling was never taken.

The co-ordination of the case for the plaintiff in this second libel action called for close and careful teamwork. Robert DiGiorgio was assigned to the team by the Corporation by virtue of his position as labor relations and publicity director. A junior associate of Brobeck, Phleger and Harrison, Malcolm Dungan, was responsible for the research and the legal documents. It was Dungan who prepared the complaint filed on November 8. Five days later Subcommittee Number 1 opened.

THE BAKERSFIELD HEARINGS

In the 80th Congress the workload of the House was distributed among more than one hundred subcommittees.[37] These *ad hoc* subcommittees, usually composed of three majority and two minority Members are traditionally appointed by the chairman of the standing committee. The chairman of the subcommittee is always a member of the majority party. To him the chairman of the standing committee entrusts a portion of the great power with which he is vested by the rules of the House and the seniority system. The first skirmishes of the battles on the floor of the House take place on these subcommittees. To every Member of the House his assignment to a standing committee is crucial; his appointment to a subcommittee can make the difference between obscurity and repute among his colleagues. His votes on a subcommittee can deflect the runnels of congressional decision, attach his name to some current national issue, attract the notice of the news media and give him solid credentials with those who co-opt the future favorites of power.

As a member of a subcommittee, the congressman is the drudge of the House. He promptly learns that the subcommittee system is the alternative to anarchy in the business of the House, the practical answer to chaos. If he is a minority member, and short on seniority, he may have to serve time under a cross-grained, wily, unreasonable arbitrary veteran of the opposition, perhaps wondering at times why anarchy and efficiency must at times be reconciled with senility.

When this daily round of hard work and menial obscurity can be broken by an investigation, the big moment of the congressman arrives. Investigations are authorized by the rules of Congress.[38] There were some six hundred of them between the 1790s and the 1940s. Originally intended to provide Congress with the means for gathering facts for legislation, to check out the executive branch and to inquire into its own internal affairs, the investigative process always manifested a fourth power—that of molding public opinion. The brief but scandal-propelled prominence of Senator Joseph P. McCarthy proved, indeed, that such a power could be the principal use of a congressional investigation. As Taylor observed, "in skillful and unscrupulous hands, a legislative investigation is truly a most potent and versatile engine of destruction."[39] Congressman Elliott's demand for an investigation of the DiGiorgio strike "to put an end to it once and for all" was plainly in the McCarthy style.

Chairman Lesinski had announced publicly on 22 July 1949 that an investigation would be made and hearings would be held near the scene of the strike. In a letter of authorization dated October 7, Bailey, as chairman of Subcommittee Number 1, was "authorized and directed to investigate conditions to provide for the education of children . . . residing in localities overburdened with increased school enrollments resulting from Federal activities . . . as outlined in H. R. 4115." Bailey was "further authorized and directed to conduct a thorough study and investigation of labor-management relations at the DiGiorgio Fruit Corporation known as the Di-Giorgio Farms in DiGiorgio, California." At the completion of the study and investigation Bailey was instructed to "prepare a report to the Congress."[40]

Bailey called the Subcommittee to order at ten o'clock on the morning of 12 November 1949, at the Bakersfield Inn. It was a charming setting for a hearing on a labor disturbance. The bougainvillea that November still hung in small cascades of lavender over the red-tile roofs of the guest bungalows. The crowns of the palm trees raised their graceful green sprays around the blue waters of the swimming pool. Around them and between the luxuriant hedges and shrubs the cement paths curved and were lost in the private retreats of the caravansary.

Chairman Bailey presided at a large table at one end of the hearing room. To his left sat the Hon. Richard M. Nixon, to his right the Hon. Tom Steed. Congressman Thruston B. Morton and Congressman Leonard Irving, the remaining two members of the subcommittee, did not attend the hearings. The majority clerk, Frank Boyer, and the clerk for the minority, John O. Graham, completed the official panel. A court reporter sat next to the witness chair recording the proceedings.

In front of Bailey and his colleagues was the audience of some hundred persons, the seating arrangement neatly dividing their partisan interests. The majority of those present were representatives and spokesmen for large-scale farming, an enlarged cast of the Special Citizens of Kern County, joined now by influentials like Robert Schmeiser of the Associated Farmers, whose connections formed the network of agribusiness of California.

With a quorum verified—Bailey, Nixon and Steed—the chairman explained that the proceedings would be formal under the rules of the House. In addition to hearing the oral testimony, the subcommittee viewed two films, *Poverty in the Valley of Plenty* and a company production called *The DiGiorgio Story.* Robert DiGiorgio received the congressmen at the ranch on the second day of the hearings, at which time employees of the Corporation were interviewed and examined on their opinions of the strike. The Hon. Thomas H. Werdel, representative of the host district, drifted in and out of the sessions. He was not a member of the subcommittee.

During the noon recess of the twelfth in the patio adjoining the hearing room copies of the complaint of the DiGiorgio lawsuit against Flannery et al. were served on H. L. Mitchell, Henry Hasiwar, Jimmy Price and Ernesto Galarza. The complaint was a mimeographed document of nine pages with the summons attached.

Formally, the subcommittee hearings were in the control of a Democratic chairman, Bailey, supported by a Democratic colleague, Steed, and under the partisan watch of the Republican minority in the person of Nixon. Of the two absentees, Irving and Morton, only Morton was to play a role in future events.

Werdel, seated at the head table by congressional courtesy, had been elected to Congress in 1948. A lawyer with a corporate practice in Bakersfield, he served several years in the State legislature. His partner was Vincent DiGiorgio, a relative of Mr. Joseph's. A tall, heavily-fleshed man, Werdel did not enjoy using his influence openly, but preferred to bring it to bear in quiet ways. He did not testify at the hearings, but rather attended them as an observer, without being heard at all and being noticed as little as possible. His political ambitions were tied closely to the America First party and to the well-financed approval of Kern County's Special Citizens. On their platform of honesty, economy, loyalty and the ordinary virtues[41] Werdel stood. In speeches in the House, he denounced strikes as "periodic interference with the family income," and he stood up to "the bureaucratic

Cossacks riding through the halls of Congress" who opposed his bills to discipline the trade-unions.

The junior Democrat on the subcommittee who heard testimony and visited the Farms was Tom Steed, from the fourth congressional district of Oklahoma. Born Thomas Jefferson Steed on a farm near the town of Rising Star, he was a newspaper reporter, editor and automobile salesman. He was elected to the House in 1948, and modestly recognizing his unexceptionalness he dropped the Thomas Jefferson and became plain Tom Steed, the representative for a district of small family farmers, the American tillers of the soil who were a continent and a social class apart from agribusiness. Steed listened to the testimony with just enough alertness to avoid involvement in issues which would be meaningless—and perhaps alarming—to his constituents. For him attendance at Bakersfield was one of the drudgeries for a junior committeeman.

In contrast Nixon was in fine fettle for his role. He had graduated from Whittier College, near Los Angeles, in 1934 and from Duke University Law School in 1937. After service in the Navy and as government attorney in Washington, he was elected to the House in November 1946 from the twelfth congressional district of California. His election majorities in the district were impressive if not phenomenal—56 percent in 1946, 86 percent in 1948. Although he rated only number 44 in Republican seniority in the 81st Congress he was climbing rapidly above his contemporaries. He owed this to his appointment to the House Un-American Activities Committee, where he gained solid footing. He was appointed chairman of a subcommittee to find out whether Whitaker Chambers or Alger Hiss was lying under oath, and became known as a particularly active conservative. His successes were notable, as with Alger Hiss; his failures went almost unnoticed, as his unproductive assignment to Robert Stripling to "make a record" on the National Farm Labor Union, Local 218.

Sitting next to his antagonist, Bailey, Congressman Nixon cross-examined Union witnesses with the practiced courtesy that had already attracted favorable notice, question-

ing the spokesmen and friends of the Corporation sympathet-
ically to underscore the points they made. Beneath Nixon's
well-brushed wavy dark hair, his nimble, alert mind was at
work. He sat forward in his chair and frequently darted
glances at that portion of the room where the Special Citizens
sat. Among them were the strongest and most influential supporters of the Nixon-for-Senator movement. They were watch-
ing their man in a crucial test and he was doing well. Here,
for them, was their political model who, by his own definition,
"owes it to himself and to the system" to "use his abilities
and his experience to the fullest." He was, moreover, at that
critical moment a freshman congressman beckoned by the
appeal of "the power and the glory."[42]

The Union stated its case first. H. L. Mitchell, its
president, stoop-shouldered and outwardly flaccid, was one
of the most durable defenders of the farm laborers in the
nation. Once more he reviewed the evils of the corporation
farming system, arguing single-mindedly for equality in bargaining power. Hank Hasiwar, the director of the strike, re-
cited the grievances, the efforts to negotiate, the boycotts,
and the misfortunes of the Union with the National Labor
Relations Board, the state agencies and the courts. C. J.
Haggerty was a character witness for the strikers, conveying
to Nixon, principally, that no union endorsed by the State
Federation of Labor could possibly be suspected of Com-
munism. The Union submitted six copies of a brief. The
thirty-page statement of the Union's case included a chron-
ology of the principal events of the strike to the date of the
hearings.

Jimmy Price, president of Local 218, closed for the
Union. Price cautioned the congressmen that "maybe you
won't hear some of the fancy words some of these people
use . . . I haven't got no high education." Price went on to
detail the complaints of the DiGiorgio strikers: men who
moved from a temperature of 32 degrees in the cooling rooms
of the packing shed into the broiling heat of 112 degrees
outside; the lack of hot water and bathing facilities in some

of the DiGiorgio housing; toilets in such shape that "sometimes you could get in there, sometimes you couldn't"; the firing of an employee who asked for a raise in wages of five cents an hour; no overtime, no unemployment insurance, no social security, no paid vacations, no regular hours.

Nixon tried to lead Price into a more favorable review of DiGiorgio's labor relations:

NIXON: What did you earn when you first came?
PRICE: I believe it was twenty-five cents.
NIXON: That was ten years ago?
PRICE: Approximately.
NIXON: Now is it eighty cents?
PRICE: Eighty cents. Yes.
NIXON: That's a little more than three times as much.
PRICE: Groceries is more than that.[43]

The Corporation's principal witness was Robert DiGiorgio. He reviewed the notable accomplishments of Mr. Joseph, the many benefactions of the Corporation to the community, the sensitive awareness of its management to the welfare of its workers, their complete negativism toward the Union, the total ineffectiveness of the strike. He testified that he would never consent "to have outsiders come in and tell us whether we will or will not have an election."

But above all Robert's testimony was a sustained attack on the Union film, *Poverty in the Valley of Plenty*. He detailed the alleged canards, misrepresentations and falsehoods he and his associates read and heard in the film. To impress the subcommittee with the seriousness of the matter, DiGiorgio put into the record official notice that the Corporation had just a few days before filed a libel action against the Union and other sponsors of the motion picture. To drive home this denunciation of the film, he introduced correspondence between Governor Warren, Mr. Joseph and Congressman Werdel which had been exchanged previous to the hearings. He also asked Bailey for permission to file an answer to the Union's brief. Bailey acceded, informing DiGiorgio that the record would remain open and that supplementary documents should be forwarded to the majority clerk, Frank Boyer.

Some prominent agribusinessmen testified to the high prestige and the solid reputation of the DiGiorgios. Gregory Harrison, the Corporation's attorney, flatly rejected the Union's offer to produce more than eight hundred signed authorization cards of DiGiorgio employees. To the Union's complaint of discrimination under the National Labor Relations Act, Harrison replied that "Congress need not purchase compliance with the laws of the United States on the basis of privileges and gratuities."[44]

A minor witness for the Corporation was Lawrence Webdell, office manager of DiGiorgio Farms. Webdell had previously told newspapermen that he knew of no DiGiorgio employees who lived in the run-down houses that marred the surrounding communities. For the subcommittee, he did estimate that some eight hundred of DiGiorgio's permanent employees lived in homes in the neighborhood. Webdell also accused H. L. Mitchell of forcing his way into the home of a non-union employee. Alexander Schullman, the Union attorney, protested and demanded that the committee "use its power to have somebody held for testifying falsely concerning that situation." Nixon's face darkened a shade in the slanting afternoon shadows of the room as he answered ominously, "There is likely to be a lot of that before this hearing is over, and not only about Mr. Mitchell." The punishment of perjurers, however, was not the main business of the hearings, so Nixon dropped the subject.

Webdell's weak feint did not sidetrack the proceedings. Robert DiGiorgio tried more insistently. He arranged for the screening of the Union's film as well as for that of his own. A print of *Poverty* was introduced as evidence and became a part of the exhibits before the subcommittee. This served no purpose of the Union, whose presentation was made by live witnesses and supported by documents which Brobeck refused to accept.

It did serve DiGiorgio's tactical aim, which was to convince the subcommittee of these propositions: that the charges in the film were directed exclusively at the Corporation; and that they were false, scurrilous, vicious and scandalous. It placed the film and its sponsors, not the labor-management relations at the Farms, on trial.

Bailey did not step into the snare. He viewed both films unperturbed, admitted them as evidence and went on with the proceedings. Steed gave no hint, on the official record, that he was any more interested in the motion picture than Bailey. He asked no questions on any aspect of it.

Nixon's reaction was positive. Before the film was screened he had gathered from a private briefing that the producers of the film "were very careful . . . to point out that most of these pictures were taken on the ranch,"[45] but the showing did not confirm his previous judgment. He agreed that the sound track "did not say" that the shacks were on the Corporation's land, but in any case, he asserted, "the implication was clear."

Another statement which the film did not make was that "there is no compensation on DiGiorgio" for injuries suffered on the job. Nixon attributed this charge to the film also by implication and marked another count of false witness against the Union. He was to leave Bakersfield with "no doubt in my mind whatever as to its implications."[46]

Although Nixon swiftly saw these implications, he did not detect one that intruded itself into the record by way of DiGiorgio's testimony, one which raised a legal issue of some delicacy.

Both Robert DiGiorgio and Nixon were attorneys. Robert had informed the subcommittee, with emphasis, that the Corporation had just filed a suit for defamation against the producers and sponsors of *Poverty*.[47] The film, therefore, was on trial before the Superior Court of Los Angeles County. It was to be presumed that DiGiorgio, his attorneys and Nixon were familiar with Canon 20 of the Proposed State Bar rule on civil procedure during trial. This canon, approved by the California State Bar, declared that "A member of the State Bar whether engaged in private practice or public employment shall not, directly or indirectly make . . . any press release statement or other disclosure of information, whether of alleged facts or opinion, for publication or other release to the public in any newspaper or other documentary medium, or by radio, television or other means of public information relating to any pending or anticipated civil action or proceeding . . . calculated, or which may reasonably be expected, to interfere in any manner or to any degree with a fair trial in the courts or with due administration of justice."[48] In the *Times-Mirror* case (1940) it had been held that one of the duties of the courts was "to give every suitor . . . assurance that no . . . hostile influence shall operate against him while his cause is under consideration."[49]

It was an old doctrine, confirmed by often-quoted authorities like Odgers, for whom there was nothing more pernicious "than to prejudice the minds of the public against persons concerned as parties in the causes."[50]

The witnesses for the Union at the hearings had, without benefit of counsel, considered the point and concluded that neither in their testimony nor in the Union's brief would the charges made in the DiGiorgio complaint be refuted. It was decided to reserve the defense for the court proceedings and to rest for the time being on brief declarations as to the intent of the film. To Nixon's question "Do you intend for the picture to leave the implication that those houses were on DiGiorgio Farms?" Mitchell replied: "No, I don't think that was even intended or certainly not stated in either the picture or the sound track."[51] Mitchell's direct challenge was evaded by Nixon, DiGiorgio and DiGiorgio's attorney, Harrison.

On Sunday November 13 Bailey closed the hearings. "It will not be known," he announced, "what our recommendations will be in this matter until we have gone over that record and studied the testimony and given it due consideration." By "that record" he meant the testimony that the official reporter at his side had been busy taking in shorthand. Her notes would be typed up; delivered to Boyer, the majority clerk; sent to the Government Printing Office in Washington; printed, and the volumes delivered to the committee chairman who would release them. It would be upon review and study and due consideration of that document that the report required by Lesinski's instructions would be issued.

This, at any rate, was the formal course laid down by custom and the rules of the House for such important particulars. In this instance it was avoided. Four freshman congressmen—Nixon, Morton, Steed and Werdel—the Special Citizens, Joseph DiGiorgio and other members of the Corporation strained at the slow pace of House procedure. To them it was an obstacle course to be avoided, so the congressmen produced the

NIXON-MORTON-STEED-WERDEL REPORT

At the close of the session of the House on 9 March 1950, Congressman Werdel was recognized by the Speaker. He asked for and was given permission "to extend his remarks in the Appendix of the *Record* and include a majority report filed by the subcommittee on which he serves."[52]

The right to extend remarks "affords Members the opportunity to explain their attitude on pending questions and so give constituents a basis on which to approve or disapprove . . . and apprises the country at large of local sentiment."[53] By virtue of this rule, serious and informative matter additional to the proceedings on the floor can and often does come to public attention.

Extensions of remarks have become a form of high congressional courtesy that can also be put to uses less practical though not less expensive. Congressmen permit one another to extend their remarks in the Appendix, to escape having to listen to them on the floor of the House. It is a device even more frequently used to please in print, at public expense, a constituent who has composed an otherwise unpublishable poem, a recipe for bean soup, an editorial that shook Toonerville to its foundations or a public address that was never delivered. Since every Member of the House will have occasion to extend his political views or to circulate the whimsies of friends or constituents, unanimous consent for an Extension of Remarks, such as Werdel was given on March 9, is a routine matter.

There is not a Member of the House but who at one time or another could and would use the Extensions in such inoffensive ways. Undoubtedly also it was agreed with Speaker Champ Clark that it was preferable to let the speeches and articles be printed rather than be compelled to listen to them. It was "a mass of worthless matter which composes nearly one-half of the Congressional set" of records.[54]

The worthless matter was allowed, but only on the condition that it occupy a separate and unequal, segregated and inferior place among the Congressional papers. Thus the standing rule of the House is: "I. Arrangement of the daily *Record*. The public printer will arrange the contents of the daily *Record* as follows: First, Senate proceedings; second, House proceedings; third, the Appendix." That the Appendix did not contain the proceedings of the Chamber was further emphasized: "When either House has granted leave to print (1) a speech not delivered in either House, (2) a newspaper or magazine article, or (3) any other matter not germane to the proceedings, the same shall be printed in the Appendix."[55]

Long the target of criticism from Members and the public who complained both of the trifling subjects in the Extensions and the expense of printing them, the House never brought itself to the point of abolishing the practice entirely. It did, however, ease its conscience and the public purse somewhat by discontinuing the publication of the Appendix in a bound volume for permanent reference. This was done through a resolution adopted by the Joint Committee on Printing on 22 June 1953, excluding all extraneous matter and excessive bulk "from the permanent form of the *Congressional Record*." The last bound volume of Extensions was Number 99, Part 12, 2 July 1953 to 18 August 1953, 83rd Congress, First session. The closest thing to a valedictory were some insertions in that last volume entitled "Death Stalks the New Deal," "The William the Silent Award", and "It Tolls for Thee." Thenceforth the congressional oddities would appear but once in the daily edition of the *Record*.

The rules of the House of Representatives permit congressmen to order reprints of their Extensions of Remarks, in quantities of not fewer than one thousand copies, ordered and paid for by the interested congressman. The order goes to the Government Printing Office while the type of the daily edition of the *Congressional Record* is still in the forms, and the reprint is arranged as a mailer or flier. The congressman adds an appropriate headline. The most trivial contents of an extension gain something in elegance from the format of a reprint. The standard running head gives the source as the "Proceedings and Debates" of Congress and the Great Seal of the United States of America is stamped on one corner of the front page. Above it there is a legend: "Not printed at government expense." At the top of the first column there appears the name of the Honorable Member of the House whose Extension of Remarks follows.

Congressman Werdel, soon after the publication of the Nixon-Morton-Steed report in the Appendix, ordered reprints and delivered them to the Corporation. They were captioned "Congressional Committee Bares Facts on Alleged DiGiorgio Ranch Strike." Like all such prints it was intended for wide distribution. Many copies undoubtedly would come into the hands of citizens who would not know that Extensions of Remarks are not proceedings in the House, nor are they taken from debates on the floor. None but the most expert in congressional procedure would know that the seal and the running head were as appropriate as a notary's seal on a menu.

This borrowed dignity in fact gives reprints much of their appeal. It also provided, in the case of the DiGiorgio Fruit Corporation, an appearance of credibility, officialism and authenticity.

The Corporation enlisted these assets in a continuing though confidential distribution of the Nixon-Morton-Steed reprints. Copies were given out as Werdel delivered them fresh from the Government Printing Office. The distribution, by mail and by hand, continued for nearly fifteen years.*

Werdel's Extension was printed in the daily edition of the *Congressional Record* of 10 March 1950 in the Appendix. It consisted of some forty-four hundred words of close print filling nine columns. The contents were divided in two parts. The first six paragraphs in column 1 were devoted to Werdel's own prefatory remarks, and the last section, to the text of what Werdel called "the report." This text was preceded not by a letter of submittal from the chairman of the subcommittee to that of the full committee but by the letter of authorization which Bailey had produced in Bakersfield four months before—an unprecedented departure from House custom. Werdel said in his preface that the report was not yet in print, which meant that it was not yet in form for official submission to the House.

In his preface Werdel said he wished to enlighten the House about a false and libelous film that had been fabricated by one Harry W. Flannery and his associates "for thirty pieces of silver." Werdel went on to say that the fabrication had been used "to collect hundreds of thousands of dollars from working men throughout the country to finance a purported strike that did not exist." The authors and sponsors of *Poverty*— for that was the name of the film—were "corrupt men deliberately bearing false witness." They had perpetuated a fraud "to the advantage of a handful of men." They had com-

---

*Robert DiGiorgio, Deposition. 16 December 1964, p. 16, The Corporation's use of the Werdel reprint from 1950 to 1966 illustrated with uncanny accuracy the comment of the Court in *Winrod v. McFadden*, 67 Fed. Sup. 251, decided in 1945: ". . . the publisher could with impunity, print a large number of extra copies of an issue containing libelous matter, retain them on hand and from time to time through the years mail them to members of the general public. The original publication may have been forgotten, but the continuous mailing of same by the publisher year after year would reiterate and emphasize the libel and could possibly after repeated mailings cause more damage to the person against whom the libel was directed than the original publication." The Werdel reprint contains five libelous charges against Union officials: bearing false witness, deliberately fabricating falsehoods for 30 pieces of silver, collecting hundreds of thousands of dollars for a nonexistent strike, committing fraud and perverting the processes of the Congress of the United States.

mitted "a disservice to the legitimate American labor movement."

Werdel then introduced the "report" which, he asserted, had been prepared by Bailey's Subcommittee Number 1 based on the Bakersfield hearings. "I am including the report in the *Record*," he explained, "inasmuch as it may be several weeks before it is distributed in printed form by the subcommittee. It follows."[56]

What followed was a devastating attack not only on the film but on the National Farm Labor Union, the striking members of Local 218 and their officers.

External evidence was not necessary to bring out the contradictions and inconsistencies within the document itself. It said that the DiGiorgio employees had no grievances, yet it listed them. It said first that there was no strike and then that the strike "at least theoretically continues to the present time." It said that there was no picket line, and then it declared that the picket line "may be regarded as a relatively peaceful one." It based the authorization for the investigation first on House Resolution 2032 and then on House Resolution 75. It stated that no Union witness testified to anything which even approximated the charges depicted in the film, and it also stated that officials of the Union testified that the film gave a true picture of DiGiorgio Farms conditions. It referred to evidence received which "shows that a strike of any serious proportions in agriculture would choke off interstate commerce in necessary food stuffs" and then it pointed out that the picket line had failed to affect the operations of the fruit corporation. It cited evidence proving that "the sole issue is recognition" and then referred to "much testimony" concerning other issues.

The rapporteurs concluded that "insofar as it [the film] purports to represent conditions existing on DiGiorgio Farms . . . [it was made] and was presented to the committee in disregard of the truth." The major charges set forth in the DiGiorgio complaint filed on November 8 were found to be true. The horrendous housing in which employees were forced to live; the cold-water showers; the open fires; the failure to pay wages for a full working day; the rent for washing ma-chines; the lack of workmen's compensation; the smuggling of Wetbacks—these conditions did not exist on the DiGiorgio ranch. The film "said" they did. "No one could doubt that these charges were levelled straight at the corporation. . . . All of these representations are false."

Although frequently referring to evidence, the report lashed the Union and its film on the basis of "unmistakable innuendos" as well as on words explicitly "said" in the sound track. There was not, for the Union, any escape from this crossfire of congressional logic seemingly based on docu-mentary evidence as well as on inferences.

In vain Mitchell and Hasiwar denied that the primary target of the film was the Corporation, and affirmed that it was intended as an attack on conditions prevailing throughout the industry. The report waived this aside, adducing that "the educational director and the western representative insist that the film is a true picture of the DiGiorgio Farms." Although there was no evidence in the record to this effect, there was, in their judgment, ample proof that the film was "a shocking collection of falsehoods almost wholly unrelieved by any re-gard whatever for the truth and the facts."

As to the strike itself, the Union men fared no better. There was "no strike, no grievances, no pickets." The sub-committee considered the testimony given by Price and other Union witnesses irrelevant, extraneous matter with no more merit than "afterthoughts and makeweights."

The report rounded out its indictment of *Poverty* and the strike with these words: "The processes of the Congress of the United States have been perverted and misused by the National Farm Labor Union in order to furnish a sounding board for its claims. The committee should certainly not be without power to prevent the recurrence of this kind of abuse of its functions and impositions upon its energies."

The rapporteurs were the Hon. Richard Nixon, the Hon. Thruston B. Morton and the Hon. Tom Steed, so identi-fied by their names in print in that order at the bottom of Werdel's Extension in the Appendix.

This typographical detail was to become a major issue in the years to come. Werdel stated in his preface that the report had been "signed." The names in print were for the time being the closest to holographic evidence that he could produce.

Werdel also characterized it as a "majority report." "I recommend as the majority report," he wrote, "of the subcommittee . . . to all the Members of the House" what he was about to insert in the Appendix.

It was also Werdel's intention to give the insertion in the Appendix every appearance of an official report, an official document of the subcommittee, and of the full Committee on Education and Labor. It was for this reason that he extended himself in the prefatory remarks, which are usually a laconic sentence or two by the extending congressman. Only the unwary could be impressed, not the Members of the House, who were thoroughly familiar with the character of official House reports and the surplusage that they themselves often put into the Appendix.

A detail that would not have escaped the critical congressional eye was the document that Werdel used to introduce the fearsome report. Immediately after the title—Agricultural Labor at DiGiorgio Farms, California—he had inserted the letter of authorization from Lesinski to Bailey of 7 October 1949. House reports, when submitted, are prefaced by a letter of submittal, which concludes the assignment as unmistakably as the letter of authorization begins it.

In response to pressure from his electors, Werdel had evidently given an informal twist to the process by which reports are prepared and submitted, the process which Bailey had explained in Bakersfield. Nixon recalled that Werdel had often asked about the progress of the publication of the hearings and the promised report.[57] Referring in his prefatory remarks to his district, Werdel wrote: "Public opinion in the area of the DiGiorgio Ranch is incensed over the falsehoods embraced in the said moving picture and narration. . . . That area is desirous of immediately correcting the infavorable publicity resulting from the libelous action." Whose opinion

Werdel was referring to, and the degree of its indignation, had already appeared in the visit of the Special Citizens to the Farms and the subsequent publication of *A Community Aroused.*

The publication of Werdel's Extension of Nixon, Morton and Steed took the Union completely by surprise. There had been no correspondence or discussion between its officers and the staff of the subcommittee since the Bakersfield hearings. On March 11 Congressman Shelley of San Franoisoo gave the Union its first Information regarding Werdel's action. Mitchell then talked with Walter Mason, lobbyist for the American Federation of Labor. Together they met with Bailey, who promised to answer Werdel. Union officers telegraphed Werdel inviting him to repeat his charges off the floor of the House, an invitation which Werdel ignored; he kept a safe distance within the aura of constitutional privilege which surrounds all congressmen.

Thus protected, the report began immediately to produce drastic effects. It settled like an invisible noose around the lone picket at the DiGiorgio gates. A few violent yanks of publicity and some twists in private negotiations lifted the picket, her box, her sign and her umbrella completely out of sight.

25. *Oakland Tribune,* 26 February 1948.
26. *Hearings.* Bakersfield, 12-13 November 1949, p. 644.
27. *Hearings.* House Resolution Number 2032, 999-1004.
28. MacNeil. *Forge of Democracy,* p. 159.
29. *Congressional Quarterly.* Vol. III, 1947, p. 180.
30. *Congressional Record.* 22 March 1948, pp. 3287, 3288, 3293.
31. *Congressional Record.* Appendix, 29 March 1948, p. A-2058.
32. *Congressional Record.* 24 June 1949, p. 8396.
33. *Ibid.,* p. 8396. *Congressional Record,* 26 September 1951, p. 12175.
34. Complaint for libel. *DiGiorgio Fruit Corporation v. Harry W. Flannery et al.* Number 566888, 8 November 1949
35. 53 C J S sections 255-256.
36. 33 American Jurisprudence, section 237.
37. Miller. *Member of the House.* p. 145.
38. *Jefferson's Manual and Rules of the U.S. House of Representatives.* 81st Congress. Section 739.
39. Taylor. *Grand Inquest,* p. 15.
40. *Hearings.* Bakersfield, 12-13 November 1949, p. 541.
41. Kern County Werdel Delegation Committee. Bakersfield, California. 1952.

42. *San Jose Mercury*, 13 October 1968.
43. *Hearings*. Bakersfield, 12-13 November 1949, p. 700.
44. Ibid., p. 682.
45. Ibid., p. 557.
46. Ibid., p. 656.
47. Ibid., p. 644.
48. Proposed State Bar Rule. Canon 20. "California Civil Procedure During Trial." California State Bar Association, p. 59.
49. 98 Pacific 2d., 1039.
50. *Odgers on Libel*, p. 324.
51. *Hearings*. Bakersfield, 12-13 November 1949, p. 546.
52. *Congressional Record.* 9 March 1950, p. 3157.
53. *Cannon's Procedures in the House of Representatives.* 81st Congress, p. 315.
54. *Tables and annotated Index of U.S. Public Documents.* Government Printing Office, Washington, D.C. 1902, p. 12.
55. "Laws and Rules for Publication of the Congressional Record." *Congressional Record.* 9 March 1950, A-1938.
56. *Congressional Record.* Daily edition. 81st Congress, second session. February 27—March 10, 1950. Bound volume number 96. Appendix, pp. A-1479-1947.
57. Richard M. Nixon. Deposition. 7 January 1963, p. 29.

VI / LEADERS

The Chicano Movement is a movement headed by many leaders, each seeking to achieve for his people a program dictated by the needs of the particular locale. The fact is that the Chicano Movement is many movements scattered about the Southwest, with race and a desire for social justice being the bonding agents by which the many are united loosely into one amorphous whole.

The men whose profiles are given here have emerged as nationally recognized leaders. Each has made a commitment to improve the lot of his followers and each has devised a strategy toward that end.

César Chávez, for example, has concerned himself with organizing agricultural migrant laborers, most of them Mexican-American, into a union designed to improve their social and working conditions through collective bargaining with agricultural producers in California. Rodolfo "Corky" Gonzales has made the urban Chicanos of Denver his concern, and Reies Tijerina has devoted his efforts to the rural Hispano poor of New Mexico. Since each leader is working with a different group, within a different economic and political environment, each has adopted a strategy which is appropriate for the particular time and circumstances. However, the three leaders and their respective followers, although seeking different proximate goals, are as one in seeking to improve the human condition of Chicanos everywhere in the United States.

The first selection, a detailed account of César Chávez* by Peter Matthiessen, describes not only the man but his movement as well. The selection is not only a description of Chávez but also a treatise on how to organize an inchoate human mass into a working organization capable of creating and wielding power in a stubborn fashion. It was the sinews of the union, and its stubborn will to succeed, that brought it success in the Delano strike described by Matthiessen.

*The three Chicano leaders discussed here are arranged by alphabetical order and not necessarily in order of their importance, however it might be measured.

The reader is led to believe that what brought the agricultural migrant workers in California into a union was the will of César Chávez. For the conditions that he sought to correct existed and the tactics he used to correct those conditions existed before he did. The very need to organize a union was there long before he was, but it was Chávez who responded to this need.

Corky Gonzales needs no introduction to the Chicanos of the Rocky Mountain West. He was a regional sports celebrity as early as the late 1940s when he was winning amateur championships in boxing He became a national figure to those who follow that sport. Stan Steiner has done a remarkable job in tracing Gonzales' career as he moved from sports celebrity to businessman to establishment politician to, finally, Chicano leader. Gonzales' career reveals the intensity of what being Mexican-American in the United States is like. He was "successful" by the conventional Anglo standards of measurement—he had family, material sufficiency, respect, and a responsible position—yet he was vaguely dissatisfied. As he identified the cause of that dissatisfaction, his unwillingness to trade his heritage for assimilated success, he moved away from that success to a path barely perceived but increasingly attractive. He moved toward his people.

The path he traveled is an important journey, not only for Gonzales, but for thousands of Chicanos who have traveled similar ones and who have had to face the same dilemma: to be or not to be Chicano. Not everyone making the journey has resolved the dilemma, but since Gonzales set his example, we can see, at last, the dilemma.

The reforms Gonzales lists are a good index of what it is Chicanos are seeking. They are radical only in the specifics of what he asks, they are in keeping with the direction that American public policy has been taking since the 1930s. Gonzales is working to hasten the velocity of that public policy so that it reaches Chicanos today and not tomorrow.

Reies Tijerina has been active in New Mexico in trying to return to the descendants of the original settlers lands taken from them, illegally, by unscrupulous firms and individuals. Tijerina differs from Chávez and Gonzales in that his aims are less "practical" than theirs. The return of lands to the descendants of the original settlers on the basis of ancient grants from the Spanish Crown seems more than a bit Quixotic. Yet, the action is intensely practical for it has given a focal point to the discontents felt by Hispanos in New Mexico.** It is too soon to determine whether the catalytic action provided by Tijerina in New Mexico will bring about reforms, although Dr. Nancie Gonzalez in writing about political activity earlier in the book seems to believe that it already has.

The selection on Tijerina by Peter Nabakov is about the man and not his program. It reveals the evangelical dimension of Tijerina. This dimension has been a source of strength to Tijerina by giving his activities a religious cast which is attractive to many. Yet, the religion he preached was of a non-Catholic variety which made it suspect to many of the predominantly Catholic Chicanos. Another feature of the Tijerina phenomenon is its acceptance, if not sponsorship, of violence to achieve its objectives. As with the case of the religious dimension the violence factor has attracted and repelled simultaneously.

Obviously, the two elements that these Chicano leaders share with each other is their common heritage and the social injustice experienced by their followers in the United States. Time will tell if those elements will be sufficient to bind the three leaders, and many others like them, together. Such an alliance would, on its face, make the Chicano Movement much stronger.

Yet the fact remains that the Chicano Movement has gained a great deal of strength even while being as factionalized and decentralized as it is. The conclusion must be, therefore, that unified or divided the Chicano Movement will be an active presence in the public life of the Southwestern United States for the foreseeable and indefinite future.

**The problem of what to call the Spanish-speaking population in New Mexico stems from the fact that many New Mexicans are not the descendants of Mexican immigrants. They are the descendants of the offspring of Spanish fathers and Indian mothers. They refer to themselves as *Hispanos* or *Mexicanos*. We shall refer to them as Chicanos although we recognize the analytic distinction noted above.

Cesar Chavez

Peter Matthiessen

One Sunday of August 1968, I knocked on the door of a small frame house on Kensington Street in Delano, California. It was just before seven in the morning, and the response to the knock was tense, suspenseful silence of a household which, in recent months, had installed an unlisted telephone, not as a convenience, but to call the outside world in case of trouble. After a moment the house breathed again, as if I had been identified through the drawn shutters, but no one came to the door, and so I sat down on the stoop and tuned in to a mockingbird. The stoop is shaded by squat trees, which distinguish Kensington Street from the other straight lines of one-story bungalows that comprise residential Delano, but at seven, the air was already hot and still, as it is almost every day of summer in the San Joaquin Valley.

Cesar Chavez's house—or rather, the house inhabited by Cesar Chavez, whose worldly possessions, scraped together, would scarcely be worth the $50 that his farm workers union pays for him in monthly rent—has been threatened so often by his enemies that it would be foolish to set down its street number. But on Kensington Street, a quiet stronghold of the American Way of Life, the house draws attention to itself by its very lack of material aspiration. On such a street the worn brown paint, the forgotten yard (relict plantings by a former tenant die off one by one, and a patch of lawn between stoop and sidewalk had been turned to mud by a leaky hose trailing away into the weeds), the uncompetitive car which, lacking an engine, is not so much parked as abandoned, are far more subversive than the strike signs (Don't Buy California Grapes) that are plastered on the car, or the Kennedy stickers, fading now, that are still stuck to the old posts of the stoop, or the Stop Reagan sign that decorates the shuttered windows.

Behind those drawn shutters, the house—two bedrooms, bath, kitchen and an L-shaped living room where some of the Chavez children sleep—is neat and cheerful, brought to life by a white cabinet of bright flowers and religious objects, a stuffed bookcase, and over the sofa bed, a painting in Mexican mural style of surging strikers, but from the outside it might seem that this drab place has been abandoned, like an old store rented temporarily for some fleeting campaign and then gutted again of everything but tattered signs. The signs suggest that the dwelling is utilitarian, not domestic, that the Chavez family live here because when they came, in 1962, this house on the middle-class east side was the cheapest then available in Delano, and that their commitment is somewhere else.

Chavez's simple commitment is to win for farm workers the right to organize in their own behalf that is enjoyed by all other large labor groups in the United States; if it survives, his United Farm Workers Organizing Committee will be the first effective farm workers union in American history. Until Chavez appeared, union leaders had considered it impossible to organize seasonal farm labor, which is in large part illiterate and indigent, and for which even mild protest may mean virtual starvation. The migrant labor force rarely remains in one place long enough to form an effective unit and is mostly composed of minority groups which invite more hostility than support, since the local communities fear an extra municipal burden with no significant increase in the tax base. In consequence, strikes, protests and abortive unions organized ever since 1903 have been broken with monotonous efficiency by the growers, a task made easier since the Depression years by the specific exclusion of farm workers from the protection of the National Labor Relations Act of 1935 (the Wagner Act), which authorizes and regulates collective bargaining between management and labor, and protects new unionists from reprisal. In a state where cheap labor, since Indian days, has been taken for granted, like the sun, the reprisals have been swift and sometimes fatal, as the history of farm labor movements attests.

The provision of the NLRA which excludes farm workers was excused by the bloody farm strikes of 1934, when the Communist label was firmly attached to "agrargian reformers"; its continued existence three decades later is a reflection of the power of the growers, whose might and right have been dutifully affirmed by church and state. But since 1965, America's last bastion of uninhibited free enterprise has been shaken so hard by national publicity that both church and state are searching for safer positions. And this new hope for the farm workers has been brought not by the Communist agent that his enemies have conjured up, nor even by a demagogue, but by a small, soft-spoken Mexican-American migrant laborer who could never leave the fields long enough to get past the seventh grade.

In no more time than it would take to pull his pants on and splash water on his face, the back door creaked and Cesar Chavez appeared around the corner of the house. "Good morning." He smiled, raising his eyebrows, as if surprised to see me there. "How are you?" He had not had much sleep—it was already morning when I dropped him off the night before—but in that early light he looked as rested as a child. Though he shook my hand, he did not stop moving; we walked south down Kensington Street and turned west at the corner.

The man who has threatened California has an Indian's bow nose and lank black hair, with sad eyes and an open smile that is shy and friendly; at momento he is beautiful, like a dark seraph. He is five feet six inches tall, and since his twenty-five-day fast the previous winter, has weighed no more than one hundred and fifty pounds. Yet the word "slight" does not properly describe him. There is an effect of being centered in himself so that no energy is wasted, an effect of *density*; at the same time, he walks as lightly as a fox. One feels immediately that this man does not stumble, and that to get where he is going he will walk all day.

In Delano (pronounced "De-*lay*-no"), the north-south streets are named alphabetically, from Albany Street on the far west side to Xenia on the east; the cross streets are called avenues and are numbered. On Eleventh Avenue, between Kensington and Jefferson, a police car moved out of an empty lot and settled heavily on its springs across the sidewalk. There it idled while its occupant enjoyed the view. Small-town policemen are apt to be as fat and sedentary as the status quo they are hired to defend, and this one was no exception; he appeared to be part of his machine, overflowing out of his front window like a growth. Having feasted his eyes on the public library and the National Bank of Agriculture, he permitted his gaze to come to rest on the only two citizens in sight. His cap, shading his eyes from the early sun, was much too small for him, and in the middle of his mouth, pointed straight at us, was a dead cigar.

At seven on a Sunday morning in Delano, a long-haired stranger wearing sunglasses and sneakers, in the company of a Mexican, would qualify automatically as a trouble-maker; consorting with a *known* troublemaker like Chavez, I became a mere undesirable. The cop looked me over long enough to let me know he had his eye on me, then eased his wheels into gear again and humped on his soft springs onto the street. Chavez raised his eyebrows in a characteristic gesture of mock wonderment, but in answer to my unspoken question—for in this tense town it could not be assumed that this confrontation was an accident—he pointed at the back of a crud-colored building fronting on Jefferson Street. "That's our station house," he said, in the manner of a man who is pointing out, with pardonable pride, the main sights of his city.

A walk across town on Eleventh Avenue, from the vineyards in the east to the cotton fields in the west, will teach one a good deal about Delano, which lies in Kern

County, just south of the Tulare County line. Opposite the National Bank of Agriculture is a snack stand, La Cocina— Pepsi, Burgers, Tacos, Burritos—as well as the Angelos Dry Goods shop and the Sierra Theatre, which features Mexican films; from here to Main Street and beyond, Eleventh Avenue is lined with jewelry shops and department stores. Main Street, interrupting the alphabetical sequence between Jefferson and High, is a naked treeless stretch of signs and commercial enterprises, mostly one-story; today it was empty of all life, like an open city.

Toward High Street, Empire Ford Sales rules both sides of Eleventh, and the far corners of High Street are the properties of OK *Used Trucks and Kern County Equipment: Trucks and Tractors.* The farm-equipment warehouses and garages continue west across High Street to the tracks of the Southern Pacific Railroad; the loading platforms of the farm-produce packing sheds and cold-storage houses front the far side of the tracks, with their offices facing west on Glenwood Street. Opposite these buildings are some small cafes and poker parlors frequented by the workers—Monte Carlo Card Room, Divina's Four Deuces, Lindo Michoacan—and beyond Glenwood, the workers' neighborhoods begin. Fremont Street, relatively undeveloped, overlooks U.S. Highway 99, which bores through the town below ground level like an abandoned subway trench. An overpass across the freeway links Fremont with Ellington Street, which is littered with small cafes and markets. The wrong side of the tracks, a community of small houses, mostly Mexican-American, spreads west to Albany Street and the cotton, food and flower factories of the San Joaquin Valley.

Toward Dover Street, a car coming up behind us slowed too suddenly. Chavez, like a feeding deer, gave sign of awareness with a sidelong flick of his brown eyes, but he did not turn or stop talking. When a voice called out in Spanish, asking him if he would like a lift, he smiled and waved, then pointed at the church two streets away. *"!No, gracias! Yo voy a la misa."*

Irregularly, Chavez attends this pretty stucco church at the corner of Eleventh Avenue and Clinton Street. The church sign, Our Lady of Guadalupe, is garish and utilitarian, in the spirit of Delano, and the churchyard is a parking lot enclosed by a chain-link fence. But the place has been planted with cypress, pines and yew, which, in this early light, threw cool fresh shadows on the white stucco. In the flat angularities of their surroundings, the evergreens and red tile roof give the building a graceful Old World air that is pointed up by twin white crosses, outlined against the hot blue of the sky.

Chavez hurried on the concrete path, in the bare sun. He was wearing his invariable costume—plaid shirt, work pants, dark suede shoes—but he was clean and neatly pressed, and though he had said nothing about church, it appeared that he had been bound here all along. "Let's just go in for a little while," he murmured. He was hurrying now as if a little late, though in fact the mass was near its end. From the church door came the soft drone of liturgy, of late footsteps and a baby's cry, the hollow ring of heels on church stone, and cavernous mumbling. A cough resounded.

Slipping through the door, he moved into the shadows on the left, where he crossed himself with water dipped from a font in the rear wall. At the same time he subsided onto his knees behind the rearmost pew. In the church hush, the people had begun to sing "Bendito." All were standing, but Chavez remained there on his knees behind them until the hymn was finished. Alone in the shadows of the pew, the small Indian head bent on his chest and the toes of his small shoes tucked inward, he looked from behind like a boy of another time, at his prayer beside his bed.

When the hymn ended, Chavez rose and followed the people forward to receive the blessing. A Franciscan priest in green cossack and white surplice loomed above him under the glowing windows. Then he turned left, passing an American flag that stood furled in the far corner, and returned down the outside aisle. Touching the water, he crossed himself again and followed the people out the door into the growing day. To the side of the door, under the evergreens, he waited to talk to friends; meanwhile others in the congregation came forward to greet him.

"*!Cesar, como esta?*"

"*!Estoy bien!*"

"*!Bueno—dia—*" !

"*Buenos dias!*"

"*?Como esta?*" another man said.

"*!Oh,*" Chavez answered, "*batallando con la vida!*"— "I am still struggling with life." He grinned.

A Filipino in his sixties came up with a fine wordless smile and pumped Chavez's hand in both his own. "That's one of the brothers," Chavez explained when the old man had gone; the term "brother" or "sister" is used to describe a Union member, but it also has the connotation of "soul brother," and is so used by Chavez when addressing strangers.

Father Mark Day, a young Franciscan priest who was assigned to the farm workers in 1967, came up and greeted Chavez heartily. The following Sunday, he said, the Catholic churches of Delano would speak out in favor of the workers' right to form a union; hearing this, Chavez merely nodded. Since 1891, papal encyclicals have affirmed the workers' right to organize—Pope John XXIII had even spoken of their right to strike—but in Chavez's opinion Catholic help has too often taken the form of food baskets for the needy rather than programs that might encourage independence: a union and a decent wage would enable the worker to escape from demeaning and demoralizing dependence on welfare and charity. Although individuals in the clergy around the country had lent sympathy to the farm workers very early, and many outside church groups, particularly the Migrant Ministry, had long ago come to his support, with personnel as well as money, the clergy, Catholic as well as Protestant, had denounced the grape strike or dodged the issue for fear of offending the growers, most of whom are Catholics of Italian or Yugoslav origin and contribute heavily to the Church. In fact, when Chavez's organization, the National Farm Workers Association, began the strike in 1965, the growers were able to pressure the Church into forbidding NFWA to use the parish hall of Our Lady of Guadalupe. ("I find it frankly quite embarrassing," Father Day has said, "to see liberals and agnostics fighting vehemently for social justice among agricultural workers while Catholic priests sit by and sell them religious trinkets.") Though more and more embarrassed by the example of outside clergy of all faiths, many of whom had marched in the Union picket lines, it was only recently that the Delano clergy abandoned its passive stance and joined in attempts to reconcile the growers to the Union. Now Father Day spoke of the large Zaninovich clan, some of whom came to mass here at Our Lady of Guadalupe. "If they would just get together with their workers," he said, "we wouldn't have any problems."

Chavez looked doubtful, but he nodded politely. "Yes," he said after a moment, "this church is really coming to life." With Chavez, it is sometimes hard to tell when he is joking and when he is serious, because he is so often both at the same time.

More people greeted him, *"?Va bien?" "!Esta bien!"* Most of the people are jocular with Chavez, who has a warm, humorous smile that makes them laugh, but after the joking, a few stood apart and stared at him with honest joy.

A worker in a soiled white shirt with a fighting cock in bright colors on the pocket stood waiting for a hearing. Though Chavez is available to his people day and night, it is on Sunday that they usually come to see him, and his Sundays are all devoted to this purpose. ". . . *buscando trabajo,"* I heard the worker say when he had Chavez's ear: he was looking for work. He had just come in from Mexico, and the visa, or "green card," that he carried in his pocket is the symbol of the most serious obstacle that Chavez's strike effort must face: the century-old effort of California farmers to depress wages and undercut resistance by pitting one group of poor people against another.

By the 1860's the local Indians used as near-slaves in Spanish California had been decimated; they were largely replaced, after the Gold Rush, by Chinese labor made available by the completion of the Southern Pacific railroad. But the thrifty Chinese were resented and persecuted by the crowds of jobless whites for whom the Gold Rush had not panned out, and also by small farmers, who could not compete with the cheap labor force, and when their immigration was ended by the Exclusion Act of 1882, the big farmers hired other immigrants, notably Japanese. The Japanese undercut all other labor, but soon they too were bitterly resented for attempting to defend their interests. Even worse, they were better farmers than the Americans, and they bought and cultivated poor ground that nobody else had bothered with; this impertinence was dealt with by the Alien Land Law of 1913, which permitted simple confiscation of their land. (The land was subsequently restored, then confiscated again after Pearl Harbor.)

The next wave of farm laborers in California contained Hindus (Sikhs), Armenians and Europeans; they slowly replaced the Japanese, who by 1917 were referred to as the "yellow peril," and after the war, for patriotic reasons, were kicked out of their jobs to make room for red-blooded Americans. Meanwhile, the European and Armenian immigrants, less beset than the Asiatics by the race hatred that has advanced the economy of California from the start, were gaining a strong foothold; many were the parents of the Valley farmers of today.

Throughout the nineteenth century, Mexican peasants had crossed the border more or less at will. After the Mexican Revolution of 1910, the starving refugees presented the growers with a new source of cheap labor which, because it was there illegally, had the additional advantage of being defenseless. Cheap Mexican labor was pitted against cheap Filipino labor; the Filipinos were brought in numbers in the twenties. Many of the Mexicans were deported after 1931, when the Okies, Arkies and up-country Texans swarmed into California from the dust bowls; the Depression had caused a labor surplus beyond the wildest dreams of the employers, and an effort was made to keep the border closed.

Still, Mexicans were predominant in the farm labor force from 1914 until 1934. In these years, because of their illegal status, they tended to be more tractable than other groups; the famous farm strikes of the thirties occurred more often among Anglos and Filipinos. Despite their quiet nature, the Filipinos refused to scab on other workers or underbid them. "The Filipino is a real fighter," Carey McWilliams wrote in *Factories in the Fields*, "and his strikes have been dangerous." Few Filipino women had immigrated, and the ratio of men to women was 14 to 1; predictably, the growers dismissed the Filipinos as "homosexuals." McWilliams quotes the *Pacific Rural Press* for May 9, 1936, which called the Filipino "the most worthless, unscrupulous, shiftless, diseased semi-barbarian that has ever come to our shores." After the Philippine independence act of 1934, further importation of the spirited Filipinos came to an end, and their numbers have been dwindling ever since.

By 1942 the Chinese were long since in the cities, the Japanese-Americans had been shut up in concentration camps, the Europeans had graduated from the labor force and become farmers, and the Anglos had mostly drifted into the booming war economy of factories and shipyards; the minority groups that remained were not numerous enough to harvest the enormous produce that the war demanded.

The farm labor emergency was met by a series of agreements with the Mexican government known collectively as the *bracero* program, under the terms of which large numbers of day laborers, or *braceros*, were brought into California and the Southwest at harvest time and trucked out again when the harvest was over. The *bracero* program was so popular with the growers that it was extended when the war was over. In Washington the lobbyists for the growers argued successfully that Americans would not do the hard stoop labor required in harvesting cotton, sugar beets, and other crops; hence the need for the extension of the *bracero* program. Everyone conveniently forgot that the white fruit tramps of the thirties had done plenty of stoop labor and that domestic workers of all colors would be available to the farms if working conditions were improved. But the Mexicans, whose poverty was desperate, worked hard long days for pay as low as 60 cents an hour, and were used to undermine all efforts by domestic workers to hold out for better treatment; by 1959 an estimated four hundred thousand foreign workers (including small numbers of Canadians in the potato fields of Maine, and British West Indians in the Florida citrus groves) were obtaining work in an America where millions were unemployed.

Already the churches and citizens' groups were protesting the lot of the farm workers, and the domestic migrant laborers especially, and at the end of 1964 Public Law 78, the last and most notorious of the *bracero* programs, was allowed to lapse. (This was the year in which a long-accumulating sense of national guilt had permitted the passage of significant poverty and civil rights legislation, and it would be pleasant to assume that P.L. 78 was a casualty of the new humanism, but congressional concern about the outflow of gold was probably more important.)

The death of P.L. 78 was the birth of serious hope for a farm union, but by 1965, when the grape strike began, the growers had found another means to obtain the same cheap labor. Under Public Law 414 (the Immigration and Nationality Act of 1952, also called the McCarran-Walter Act), large numbers of foreigners were permitted to enter the United States as "permanent resident aliens" on a special green visa card. "Green-carders" could become citizens after five years' residence (and hold social security, pay taxes, and be drafted while they waited), but since the Mexican may earn fifteen times as much for a day's work in the United States ($30 versus 25 pesos, or about $2), most have declined this opportunity in favor of "commuting," i.e., they cluster around the border towns and take their high harvest wages—an estimated $15 million worth in 1967—back to Mexico.

Today almost half the membership of Chavez's union hold green cards; they are welcome so long as they do not work as scabs. The law specifies that no green-carders may work in a field where a labor dispute has been certified, or where a minimum wage (now $1.40 an hour) has not been offered first to domestic workers, but enforcement of this law has been desultory, to say the least. Many Mexicans, with the active encouragement of the growers and the passive encouragement of the Border Patrol of the U.S. Immigration Service, have joined the numerous "wetbacks" (that is, the illegal immigrants) as strikebreakers. As long as they are excluded from legislation that guarantees collective bargaining, the farm workers have no formal means to force employers to negotiate. When their strike against the grape growers was subverted by imported scabs and antipicketing injunctions, they were driven to what the growers call an "illegal and immoral" boycott. Originally this boycott was directed against one company, the Joseph Giumarra Vineyards, Inc., but Guimara began selling its products under the labels of other companies, and in January 1968 the present consumer's boycott against all growers of California table grapes was begun.

In the autumn of 1968, according to the Fresno *Bee* of November 3, an estimated twenty to thirty thousand wetbacks were working in the Valley; though their presence is illegal, there is no penalty for hiring them, and since they are both economical and defenseless, the growers replace their domestic force with *alambristas* (fence jumpers) at every opportunity. "When the *alambrista* comes into a job," one of them is quoted as saying, "the regular workers are out, just like that." The Immigration Service picked up five hundred and ten wetbacks in the Delano area in August alone—about one fortieth of the lowest estimated number.

Loosely enforced, P.L. 414 is no improvement over P.L. 78, and it poses a moral problem as well as an economic one: Mexican-Americans, most of whom have parents or grandparents south of the border, have deep sympathy with Mexican poverty and do not wish to get Mexicans into trouble by reporting them to *la Migra*, as the Border Patrol is known. Besides, many green-carders are innocent, having been hired without being told, as P.L. 414 requires, that their employer was the object of a strike; some of these people, poor though they are, have walked off the job in a strange country when they learned the truth, but most are in debt for transport and lodging before they ever reach the fields, and their need— and that of their families at home—is too great to permit so brave a gesture.

The man with the fighting cock on his shirt was a Union green-carder who did not wish to cross the picket lines. But at that time there were more Union workers than Union jobs—only three growers in the Delano area had signed contracts with the United Farm Workers Organizing Committee— and Chavez encouraged the man to take a job wherever he could find it. He did not have to encourage the green-carder to help the Union on the job by organizing work slowdowns; the man was already complaining that social security payments had been deducted from his last pay checks, even though no one had asked for his social security number.

Workers who cannot read, like this man, feel that they are chronic victims of petty pay-check chiseling on the part of both labor contractors and growers, not only on illusory social security but on unpaid overtime and promised bonuses. (In the first six months of 1967, the Department of Labor discovered that nearly two hundred thousand American laborers were being cheated by their employers, mostly on unpaid overtime and evasion of the minimum wage; this figure is probably only a fraction of the actual number of victims.) Chavez feels that the labor contractor, who sells his own people in job lots to the growers, is the worst evil in an evil system that is very close to peonage; the contractor would be eliminated if the growers agreed to get their labor through a union hiring hall.

"Those people make a lot of money that way," Chavez said. "A *lot*." At this moment, he looked ugly. "In the Union, the workers get an honest day's pay, because both sides understand the arrangement and accept it. Without a union, the people are always cheated, and they are so innocent." In silence, we walked on up Eleventh Avenue to Albany and turned south along the cotton fields. It was eight o'clock now, and the morning was hot. The flat farmland stretched away unbroken into dull mists of agricultural dust, nitrates and insecticides, still unsettled from the day before, that hid the round brown mountains of the Coast Range.

Chavez said that many of the green-carders—and especially those who would return to Mexico—felt they could beat the Union wage scale by working furiously on a piece-rate basis; others did not join the Union out of ignorance—they had never heard of a union—or fear of reprisal. "It's the whole system of fear, you know. The ones we've converted—well, out at Schenley we have a contract, and P. L. Vargas, on his ranch committee—there was a guy named Danny. Danny was so anti-Union that he went to the management at Schenley and said, 'Give me a gun; I'll go out and kill some of those strikers.' He just hated us, and he didn't know why. Today he's a real good Unionist; he has a lot of guts and does a lot of work, but he still doesn't know why. He was working inside when we came with the picket line, and he wouldn't walk out, and I guess he felt guilty so he went too far the other way. And also, he told me later, 'I didn't know what a union was, I never heard of a union; I had no idea what it was or how it worked. I came from a small village down in Mexico!' You see? It's the old story. He was making more money than he had ever seen in Mexico, and the Union was a threat.

"Anyway, we won there, and got a union shop, and all the guys who went out on strike got their jobs back. And, man, they wanted to clean house, they wanted to get Danny, and I said no. "Well, he doesn't want to join the Union! And the contract says if he doesn't join the Union, he can't work there!' So I challenged them. I said, 'One man threatens you? And you've got a contract? Do you know what the real challenge is? Not to get him out, but to get him *in*. If you were good organizers you'd get him, but you're not—you're lazy!' So they went after Danny, and the pressure began to build against him. He was mad as hell, he held out for three months, and he was encouraged by the Anglos, the white guys—they had the best jobs, mechanics and all, and they didn't want to join the Union either. But finally Danny saw the light, and they did too. That contract took about six months to negotiate, so by the time we got around to setting up a negotiating committee, Danny had not only been converted but had been elected to the committee. So when the committee walked in there, P. L. was one of them and Danny was another, and the employers stared at him: 'What are you doing here, Danny?' " Chavez laughed. "And now he's a real St. Paul; he'll never turn against the Union because he knows both sides. People who don't know, and come on so enthusiastic and all at first, they may be turncoats one day, but not the ones like Danny. That's why the converted ones are our best men.

"You know how we make enemies? A guy gets out of high school, and his parents have been farm workers, so he gets a job, say, as a clerk at the Bank of America. This way, you know, he gets into the climate, into the atmosphere"— Chavez shook his head in bafflement—"and I'll be damned if in two years they haven't done a terrific job on him, not by telling him, but just by . . . by *immersion*, and before you know it the guy is actually saying there's no discrimination! 'Hell, there's no poverty!' See? He knows his place. Or he gets a job at a retail store and then feels threatened because our people are making more than he does. 'Look,' he says, 'I went to high school for four years, so how come these farm workers are making more than I do?' That *really* hurts. Either way he is threatened by the Union."

On the left as we walked south on Albany were the small houses of large families, mostly Mexican. Though these houses are simple, their neatness reflects a dignity that was not possible in the labor camps, which have always been the ugliest symbol of the migrant workers' plight. "Besides being so bad, they divide the families," Chavez said. "We don't want people living out there, we want them in their own houses. As long as they're living in the camps, they're under the thumb of the employer." He nodded toward the small houses. "In Delano the need for housing is being met, even for the migrants. I mean, if we won the whole thing tomorrow, signed contracts with all the growers, we'd have to use some of the camps for a little while, but right now the people in the camps are strikebreakers." I kicked a stone, and he watched it skid into the field. "We're going to get rid of those camps," he said, as if making himself a promise.

A car passed us, bursting with cries, and rattled to a halt a short way beyond. Two workers were driving a third to the Forty Acres, the site of the proposed new Union headquarters, and to my surprise—we had been headed for the Union offices at the corner of Albany and Asti streets— Chavez suggested that we ride out there. The car turned west at Garces Highway and rolled two miles through the cotton and alfalfa to a barren area of mud, shacks and unfinished construction on the north side of the road. Here the car left us and went back to town, and the third man, a solitary Anglo tramp, a renegade from the thirties who helps the farm workers whenever he comes to town, shouted cheerily at Chavez and marched off to water some scattered saplings that shriveled slowly in the August heat.

"We've planted a lot of trees. Elms, mostly, and Modesto ash—only the cheapest kinds." Chavez stood with his back to the road, hands in hip pockets, gazing with pleasure at the desolation. The Forty Acres lies between the state road and the city dump. Useless for farming in its present condition, the property was obtained in 1966 from a widow who could not afford to pay the taxes on it. "Don't get me started on my plans," he said. To Chavez, who envisions the first migrant workers center, the place is already beautiful; he comes here regularly to walk around and let his plans take shape. "There's alkali in this land," he said. "We're trying to get something growing here, to cut down the dust."

At the Forty Acres, near the highway, an adobe building which will house gas pumps, auto repair shop and a cooperative store had recently been completed, though it was not yet in use: the shop was heaped high with food stores for the strikers, donated by individuals and agencies all over the United States. Just across from it is the windowless small room in which Chavez lived during the twenty-five-day fast that he undertook in February and March 1968. Behind this building was a temporary aggregation of shacks and trailers which included the workers clinic and the Union newspaper, *El Malcriado* (the "rebellious child," the "nonconformist," the "protester"—there is no simple translation), which issues both English and Spanish editions every fortnight. Originally *El Malcriado* was a propaganda organ, shrill and simplistic: it saw Lyndon Johnson as a "Texas grower" careless of the lives of the Vietnamese "farm workers." Today it is slanted but not irresponsible, and it is well-edited.

One green trailer at the Forty Acres, bearing the logond Mobile Health Center, was the contribution of the International Ladies' Garment Workers Union; its medical staff, like that of *El Malcriado* and most of the rest of the UFWOC operation, is made up entirely of volunteers. So is the intermittent labor being done on the headquarters building, a gray shell in the northwest corner of the property. The work was supervised by Chavez's brother Richard, who had been sent off a few days before to help out with the boycott in New York. "The strike is the important thing," Chavez said, moving toward this building. "We work on the Forty Acres when we get a little money, or some volunteers." The day before, six carpenters from a local in Bakersfield had given their Saturday to putting up gray fiberboard interior walls, and Chavez, entering the building, was delighted with the progress. "Look at that!" he kept saying. "Those guys really went to town!" The plumbing had been done by a teacher at Berkeley, and two weeks before, forty-seven electricians from Los Angles, donating materials as well as labor, had wired the whole building in six hours. "I've never seen forty-seven electricians," I admitted, trying not to laugh, and Chavez grinned. "You should have seen it," he assured me. "I could hardly get into the building. Everywhere I went, I was in somebody's way, so I just went out through the window."

The building will combine Union offices and a service center, where workers can obtain advice on legal problems, immigration, driver's licenses, tax returns, and other matters. We inspected the credit union, legal offices, the hiring hall-and-auditorium, the dining hall, kitchen and rest rooms.

In the northeast corner were small cubicles for the Union officers. "Everybody was out here claiming his office." Chavez smiled, shaking his head. "We've outgrown this building even before we move into it, and I guess they thought that somebody was going to get left out." He grunted. "They were right." We had come to the cubicle in the corner. "This is mine, I guess," he said, "but now they don't want me here." I asked why. He was silent for a little while, looking restlessly about him. "I don't know." He shrugged and took a breath, as if on the point of saying something painful. "They're very worried about security or something. I don't know." Stupidly, I failed to drop the subject. "I guess the corner is more exposed," I said. "They want you somewhere inside."

Chavez walked away from me. "This is the conference room," he called, from around a corner. "This will save a lot of time. People are constantly coming in, you know . . ." His voice trailed off, resumed again. "The way things are going, we don't have enough office space for the newspaper or the ranch committees . . . Oh! Look at that!" He was turning a complete circle. "Those guys *really* went to town! It's entirely changed!" He finished his circle, beaming. "The first center for farm workers in history!" (A year later Richard Chavez took me out to see the progress at the Forty Acres, which was negligible. "We're so damn busy," Richard said, "and there's always something that needs the money more.")

Outside again, we walked around the grounds, in the hot emptiness of Sunday. "Over there"—he pointed—"will be another building, a little training center there, kind of a . . . a study center for nonviolence, mostly for people in the Union, the organizers and ranch committees. Nonviolent tactics, you know—to be nonviolent in a monastery is one thing, but being nonviolent in a struggle for justice is another. And we'll stress honesty. Some of these guys will be getting a lot of power as the Union develops, and some will be very good and some won't know how to handle it. If someone in the hiring hall is willing to take a bribe to put one guy ahead of another on a job, he may also be willing to steal a hundred dollars from the Union, or accept a hundred dollars for an act of violence. There's all kinds of chances for corruption, and things can go to hell fast—we've seen that in other unions. So the best way to teach them is by example."

His glance asked that I take what he was about to say as nothing boastful. Chavez is a plain-spoken man who does not waste his own time or his listener's with false humility, yet he is uncomfortable when the necessity arises to speak about himself, and may even emit a gentle groan. "I mean, you can write a million pamphlets on honesty, you can write books on it, and manuals, and it doesn't work—it only works by example. I have to give up a lot of things, because I can't ask people to sacrifice if I won't sacrifice myself." He was glad to change the subject. "We have some great guys in this Union, some really great guys. We've put together farm workers and volunteers, people who just wanted to do something for the cause. We have so many volunteers that we save only the best; they come and go, but the good ones never go. You don't say 'Stay!' They stay of their own accord!

"In a way we're all volunteers; even the ones—the lawyers and everybody—whose salaries are paid by outside people; they're not making money. You start paying the strikers for what they should do for themselves, then everything is done for money, and you'll never be able to build anything. It's not just a question of spending money, and anyway, we haven't got it. But the farm workers stand to benefit directly from the Union; it's their union, and we've been able to get that across to them—really, you know, it's working beautifully. Most of us work for five dollars a week. Outside people, the Teamsters and everybody, thought we were crazy, but it's the only way we can stay in business. It's a long, long haul, and there isn't any money, and if we start paying wages, then it means that only a *few* can be hired, and a few can't do as much as many.

"It has to be done this way. I've been in this fight too long, almost twenty years, learning and learning, one defeat after another, always frustration. And then of course, raising a family—you have to get your family to suffer along with you, otherwise you can't do it. But finally we're beginning to see daylight, and that's a great reward. And then, you see, these farm workers will never be the same. If they destroyed our union today, these people would never go back to where they were. They'd get up and fight. That's the *real* change."

Under the eaves of the garage, in the shade of the north wall, a blue wooden bench stood against the adobe. We sat there for an hour or more, cut off by the cool clay walls from the howl of the highway. To the west was a marginal dark farm—all dying farms look dark—with a lone black-and-white cow in the barnyard, and a sign, itself in need of repair, that advertised the repair of auto radiators. Across the property to the north, dead cars glittered on the crown of the city dump; heaped high like a bright monument to progress, the cars form the only rise in the depressed landscape of Delano.

The adobe walls and red tile roofs of the Forty Acres were Chavez's own wish, to be repeated in the other buildings as they take shape: the idea comes from the old Franciscan missions, and from an adobe farmhouse of his childhood. "The people wanted something more modern—you know, kind of flashy—to show that they had a terrific union going here, but I wanted something that would not go out of fashion, something that would last." Eventually the entire Forty Acres will be surrounded by a high adobe wall, which will mercifully shut out its grim surroundings. The flat hard sky will be broken by trees, and he dreams of a fountain in a sunken garden, and a central plaza where no cars will be permitted.

Chavez drew his hopes in the old dust with a dead stick. Inside the walls, paths will lead everywhere, and "places for the workers to rest. There will be little hollows in the walls—you know, niches—where people can put little statues if they want, or birds and things. We'll have frescoes. Siqueiros is interested in doing that, I think. This place is for the people, it has to grow naturally out of their needs." He smiled. "It will be kind of a religious place, very restful, quiet. It's going to be nice here." He gazed about him. "I love doing this—just letting it grow by itself. Trees. We'll have a little woods." Arizona cypress had already been planted along the property lines, but in the August heat many of Chavez's seedling trees had yellowed and died.

Car tires whined to a halt on the highway and crunched onto the flats of the Forty Acres. Chavez became silent; he sat stone-still against the wall, gazing straight out toward the glistening dump. When the car came past the corner of the building into his line of sight, he smiled. The driver was Ann Israel of the Spectemur Agendo Foundation of New York, who had introduced us originally. We all waved. "I heard you were out here," she called. "Do you want a lift back into town?"

Chavez shook his head. "That's all right, thanks," he said. "We can walk." For a moment Mrs. Israel looked as astonished as I felt—not so much that the walk back was a long one on the hot August highway but that Chavez felt relaxed enough to take the time away. But the day before, in Bakersfield, he had won a crucial skirmish with the growers; though he gives an almost invariable impression of great calm, he was more relaxed this morning than I had ever seen him. After a week's immersion in injunctions, boycotts, restraining orders, suits and strikes, he seemed glad to talk about trees and red-tiled missions, and to remain seated peacefully in the shade of his adobe wall, on a blue wooden bench.

Mrs. Israel perceived this instantly and made no effort to persuade him to accept a ride. Chavez smiled fondly after her as she waved and drove away. A pretty girl in her thirties, Mrs. Israel is both tough-minded and kind, and she has been a good friend to the farm workers, finding support for them in other foundations besides her own. In June she had got me to edit an outline of insecticide abuses for possible use in a farm workers' ad, thus transforming my vague endorsement of the California grape strike into active participation. At that time she also told me that she was going to Delano in mid-summer, to see at first hand what her foundation was considering supporting; if I cared to come along, she said, she would introduce me to Cesar Chavez.

Because he is such an unpublic man, Chavez is one of the few public figures that I would go ten steps out of my way to meet. Besides, I feel that the farm workers' plight is related to all of America's most serious afflictions: racism, poverty, environmental pollution, and urban crowding and decay—all of these compounded by the waste of war.

In a damaged human habitat, all problems merge. For example, noise, crowding and smog poisoning are notorious causes of human irritability; that crowded ghettos explode first in the worst smog areas of America is no coincidence at all. And although no connection has been established between overcrowding and the atmosphere of assassination, rat experiments leave little doubt that a connection could exist: even when ample food and shelter are provided, rats (which exhibit behavioral patterns disconcertingly similar to those of man) respond to crowding in strange and morbid ways, including neuter behavior, increased incidence of homosexuality, gang rape, killing, and consumption by the mothers of their young. But because the symptoms of a damaged habitat are social, a very serious problem of ecology (it seems fatuous to say "the most serious problem the world has ever known," not because it is untrue but because it is so obvious) will be dealt with by politicians, the compromisers and consensus men who do not lead but merely exploit the status quo. The apparatus of the status quo—the System is a partisan term but must do here for want of a better—not to speak of System ethics, is not going to be good enough when food, oxygen and water become scarce. Although it seems likely, in purely material needs, that the optimisms of the new technologies will be borne out, most men in 1985 will have to live by bread alone, and not very good bread, either. Famine is already as close as Kentucky and the Mississippi Delta, and apart from that, there is hard evidence of environmental stress—noise, traffic, waiting lines, sick cities, crime, lost countrysides, psychosis. Meanwhile, the waste of resources continues, and the contamination of the biosphere by bomb and blight.

Before this century is done, there will be an evolution in our values and the values of human society, not because

man has become more civilized but because, on a blighted
earth, he will have no choice. This evolution—actually a
revolution whose violence will depend on the violence with
which it is met—must aim at an order of things that treats
man and his habitat with respect; the new order, grounded
in human ecology, will have humanity as its purpose and the
economy as its tool, thus reversing the present order of the
System. Such hope as there is of orderly change depends on
men like Cesar Chavez, who, of all leaders now in sight, best
represents the rising generations. He is an idealist unhamp-
ered by ideology, an activist with a near-mystic vision, a
militant with a dedication to nonviolence, and he stands free
of the political machinery that the election year 1968 made
not only disreputable but irrelevant. . . .

The Poet
in the Boxing Ring
Stan Steiner

He "lurked like a cat for the kill." The ritual lingo of the boxing ring described the fighting style of a young intellectual who read Lorca in the dressing room, and who fought seventy-five professional bouts and won sixty-five of them. He fought with the desperation of a kid from the barrios. The crowds savored the blood that dripped from his eyes, his lips, his bronzed face. "A crowd pleaser," one boxing buff recalls.

"Rodolfo is a gentle man," his wife says. "He is a poet.". . .

The Championship of the World was almost his. *Ring Magazine* hailed him as one of the five best boxers of his weight. He was rated the third ranking contender for the World Featherweight title by the National Boxing Association. When Gonzales was still in his teens he had won the National Amateur Championship and the International Championship as well. In the Lysoled corridors of the pugilistic kingdoms of the Mafia he was fingered as the coming "King of the Little Men." He was a"hungry fighter," the connoisseurs of flesh wrote in the sports pages. They did not know he was a poet.

He is a "poet of action" in the ring, the boxing writers wrote unwittingly. Lithe, his mind quick as his body, he reacted like the reflex of a muscle, He was later to write of a young boxer, Manny, in one of his plays, "His movements are smooth, casual, and catlike." It may have been a self-portrait.

The Golden Boy of the boxing legend, he was to become the new voice of the Chicano movement. He was the idol of his generation, and he shared their frustrations. He was the embodiment of the confused barrio youth, the urban Chicanos. . . .

Where was he going? He did not know. "It's a long road back to yourself when the society has made you into someone else," he now says. "But I was determined to find my way, to rediscover my roots, to be the man I am, not the emasculated man that the Anglo society wanted me to be."

Rodolfo "Corky" Gonzales lived all the lives that "divide our hearts and emasculate our souls." In his young manhood he became an insurance salesman, a romantic poet, a big-city politician, a campesino in the fields, a soldier, a lumberjack, a playwright, the landlord in the ghetto, the leader of the Poor People's March on Washington, D.C., a high-ranking government official, a lone crusader, the father of eight children, the hero of the newspapers—and the villain, the All-American Boy, the victim of police riots, the descendant of the conquistadors, the "foreign Communist agitator," a political ward heeler, a successful businessman, and a revolutionary.

"The young Chicano is the most complex man in the country." He smiles, self-effacingly. "I guess that means me, too."

He was born in the barrios of Denver, a kid of the streets. Yet he grew up on the earth as well as the cement pavements, for his father was a Mexican emigrant, who worked as a campesino and coal miner in southern Colorado. As a boy he worked in the sugar-beet fields, beside his father, at the age of ten.

"Yes, I am a city man," he says. "But I did a lot of farm work. I have relatives in the villages in the San Luis Valley. Every spring and summer, as a boy, I worked in the fields. Every fall and winter I lived in the city slums."

Schools did not educate him. He learned of life in the fields and barrios. "The teachers taught me how to forget Spanish, to forget my heritage, to forget who I am," he says bitterly. "I went to four grade schools, three junior highs, and two high schools besides, because of our constant moving to the fields and back to the city." Even so, he graduated from high school at sixteen. He remembers working in a slaughterhouse at night and on weekends, so he could afford to go to school. He walked in so much blood that his shoes were always stained.

"I became a fighter because it was the fastest way to get out of the slaughterhouse. So I thought." He laughs. . . .

He came home to "be their leader." A hero, Gonzales went into politics, opened a free boxing gymnasium for ghetto youth, was befriended by the mayor, became an after-dinner speaker on inspirational themes. "Like all boys growing up in this society, I identified success by wanting to be an important person loved by everyone."

He became a businessman. In one year he was owner of an automobile insurance agency and owner of a surety-bond business. Within three years, by 1963, he was General Agent for the Summit Fidelity and Surety Company of Colorado.

Once again he was too successful. He was the pride of the barrio. "Corky beat the Anglos with his fists, then he outsmarted them with his brains," a neighbor says. The fair-haired boy wherever he went, the "different" Mexican, he was beckoned with offers of political jobs. Los Voluntarios, a political action group, had been organized in Denver with Gonzales as chairman. "The sleeping giant was awakening."

The poet with scarred eyelids became a ward heeler. He was the first Chicano ever to be a district captain in the Denver Democratic Party at the age of twenty-nine. "Corky has charisma," says a City Hall hanger-on. "He zooms. That boy was a comer." In the presidential election of 1960 he was Colorado coordinator of the "Viva Kennedy" campaign, and his district had the highest Democratic vote in the city. He was rewarded for his victory. On a table in his old barrio office, beneath a flamboyant mural of the Statue of Liberty, her breast bared as she lay half-naked and raped by corruption, there was an array of bronzed and golden sports trophies, in the midst of which there was a photograph of the late President standing beside the ex-featherweight, and inscribed, "To Corky—John F. Kennedy."

In no time he was a one-man directory of poverty agencies. He was on the Steering Committee of the Anti-Poverty Program for the Southwest, on the National Board of Jobs for Progress (S.E.R., a major funding group for the barrios), on the Board of the Job Opportunity Center, President of the National Citizens Committee for Community Relations, and Chairman of the Board of Denver's War on Poverty.

Gonzales was rumored to be in line for state or even national office. The line was long. The Chicano was last in line. On the rising aspirations of the young and pugilistic barrio go-getter there was a political ceiling. And he was not yet poet enough to celebrate his frustrations. The poverty programs had disappointed him, much as party politics had disenchanted him. In the barrios the jobs were just as scarce, the poor just as poor. He attended conferences by the dozens, perhaps feeling the same as he imagined the delegates to the White House's Cabinet Committee hearings on Mexican American Affairs in El Paso, Texas, felt: "well-meaning, confused, irate, and insulted middle-class Chicanos who knew they were being had when they were asked to swallow and digest the same old soup and cracker disks fed by the politicians, with Johnson and Humphrey at the head of the line. Lacking was any positive direction or militant action. . . . What resulted was a lot of brave words, promises, motions—and no action."

Conferences and more conferences; how many times can he talk about poverty? The young man has heroic daydreams. . . .

On the bus going from Denver to El Paso to hear the President and his Cabinet, he envisions a mirage of revolution looming out of the gas-station desert towns: "We could have been a guerrilla force riding to keep a date with destiny, if only the time and place and emotions of the people were right." But there is soup and crackers awaiting them. . . .

"The politics of the Anglo emasculates the manhood of a man of La Raza. It makes him impotent, a Tió Taco, an Uncle Tom. I was losing my cool," Gonzales says.

"I was used by the Democratic Party. I was used because I had a rapport with my people. Working in the two-party system I found out one thing, and I found it out very late. My people were exploited and men like I was are . . ." he falters, biting off the sentence. "But I was never bought. I could have accepted a number of payoffs from politicians and administrators. I never accepted one of them. Our people who get involved become political monsters." He pauses again and says, "Whores.". . .

The Golden Boy was ending his odyssey. When a Denver newspaper attacked him as "almost a thief," it was an insult to his dignity, a betrayal, he thought, of his "manhood." The poverty officials in Washington defended him, denying the accusation, but his friends in City Hall were strangely still. His scathing letter of resignation to the Democratic County Chairman, Dale R. Tooley, reverberated in the barrios of the Southwest:

> The individual who makes his way through the political muck of today's world, and more so the minority representatives, suffers from such an immense loss of soul and dignity that the end results are as rewarding as a heart attack, castration, or cancer! . . . You and your cohorts have been accomplices to the destruction of moral man in this society. I can only visualize your goal as complete emasculation of manhood, sterilization of human dignity, and that you not only consciously but purposely are creating a world of lackeys, political boot-lickers and prostitutes.

He resigned from the boards and councils of the War on Poverty one by one. He went "home again," he says. "Now I am closer back to home than I ever have been in that I am financially just as bad off as any Chicano," he says. . . .

The odyssey was ended. In an old red-brick building in the condemned barrios of downtown Denver, in 1965, the ex-almost-champion and past-president-of-everything founded *La Crusada Para la Justicia*, the Crusade for Justice. Gonzales declared this was "a movement born out of frustration and determination to secure equality with dignity."

In the politics of the Crusade for Justice there would be no wheeling and dealing. There would be no compromise with stereotypes. "To best serve our particular ethnic and cultural group our organization must be independent, and must not be dependent on the whims and demands of private agencies which are establishment-controlled and dominated. The services offered will not have the taint of paternalism, nor will the feeling of inferiority be felt when securing need, help and guidance."

In a few years, the Crusade was so influential that "the Anglos come to us for our help," Gonzales says. He tells how Archbishop James Casey of Denver came, uninvited, to the Easter "Mexican Dinner" they held. The Archbishop donned a tourist sombrero, told the guests, "Cherish your history, your culture, and preserve your wonderful language," and donated $100 to the Crusade's Building Fund.

The Crusade bought an old church in downtown Denver that resembled a miniature U.S. Treasury. In the colonnaded edifice there is "the most unique Mexican American center in the country," with a school of "Liberation Classes," a nursery, gymnasium, Mayan Ballroom, Chicano Art Gallery, Mexican shops, library, community dining room and community center, job "skill bank," legal aid service, Barrio Police Review Board, health and housing social workers, athletic leagues, a barrio newspaper [*El Gallo*], a bail bond service, a kitchen, and a "Revolutionary Theatre."

"No government money, no grants, no rich angels, no hypocrisy, no begging, no handouts" created El Centro Para La Justicia, boasts Gonzales. "We did it. We can do it. The Crusade is living proof of self-determination. The Crusade is not just an organization; it is the philosophy of nationalism with a human form.

"Nationalism exists in the Southwest, but until now it hasn't been formed into an image people can see. Until now it has been a dream. It has been my job to create a reality out of the dream, to create an ideology out of the longing. Everybody in the barrios is a nationalist, you see, whether he admits it to himself or not. It doesn't matter if he's middle-class, a *vendito* [vendido], a sellout, or what his politics may be. He'll come back home, to La Raza, to his heart, if we will build centers of nationalism for him."

In the Southwest, "nationalism is the key to our people liberating themselves," he says.

"Colorado belongs to our people, was named by our people, discovered by our people and worked by our people. We slave in the fields today to put food on your table. We don't preach violence. We preach self-respect and self-defense . . . to reclaim what is ours.

"I am a revolutionary," he says, "because creating life amid death is a revolutionary act. Just as building nationalism in an era of imperialism is a life-giving act. The barrios are beginning to awaken to their own strength. We are an awakening people, an emerging nation, a new breed."

Rodolfo "Corky" Gonzales feels that he has found himself among his people. He is a unique revolutionary in a time of ugliness and hatred in that he devotes his efforts to building his community. He is the happiest revolutionary in the country.

"Now I am my own man. I don't need to prove myself to the Anglos," he says.

"*Machismo* means manhood. To the Mexican man *machismo* means to have the manly traits of honor and dignity. To have courage to fight. To keep his word and protect his name. To run his house, to control his woman, and to direct his children. This is *machismo*," Gonzales says. "To be a man in your own eyes.

"If you are afraid of the Anglo he is like an animal. The human being is an animal; when you are afraid he attacks you, he punishes you, but if you are not afraid of him he respects you. The Anglo respects you only when you have power and respect yourself.

"We have been withdrawn. We have been quiet. And this has been mistaken for being afraid. We are not afraid. Look at the Congressional Medals of Honor our people have. It shows that when it comes to *machismo* there is no match for La Raza. We have been withdrawn from this society to protect our culture, the values we have—not because we are cowards. Now we have to show them that we are strong. We have to use more forceful methods."

Gonzales is not talking of violence and nonviolence. The luxury of that choice he feels exists for those who have power to control and order their environment. It is meaningless in the barrio, as in the boxing arena, where violence is a normal act of everyday life that people are powerless to halt.

"Power is respected in this society," he says. "The black militants say the Negro needs black power to offset white power, and we need brown power to offset Anglo power.

"Are we endangering the economic system, the political system, by saying that? I think the system should be endangered. It is a system that is built upon racism and imperialism. That is why the low-income people and the minority people across the nation are rebelling. Unless the system changes, there will be more rebellions. Those who advocate change will save the country, not destroy it. Those who are resisting change are destroying the country.

"If there is no change by peaceful assembly, by demonstrations, by sitting down to discuss changes, then there will be frustration. Out of the frustration will come real violence, not riots. Unless everyone gets an equal share in this country, there won't be any country."

In Washington, D.C., during the Poor People's March, where he and Reies Tijerina led the Chicanos of the Southwest, Gonzales created a plan for the future, "the Plan of the Barrio.". . .

We are basically a communal people . . . in the pattern of our Indian ancestors. Part of our cultural rights and cultural strengths is our communal values. We lived together for over a century and never had to fence our lands. When the gringo came, the first thing he did was to fence land. We opened our houses and hearts to him and trained him to irrigated farming, ranching, stock raising, and mining. He listened carefully and moved quickly, and when we turned around, he had driven us out and kept us out with violence, trickery, legal and court entanglements. The land for all people, the land of the brave became the land for the few and the land of the bully. . . .

Robbed of our land, our people were driven to the migrant labor fields and the cities. Poverty and city living under the colonial system of the Anglo has castrated our people's culture, consciousness of our heritage, and language. Because of our cultural rights, which are guaranteed by treaty, and because the U.S. says in its constitution that all treaties are the law of the land . . .

Therefore we demand: Housing.

We demand the necessary resources to plan our living accommodations so that it is possible to extend family homes to be situated in a communal style . . . around plazas or parks with plenty of space for the children. We want our living areas to fit the needs of the family and cultural protections, and not the needs of the city pork barrel, the building corporations or the architects.

Education: We demand that our schools be built in the same communal fashion as our neighborhoods . . . that they be warm and inviting facilities and not jails. We demand a completely free education from kindergarten to college, with no fees, no lunch charge, no supplies charges, no tuition, no dues.

We demand that all teachers live within walking distance of the schools. We demand that from kindergarten through college, Spanish be the first language and English the second language and the textbooks to be rewritten to emphasize the heritage and the contributions of the Mexican American or Indio-Hispano in the building of the Southwest. We also demand the teaching of the contributions and history of other minorities which have also helped build this country. We also feel that each neighborhood school complex should have its own school board made up of members who live in the community the school serves.

Economic Opportunities: We demand that the businesses serving our community be owned by that community. Seed money is required to start cooperative grocery stores, gas stations, furniture stores, etc. Instead of our people working in big factories across the city, we want training and low-interest loans to set up small industries in our own communities. These industries would be co-ops with the profits staying in the community.

Agricultural Reforms: We demand that not only the land which is our ancestral right be given back to those pueblos, with restitution for mineral, natural resources, grazing and timber used.

We demand compensation for taxes, legal costs, etc., which pueblos and heirs spent trying to save their land.

Redistribution of the Wealth: That all citizens of this country share in the wealth of this nation by institution of economic reforms that would provide for all people, and that welfare in the form of subsidies in taxes and payoffs to corporate owners be reverted to the people who in reality are the foundation of the economy and the tax base for this society.

Land Reform: A complete re-evaluation of the Homestead Act, to provide people ownership of the natural resources that abound in this country. Birthright should not only place responsibility on the individual but grant him ownership of the land he dies for."

On Palm Sunday, 1969, in the secular temple of La Crusada Para la Justicia the elated Rodolfo "Corky" Gonzales convened a national gathering of barrio youth. He called it, with a flourish, the Chicano Youth Liberation Conference. The young campesino activists, university graduate-school Chicanos, barrio gang members, *vados* [sic] *locos* from the streets, clever young government "Mexican Americans" incognito, and the wealthy children of the descendants of Spanish dons came to the temple-like building in downtown Denver to attend workshops in philosophy, self-defense, poetry, art, and identity. In all, more than 1,500 Chicanos come from as far away as Alaska, where no one thought there was any La Raza, and from Puerto Rico, and from all the states in between. They came from one hundred youth and student groups.

The conference of "music, poetry, *actos*, *embrazos*, tears, *gritos*, and the Chicano cheer: *'Raza, Raza, Raza, Raza,'* " went on for five days and nights. Afterward a youth wrote, "the building is just an ordinary building, but what counts is when you step through its doors. In this building we are not separated by the gringos. We are one."

" 'Conference' is a poor word to describe those five days," wrote Maria Varela, in *El Grito del Norte*. "It was in reality a fiesta: days of celebrating what sings in the blood of a people who, taught to believe they are ugly, discover the true beauty in their souls during years of occupation and intimidation. Coca-Cola, Doris Day, Breck Shampoo, the Playboy Bunny, the Arrow shirt man, the Marlboro heroes, are lies. 'We are beautiful'—this affirmation grew into a *grito*, a roar, among the people gathered in the auditorium of the Crusade's Center."

In the streets of Denver there were cries of youthful pain. The week before the Liberation Conference began some teen-agers walked out of the city's West Side High School to protest the insults of a teacher who had told his class, "Mexicans are dumb because they eat beans. If you eat Mexican food you'll become stupid like Mexicans." Students objected to his sense of humor and requested that the teacher be transferred. After a rally in the park the high school boys and girls tried to re-enter their school to present their demand to their principal. Two hundred and fifty policemen barred their way.

Soon there was a "riot." The ex-boxer hurried to the school. "Fearing the police were going to hurt the students I rushed forward to take a bull horn," Gonzales recalls. "I shouted to the young people to leave. The police were beating men, women, and children, indiscriminately." Gonzales' young daughter was one of those caught in the melee. "I heard my daughter Nito Jo scream. She was being mauled by a six-foot policeman." There were thirty-six Chicanos arrested.

Denver's barrios had never seen the kind of riots that had been desecrating ghettos in other cities. The people of the community walked to the school the following day to protest, in dismay as much as in anger. Some two thousand came, kids and parents, brown and black and white, teachers as well as students.

When the demonstration was over the police began to move in on those who lingered. There were curses hurled. In moments a battle erupted and dozens of police cars, riot police equipped with chemical Mace and a police helicopter, were ordered into the fray against the taunting teen-agers. "Some say it was a riot. It wasn't. It was more like guerrilla warfare," says one eyewitness. The helicopter dropped tear gas on the youths. "But the wind was blowing the wrong way and they [the police] ended up gassing their own men. This also happened with the Mace. The police were practically Macing their own faces," says another eyewitness.

George Seaton, the Denver Chief of Police, reported that twenty-five squad cars were damaged, "some extensively," and at least "seventeen police were assaulted, injured, and hospitalized." It was the worst street fighting in the modern history of the city.

"What took place after many people left was a battle between the West Side 'liberation forces' and the 'occupying army.' The West Side won," said Gonzales. He told the high school students, "You kids don't realize you have made history. We just talk about revolution, but you act it by facing the shotguns, billies, gas, and Mace. You are the real revolutionaries."

It was barely a year before that the Crusade for Justice leader had told me that he thought there would be no riots in the barrios. "The riots across the nation lead to the self-destruction of man. He acts like an animal," Gonzales had said. "I don't think it is in the Mexican temperament to riot, or to hurt your neighbor that way. Our way would be to pinpoint our enemy, where we wanted to attack him—not to riot."

Riots were "circuses," Gonzales had said then. He described the urban upheavals as the products of the "dehumanized cities," where life itself was riotous and people had no hope. "Why do blacks riot? Because they see no way out, because they feel trapped in the ghettos, because that is how mass society acts. I respect the suffering of the blacks. We have both suffered. We work together. But we work differently because we are a different people.

"Our culture is such that we don't like to march, to protest. We don't like to be conspicuous. We don't like to seem ridiculous in the public eye. That is *machismo.* That is a man's sense of self-respect. We are not nonviolent. But in the barrio self-determination means that every man, every people, every barrio has to be able to take care of themselves, with dignity.

"We are men of silent violence," Gonzales had said. "That, too, is *machismo.*"

He voiced these thoughts in the summer of 1968, not in the spring of 1969. In the streets of the barrios of Denver something new had happened to the young Chicanos.

In the fiesta of the Chicano Youth Liberation Conference there emerged the "Spiritual Plan of Aztlán" that opened a new road for the odyssey of Rodolfo "Corky" Gonzales. The name of Aztlán had been that of the ancient nation of the Aztecs. Now the young Chicanos who had come from throughout the Southwest of the United States voted, almost unanimously, to revive the spirit of that defeated nation.

On the flowered and festooned platform the ex-boxer, former poiltician, and once-successful businessman, who had not so long ago sought so desperately to escape from the barrio, was the heroic host to the "Spiritual Plan of Aztlán":

> *In the spirit of a new people that is conscious not only of its proud historical heritage but also of the brutal "gringo" invasion of our territories, we, the Chicano inhabitants and civilizers of the northern land of Aztlán, whence came our forefathers, reclaiming the land of their birth and consecrating the determination of our people of*

the sun, declare that the call of our blood is our power, our responsibility, and our inevitable destiny.

We are free and sovereign to determine those tasks which are justly called for by our house, our land, the sweat of our brows, and our hearts. Aztlán belongs to those who plant the seeds, water the fields, and gather the crops, and not to the foreign Europeans. We do not recognize capricious frontiers on the Bronze Continent.

Brotherhood unites us, and love for our brothers makes us a people whose time has come and who struggles against the foreigner "gabacho" who exploits our riches and destroys our culture. With our heart in our hands and our hands in the soil, we declare the Independence of our Mestizo Nation. We are a bronze people with a bronze culture. Before the world, before all of North America, before all our brothers on the Bronze Continent, we are a nation, we are a union of free pueblos, we are Aztlán.

March 1969

Por La Raza Todo   Fuera de la Raza Nada

The Growth of a Leader

Peter Nabokov

. . . Born on a mound of cotton sacks in a field near Fall City, Texas, on September 21, 1926, [Reies] Tijerina received his first insult from the Anglo world that very day. The infant who was later to champion the "new breed" offspring of Spanish and Indian union—who coined the phrase "Brown Power"—was listed as "white" on his Karnes County birth certificate.

The surname Tijerina would appear to translate as "little scissors" rather than the evocative "tiger," but Tijerina characteristically gives it a more legendary origin. "It comes from the Tejas [Texas] Indian people," he says. Then he tells a folktale of a distant ancestor, a young colonial Spaniard who rebelled against his parents to marry an Indian princess, adding the Spanish suffix "ina" to the name which changed over the years from Tejerina to Tijerina.

He tells of a landholding paternal great-grandfather who was robbed of his ranch and murdered by Anglos. He says his mother's people once owned land that is now part of the King Ranch. He vividly recalls the major formative figure in his life, his father's father Santiago. But he speaks little of his meek father, Antonio, who still lives near San Antonio.

His mother, Herlinda, was strong, big-boned, and accustomed to hefting bulging cotton sacks on her back. She

Peter Nabokov, "Growth of a Leader," in *Tijerina and the Courthouse Raid* (Albuquerque: The University of New Mexico Press, 1969), pp. 193-205. Copyright The University of New Mexico Press.

had no midwife for her ten children, three of whom died as babies. Antonio Tijerina had already outlived two wives. He did not remarry when Reies's other died at 28.

Their early existence was supported by sharecropping, a way of life which became self-defeating as the young couple with their large brood were always driven away just before harvest time. Tijerina remembers three such instances when his father, "full of fright and terror," buckled under the pressure from armed ranchers to clear out. His childhood was a series of temporary shacks outside tiny farm communities: "Whiteface, Wilson, Levelland, Forestville, Poth, the names run like stripes through my mind."

But before his mother died she had passed to Reies the outlet for his high-strung psychic energy: her faith.

"My mother was very religious," he remembers, "and she read the Bible a lot. She prayed before meals and in the evening. One time they tried to hang my father—they had a rope around his neck because they wanted his crop. She took me in her arms and cried and prayed . . . . Whenever I cried my mother, to quiet me, she would take me in her arms and say, 'Come now, tell your mother what you saw in heaven.' Wasn't that strange, 'Tell your mother what you saw in heaven.' "

Herlinda Tijerina was asking her four-year-old son to recollect the first of his visions. When Tijerina tries to explain his spiritual resources, he always mentions this "death."

"I came to the table to eat one day and there was only half a cup of tea for me. It was tea made from the bark of a pecan tree . . . I went back to bed. It was like I died. I stayed in bed for twenty-four hours. All the people surrounding thought I was dead, you see, and even they were building my coffin. When I woke up I was cold and hungry. I found a piece of tortilla and started eating it. Then I told them I had been walking with Christ and I had seen the flowers and green pastures. So any time my mother wanted me to stop crying she would ask me what I had seen in heaven.

The boy apparently had frequent occasion for terror. Once a landowner's sons assaulted Antonio and slashed his thigh muscle.

"Finally he survived," says Tijerina, "but he always dragged his foot. . . . He couldn't work very good and relied on my mother. I even remember seeing her carry him on her back to the field when they cleared the land. Yes, she lifted him and carried him into the fields, and then home when he was through."

About the year of young Reies's heavenly vision he began having a more prosaic, recurring nightmare. "We were working the Stevens Ranch, five miles from Poth, Texas. I think we were picking cotton. I used to dream that this car would come driving toward our house by itself, without any driver. It would drive up without any driver and then I would shake. I would shake from fright because I was afraid he would think we had stolen it and shoot one of us. I would wake up, and trembling."

These were the Depression years, and for the Tijerinas it was "a life made of bitter hard struggling to survive." Once, on the outskirts of Forestville, Reies remembers his mother contriving a scrap metal bow and arrow and killing a jackrabbit for food. The four boys—Anselmo, Reies, Ramon, and Margarito—each did their part in scavenging for the day's table. The girls, Maria and Josefina, helped their mother keep order in their temporary one-room houses.

"Margarito would dig, how do you call them"— Tijerina fought for the word—"rats, not the kind *del pueblo*, no, *ratas del campo*, of the fields. We'd dig them out of their holes and eat them, and, you know, they're good." The barefoot boys were keen foragers in trash cans and garbage dumps, collecting rags, old rubber, iron salvage, bones, whatever they could exchange for pennies.

And they worked the sun's full hours alongside their parents. Reies began stooping in the Texas fields at the age of seven. During these days he became dearly attached to his grandfather Santiago.

"Oh, he was a lion!" he enjoys remembering. "He's the one I take after. He had barefisted fights with the Texas Rangers. You know, when he died he had rope burns on his neck. Once, when they strung him up for something someone else had done, that Mexican border judge said, 'Wait a minute, I'm not sure that's the same one.' So they cut him down. . . . You know, that old man didn't like me when I was just a kid. But when he was dying in 1947, lasted two days, he called for me. He didn't want to be with anyone else but me. When he had seen me fight injustice he had admired me."

Reies was about six years old when his mother suddenly died. "She was my conscience that stayed with me. That was all I had in my heart, [that was] what she had left me."

With her gone, the hopelessness of attempting a semblance of family life was clear. During the spring, summer, and fall the Tijerinas joined thousands of their Spanish-speaking brethren in the migrant worker stream.

"Then for five years we went to Michigan, in those two-ton trucks, you know, the migrant laborers. I remember fighting in the fields because the rancher didn't clean the fields good enough, just full of weeds and grass. Father used to scold me. When I was talking back to those big ranchers he would tremble. But I started talking back to them when I was about fourteen or fifteen. I felt driven by this inner force to defend my rights, to tell them they weren't paying us enough or doing right by us."

Until then, Tijerina had accumulated a smattering of cut-short sojourns in roughly twenty rural schoolhouses near labor camps, equaling about six months of grade school. But his untutored gifts were obvious.

"Right from my childhood I was distinguished in the art of persuasion. They called me *abogado sin libros*, 'lawyer without books.' "

During the winters the family scraped out a living around San Antonio.

"Anselmo took on himself to feed the family when he was working with the WPA when he was sixteen. Father had to be relieved because he was infested with ailments. Anselmo was a father more or less. From his paycheck of $20, for fifteen days of pick and shovel work, he was allowed a nickel. I remember once, my father didn't want him to smoke, but he bought a pack of cigarets."

Cristobal had already, at nine months, been placed in the care of the aged Indian, Nazario Vasquez. He would not rejoin his brothers until 1961.

"Margarito, we called him Mario, was the humblest of all. He couldn't talk until he was seven. Everything others would do, he would be whipped. Before the ranchers ran us out, Mario was using one of the tough plows, those middle-busters with four horses, and he plowed those 200 acres all alone. He would go to the nopales cactus and collect the pigeon eggs and after working he would cook his own meals. But after seventeen he left our house and went on his own, to El Paso and Michigan. He only learned reading and writing when he was in jail. That happened when he was picking tomatoes in Indiana."

Of his brothers, Reies grew to feel most intimate with Ramon.

"He learned reading and writing at nineteen. He is the best-looking of all of us and was chased by beautiful girls. Then he married, both he and his wife had graduated from that same Bible school where I went, in Ysleta, Texas. He's a good-living man, straight in his family life. . . . He more or less followed me, when I changed from this religious life to the political."

Reies had already been baptized into the Catholic Church, and his head buzzed with his mother's talk of God and faith. By his mid-teens he was ripe for his own entrance into the religious world, and a profession which fed his hungry talents.

"Around this time, when a Baptist preacher named Samuel Gallindo came to our company house, he handed me a New Testament. I didn't leave that room until I read it all.

Then I got my brothers around the table and read it to them a second time. I noticed the word 'justice' used as many times as words like 'love.' So I read about Abraham, David, Ishmael, and the prophets. I found many words in there to reach my heart."

Finally, at eighteen, Tijerina's intense religiosity caused him to enroll at the Assembly of God Bible Institute in Ysleta, Texas. This was his first mature commitment. He does not regret the years of suffering which had prepared him for it.

"Once a Doctor Robert Castillo, that I went to because my vocal glands were bothering me, asked if I would agree to a psychiatrist talking to me. Castillo said that my throat hurts because I think so hard, because of tension when I meditate. One thing the psychiatrist noted was that he admired that I was happy even though my childhood was surrounded by misery and hardship. But I had no hatred, no enmity, and I told the doctor, 'That was all the life I knew. We were happy in poverty. Earthly possessions didn't bother me, but I was always attracted, always preoccupied, by that fascinating power that is justice.' "

In Bible college Tijerina soon stood out for his inspirational fire. For the young man the experience meant self-discovery at last.

"And I read in the Bible there that mercy and truth met, and justice and peace hugged. So then it was the religious life for the satisfaction and yearning of my heart for justice. And my idols, or something like that, was beginning with Moses on."

The institute's superintendent, Brother Kenzy Savage, remembers the intense, hazel-eyed young pupil as "fanatical, more peculiar, in his thoughts. I guess . . . he was not orthodox . . . when he went to school he was a very sincere student. I don't know, when he left school he began to get those rather far-out ideas about how people ought to conduct themselves." Savage explained by classifying the evolving militant as a "reformer."

Tijerina himself now has mixed memories of his three years of "formal" religious training.

"They wouldn't let me graduate because I had gone out with a girl. In 1950 I was going through there and that same man wanted me to graduate, but I refused on the grounds that my past could not be erased by my later actions."

A few months after leaving Ysleta, Tijerina married a fellow student, Mary Escobar (who was not the reason for his ouster), and hit the evangelist circuit hard. Brother Savage remembers that Tijerina joined him in some "pastoring" in the Santa Fe area.

"He was a very good speaker, with a lot of spunk and spirit. I appreciated his ministry at the time."

To Tijerina, however, the calling had deeper value than oratorical satisfaction.

"In my ten years of traveling then, up and down the country preaching, I had my first son and gave him the nickname of David. He was one year old when I would walk. Many times I have in my mind recorded when I walked. My wife would feel bad, but I tried to convince her. In 1947 we walked from Illinois to Texas, with her and that little boy, Reies Jr. Usually I refused rides because I wanted to feel related to the Bible and friends to those men that had defended justice to the world. If I didn't live with life I didn't have the right to preach the words of those holy men. But the leaders of the church planned to kick me out. They didn't like my life, when I told people to stop paying their tithes."

Savage cites an "unorthodox attitude" as the reason for the revocation of Tijerina's ministerial credentials in 1950. The complete severance from the Pentecostals meant no lessening of the young man's zeal, however. "When I was dismissed I became a nondenominational minister," he says, and he continued to roam on that mission.

Depending on charity for meals and shelter, the Tijerinas wandered through the southwestern states to Louisiana, Michigan, and New York. Reies talked in dingy evangelist halls from Fresno to Brooklyn. A collection of sermons and Biblical commentaries were later privately published in Spanish. Taking his title from St. Luke, datelining each message with the tiny town of their creation, Tijerina called his 119-page book *Hallera Fe en la Tierra?* (*Will There Be Faith on Earth?*).

In the midst of his solitary crusade his domestic life became difficult. Growing weary of her husband's driven, self-denying spirituality, his wife Mary became an unwilling companion.

"When I read that Socrates' wife threw a bucket of hot water on him because he wouldn't take money, I would rejoice. Because my wife was always angry that I gave everything away, one time to Mexican nationals, you know, who hoe the beets."

To christen his career, Tijerina says, he gave away three suits, his car, and all his furniture. During the continuing years of sleeping under bridges and on friendly floors, walking through steaming western noons—his training period —he accumulated other possessions from gifts and collection plates, but these too he gave up.

"Three times I felt the need to dispense of all my possessions . . . give away free to poor people to feel at ease with my heart's desire."

"This was a time," he explains, "when my beliefs were greater than my experiences, so I had to put myself through those things, to create a different will."

By the early 1950's, Tijerina's energies began to take a new ideological direction. Chance roadside encounters with strangers who discerned political ability beneath his evangelical gifts persuaded Tijerina to pursue his goal of *justicia* through more down-to-earth means.

"How I changed from religious to political? One of the things, I remember it very clearly . . . I was walking with my wife and child out of a big church in Dallas where I had delivered a sermon that morning. The minister of the large congregation didn't even offer me a hot meal. My wife only had the dress she was wearing. We just carried a little bag for the baby's things. So we walked out of this church and this man, Anglo, picked me up and took us home and said, 'Wife, get this man a steak.' And he said to my face, 'I don't like preachers, they take advantage of the people. What I think you should do is quit talking religion. What the Spanish-American people need is a Spanish-American politician, you may be that . . . you should study law and history and help your people. . . . I learned then that deeds of love are found in men who don't teach. And I learned that there's no mercy in churches, no justice in religious people."

But impatience with the lack of engagement to be found in evangelizing was probably as much a reason for Tijerina's next move as disillusion with religion. From a traveler passing the Word to imperfect human communities, Tijerina now came to conceive of himself as a utopian colonizer, forging into a "just" society the spiritual principles he had preached. By now he had acquired a modest following. Choosing "the wildest spot in the desert," a plot between Casa Grande and Eloy, Arizona, he pooled the funds of seventeen Spanish-American cottonpicker families to buy about 160 arid acres of the former multimillion-dollar Peralta land grant at $9 an acre. Just north of the Papago Indian Reservation, the settlement was optimistically called Valle de Paz (Valley of Peace), and its families knew each other as "Heralds of Peace."

Tijerina asserts that his communizing band had Arizona state permission to construct their church, general store, and earth-roofed dugout homes. Wages were earned by the adults commuting to cotton fields every day. But life was hardly peaceful. After one of their girls was raped while waiting for a school bus, Tijerina says the community received permission from Phoenix to build their own schoolhouse and hire their own teacher. This grated on some Anglo citizens of nearby Casa Grande and Toltec.

"All of a sudden," says Tijerina, "to our astonishment, the surrounding teachers objected." Also, Tijerina's own legal defense of some of the Valle de Paz youths arrested for misdemeanors apparently irritated the local sheriff.

At the same time, says Tijerina, the price of neighboring land skyrocketed to $1,500 an acre as Rockefeller dollars poured into the "Arizona City" housing project. Whatever the actual reasons, the band of believers began suffering harassment.

"They sent high school kids to our houses while the men and women were picking cotton," Tijerina claims. "They took two years to burn all our buildings down. . . . Then a high-flying airplane flew down into our property. . . . Because of that accident one pregnant girl lost her child and an old woman went crazy."

According to Tijerina, the FBI refused to investigate the crash, pleas to Washington went unanswered, and the local sheriff's office ignored the house-burnings. Finally everything was leveled to ashes. It took the theft of some automobile parts to bring the arm of the law into the dregs of the settlement.

By March 19, 1957, Tijerina and a few followers were living in a "gypsy camp near Pete's corner," reported a lawman in Pinal County, Arizona. That was the day Reies became one of the defendants charged with grand theft, for an incident in which six feed-trailer wheels were reportedly stolen. Although the case was thrown out for lack of evidence, the next month a second grand theft charge was thrown at Tijerina for stolen hardware discovered in the Valle de Paz well. He insists the tools were planted. But while officers were investigating this they discovered that Margarito Tijerina, a prodigal who had returned to the family fold after a troublesome life in the midwest, was a parole violator from Indiana. While he was being held for return and imprisonment, a jailbreak involving a smuggled hacksaw was attempted in the Pinal County jail in early July. Reies was accused of being at the wheel of the getaway car after the alleged scheme to free his brother failed, and he was released on $1,000 bond.

During a noon recess at his hearing on this charge, Tijerina calmly strode out of the doors of the Pinal County courthouse. He kept on walking, and began his successful attempt to run out the Arizona statute of limitations. Of this chapter-closing he says simply, "We moved out of Arizona."

The next four years, before Tijerina turned up to stay in New Mexico, are hazy. "That is for *my* book, those years when I was in flight," he says to questioners. But one time he gave me a glimpse into them.

"From 1957 to 1960 I was a fugitive. I escaped from the law seventeen times. I escaped when the FBI was after me, all around me, with guns. Once I was in the only room they didn't search, right behind the door, but they didn't look in. I am an alert man. Once we were surrounded by five FBI cars in Plainview, Texas. Texas Rangers also. They had surrounded my house; my wife with six children was inside. They told her, 'If you don't tell us where your husband is, we'll arrest all of you.' I went into the bathroom where Rosina [his oldest daughter] was taking a bath and told her to show her shoulder if they came, and I stood behind the shower curtain. You wouldn't believe the stories."

For a period of three months Tijerina and armed followers hid on a Texas ranch. During this span Tijerina began wandering once again. On one trek with his family he found himself near El Monte, California, and in spiritual turmoil.

"I kept on having a struggle with my conscience, you know, my soul. I was not satisfied. I was always finding that the Bible rebuked me. I found things, not outright things, but that I was a hypocrite, that I was not doing what I could do. So in order to overcome that struggle and doubt and fear I told her [his wife] that I was going to seek a better life, a better opening, and I wouldn't leave that place until God would show me my duty."

In the manner of a Plains Indian striving for a life-guiding vision, Tijerina proceeded to find a cave hidden amidst underbrush into which he had to "crawl like a snake." Without food or water, he made his ritual bed of cotton stuffing from a car seat. There he made a discovery:

"There were not so many religions that I studied in school, there was just two strong powers, and the religion was just like gasoline. If you use Texaco or Mobil, it's all the same, it makes your motor, you know, burn, and I had very strong illuminations, and so far so good, I had found that religion now, I knew that there was no difference between Protestant and Catholic, because these and those of the different religions were all the same, they all wanted new automobiles, they all coveted the same things."

The second great power revealed to him, that of justice, had already summoned him in a previous, more prophetic dream. Around the year of Valle de Paz's founding, Tijerina was the guest of a poor family in Visalia, California, south of Fresno. One night he wandered into the countryside and unintentionally fell asleep. The next morning "the sun woke me and that white, how do you say, dew, had covered me all over. It shaked all my life, from there I turned to New Mexico. I saw frozen horses, they started melting and coming to life in a very old kingdom with old walls. Then I saw three angels of law and they asked to help me. They said they had come from a long ways, had traveled the earth and come for me. . . . Those tall pines I saw meant New Mexico. When I started doing research into the land grants I found they are not dead, they are just frozen. They are living, latent political bodies."

Before Tijerina and seven carloads of followers finally drove to New Mexico in 1960 he had already made friends there through his ministerial meanderings. He had also, during his fugitive period after 1957, dropped south into old Mexico. It was during this interlude of mental questioning and outwitting lawmen that he came to focus on the land-grant question. From September 1958 to September 1959 he spent nearly the entire year in Mexico, researching in libraries. He attempted to pass on land-grant data to the Secretary of Exterior Relations in Mexico City, with unenthusiastic response. In August 1959 Tijerina accompanied the president of the International Front of Human Rights, Dr. Benjamin Lauriano Luna, when he met Dr. Milton Eisenhower in Mexico City. A New Mexico newspaper commented that this caused, at 1,000 miles distance, a revival of the century-old dispute over the ancient southwestern lands. From March to May 1960 Tijerina and his brother Cristobal were in Mexico, and an April 11 news item in *Excelsior* described them as "residents of the land grant of Tierra Amarilla," visiting Mexico for aid in retrieving land-grant holdings.

When Tijerina came to New Mexico in 1960 he followed up his old preaching contacts for his new crusade.

"We went to seven families," he says. "I asked them to give us all the stories and documents and maps they had, but they didn't have a copy of the Treaty of Guadalupe Hidalgo. So after a few months I went to Mexico and there I found an old book, eaten by termites, with all the maps, the treaty and the protocol. Later I found the whole legal history, and then I went around to the old people, eighty and a hundred years old, and even though they didn't know each other and lived hundreds of miles apart, their stories matched."

With a little effort Tijerina could have obtained a copy of the treaty between Mexico and the United States in any New Mexico public library. But his concern about the all-important protocol, adopted after the treaty was redrafted, was his point here. It is that added and often overlooked portion which he insists reserves the old land grants to the first grantee's descendants in perpetuity.

As Tijerina began absorbing the rhythms and histories of the northern valley communities, he moved circumspectly. This was in part because of his vulnerable legal status; it was also necessary in order to prospect. His intuition told him that in these forgotten islands lay something approximating a "pure" Spanish-American heritage. His organizational efforts in the north began with caution. Shortly, in the "tall pines" and humble settlements he became assured that he had found his calling and the Athens of the Indo-Hispano world.

SELECTED BIBLIOGRAPHY

Clark, Margaret, *Health In The Mexican-American Culture* (Berkeley: University of California Press, 1959).

Galarza, Ernesto, *Merchants of Labor: The Mexican Bracero Story* (San Jose, California: The Rosicrucian Press, 1964).

————, *Spiders in the House and Workers in the Field* (Notre Dame, Indiana: University of Notre Dame Press, 1970).

————, Herman Gallegos and Julian Samora, *Mexican-Americans in the Southwest* (Santa Barbara: McNally & Loftin, 1960).

Gamio, Manuel, *Mexican Immigration to the United States* (Chicago: The University of Chicago Press, 1931).

Gonzalez, Nancie L., *The Spanish-Americans Of New Mexico* (Albuquerque: University of New Mexico Press, 1969).

Grebler, Leo, Joan W. Moore and Ralph C. Guzman, *The Mexican-American People: The Nation's Second Largest Minority* (New York: The Free Press, 1970).

Heller, Celia S., *Mexican-American Youth: Forgotten Youth at the Crossroads* (New York: Random House, 1966).

Holmes, Jack E., *Politics in New Mexico* (Albuquerque: University of New Mexico Press, 1967).

Landes, Ruth, *Latin-Americans of the Southwest* (New York: McGraw-Hill, 1965).

Madsen, William, *Mexican-Americans of South Texas* (San Francisco: Holt, Rinehart and Winston, 1964).

Manuel, Herschel T., *Spanish-Speaking Children of the Southwest* (Austin: University of Texas Press, 1965).

Matthiesen, Peter, *Sal Si Puedes—Cesar Chavez and the New American Revolution* (New York: Random House, 1969).

McWilliams, Carey, *North From Mexico: The Spanish Speaking People of the United States* (New York: J. P. Lippincott, 1961).

Nabokov, Peter, *Tijerina and the Courthouse Raid* (Albuquerque: University of New Mexico Press, 1969).

Paz, Octavio, *The Labyrinth Of Solitude: Life and Thought in Mexico* (New York: Grove Press, 1961).

Ramos, Samuel, *Profile of Man and Culture in Mexico* (Austin: University of Texas Press, 1962).

Rendon, Armando, *Chicano Manifesto* (New York: The Macmillan Company, 1971).

Robinson, Cecil, *With the Ears of Strangers: The Mexican in American Literature* (Tucson, Arizona: The University of Arizona Press, 1969).

Rubel, Arthur, *Across the Tracks: Mexican-Americans in a Texas City* (Austin: University of Texas Press, 1966).

Samora, Julian, ed., *La Raza: Forgotten Americans* (Notre Dame, Indiana: University of Notre Dame Press, 1966).

Sánchez, George G. *Forgotten People: A Study of New Mexicans* (Albuquerque: University of New Mexico Press, 1940).

Steiner, Stan, *La Raza: The Mexican Americans* (New York: Harper & Row, 1968).

ACKNOWLEDGMENTS

Traditionally, an acknowledgments page expresses the author's gratitude for assistance received on the book being published. I would like to depart from that tradition and offer, instead, thanks to a number of men who, to paraphrase the late Frank Dobie, have left "bits of themselves" in my life. None is responsible for what is of dubious quality in my life, but I am happy to share with them credit for whatever might be of value.

When I reflect on their names and contributions I find it significant that most are non-Chicano. Yet each contributed something of themselves to a Chicano when it was not yet a fashionable thing to do. This reflects, I think, what is good and valuable about American higher education—it cares little about birth, status, class, race or wealth, it does, however, value labor and effort. And the following names are of men who have labored with me as teachers or colleagues: Charles Beall, Glenn Brooks, Henry Ehrmann, Heinz Eulau, Timothy Fuller, David Finley, Judd Harmon, Antonio Jaure, Curtis Martin, Dayton McKean, the late Milton Merrill, Douglas Mertz, Robert North, Fred Sondermann, Aristeo Torres, and Mark Van Aken.